Deleuze and World Cinemas

Also available from Continuum:

Anti-Oedipus, Gilles Deleuze and Felix Guattari
A Thousand Plateaus, Gilles Deleuze and Felix Guattari
Cinema I, Gilles Deleuze
Cinema II, Gilles Deleuze
Difference and Repetition, Gilles Deleuze
The Fold, Gilles Deleuze
Foucault, Gilles Deleuze
Francis Bacon, Gilles Deleuze
Kant's Critical Philosophy, Gilles Deleuze
Proust and Signs, Gilles Deleuze
Deleuze: A Guide for the Perplexed, Claire Colebrook
Deleuze and Guattari's 'Anti Oedipus': A Reader's Guide, Ian Buchanan
Deleuze and Guattari's Philosophy of History, Jay Lampert
Deleuze and Ricoeur, Declan Sheerin
Deleuze and the Genesis of Representation, Joe Hughes
Deleuze and the Meaning of Life, Claire Colebrook
Deleuze and the Schizoanalysis of Cinema, Ian Buchan and
    Patricia MacCormack
Deleuze and the Unconcious, Christian Kerslake
Deleuze, Guattari and the Production of the New, edited by Simon O'Sullivan
    and Stephen Zepke
Deleuze's 'Difference and Repetition': A Reader's Guide, Joe Hughes
Gilles Deleuze: The Intensive Reduction, edited by Constantin V. Boundas
Kant, Deleuze and Architectonics, Edward Willatt
Thinking Between Deleuze and Kant, edited by Edward Willatt and Matt Lee
Who's Afraid of Deleuze and Guattari?, Gregg Lambert

Deleuze and World Cinemas

David Martin-Jones

continuum

Continuum International Publishing Group

The Tower Building	80 Maiden Lane
11 York Road	Suite 704
London SE1 7NX	New York, NY 10038

British Library Cataloguing-in-Publication Data
A catalogue record for this book is available from the British Library.

ISBN: HB: 978-0-8264-1693-3
       PB: 978-0-8264-3642-9

Library of Congress Cataloguing-in-Publication Data
Martin-Jones, David.
  Deleuze and world cinemas / David Martin-Jones.
    p. cm.
  Includes bibliographical references.
  ISBN: 978-0-8264-3642-9 (pbk.)
  ISBN: 978-0-8264-1693-3 (hardback)
  1. Motion pictures–Philosophy. 2. Motion pictures and globalization.
  3. Deleuze, Gilles, 1925-1995–Criticism and interpretation. I. Title.

PN1995.M37 2011
791.4301–dc22

2010028036

Typeset by Newgen Imaging Systems Pvt Ltd, Chennai, India
Printed and bound in India by Replika Press Pvt Ltd

Para Soledad

Contents

Spectacle II: *Masala*-Image

Acknowledgements

Sections of certain chapters have appeared before in earlier versions, and are reprinted here in a more developed form. Parts of Chapter 1 were published in: 'Schizoanalysis, Spectacle and the Spaghetti Western', in Ian Buchanan and Patricia MacCormack (eds), *Deleuze and the Schizoanalysis of Cinema* (Continuum, 2008). This work is reprinted with the kind permission of The Continuum International Publishing Group Ltd. Parts of Chapter 2 appeared in: 'Towards Another '-Image': Deleuze, Narrative Time and Popular Indian Cinema', *Deleuze Studies* 2: 1 (2008). This work is reprinted with the kind permission of Ian Buchanan and Edinburgh University Press http://www.eupjournals.com/journals/dis. Parts of Chapter 4 are contained in 'Decompressing Modernity: South Korean Time Travel Narratives and the IMF Crisis', by David Martin-Jones, from *Cinema Journal*, 46: 4, pp. 45-67. Copyright © 2007 by the University of Texas Press. All rights reserved.

Thanks to Ian Buchanan for providing me with the inspiration to pick up Deleuze again, and for sound advice generally. For providing extremely helpful commentary on early drafts I owe immense gratitude to William Brown, David Deamer and Kay Dickinson. Thank you to Beatriz Tadeo Fuica, Alexia Cortés Maquieria, Yun-hua Chen and William Brown for fantastic help with translations. I also thank the following people for innumerable informing debates about Deleuze and cinema since the 1990s. Antonio Carlos Amorim, Martine Beugnet, Ronald Bogue, Robert Burgoyne, Edward Branigan, Ian Buchanan, Yun-hua Chen, Felicity Colman, David Deamer, Elena Del Rio, Dimitris Eleftheriotis, David Fleming, Daniel Frampton, Colin Gardner, Amy Herzog, Matthew Holtmeier, Barbara Kennedy, András Bálint Kovács, Robert Lapsley, Laura U. Marks, Patricia MacCormack, Bill Marshall, Paola Monaldi, John Mullarkey, Serazer Pekerman, Patricia Pisters, Anna Powell, Angelo Restivo, David Rodowick, Richard Rushton, Steven Shaviro, Daniel W. Smith, David Sorfa, Damian Sutton, Sharon Tay and Hunter Vaughan.

Thanks also to a number of friends who have helped me understand what was at stake in the different cinemas I chose to discuss in this book: SooJeong Ahn, Davie Archibald, Saër Maty Bâ, Canan Balan, Wai Yee Ruby Cheung,

Andrew Dorman, Rajinder Kumar Dudrah, Elizabeth Ezra, Elisabetta Girelli, Lee Grieveson, Mark Harris, Mette Hjort, Yun Mi Hwang, Dina Iordanova, Hyangjin Lee, Tae Hun Lee, Karen Lury, Aaron Han Joon Magnan-Park, Hamid Naficy, Gary Needham, Chi-Yun Shin, Julian Stringer, Rosie Thomas, Leshu Torchin, Greg Tuck, Pasi Väliaho and Belén Vidal.

Thanks to my family, as always, for their invaluable support. Thanks to the family Montañez Morillo, and most of all, thanks to Sol.

A note regarding names. Where appropriate, and especially in chapters 3 and 4, I render names with family name first followed by given name, except where the name has been published or is widely known otherwise (such as an author's name, or a star like Jackie Chan, director like John Woo, etc.). This is in order to respect the usual conventions related to scholarship on Asian cinemas like those of Korea and China.

Introduction

Deterritorializing Deleuze

Deleuze and World Cinemas uses different cinemas from around the world to critically engage with Gilles Deleuze's philosophical work on cinema. It explores how Deleuze's ideas can be refined, adapted and developed in relation to films Deleuze did not examine, films that are viewed as products of specific historical, cultural, aesthetic and industrial contexts. In this way it provides a constructive critique of the Eurocentric conclusions that Deleuze draws in *Cinema 1* (1983) and *Cinema 2* (1985). This critique applies not only to the construction of his movement-image and time-image categories but also to the validity of this very distinction.

When considered in the current context of widespread global film production and distribution, the primary focus of the *Cinema* books on films from Europe and the USA now appears to provide a limited range of aesthetic examples with which to propose a seemingly universal consideration of time. This is especially so because Deleuze's approach to these cinemas does not engage with their context of production and distribution, factors now often considered crucial for an understanding of film aesthetics. For this reason *Deleuze and World Cinemas* reconsiders Deleuze's conclusions by broadening the range of cinemas examined, both geographically and historically. In each chapter Deleuze's ideas are engaged with in relation to a different cinema, demonstrating the need to reconsider Deleuze's work in various contexts, and thereby illuminating some of the major difficulties with the *Cinema* books. For the purposes of this work, these difficulties are: the relative nature of the formally defined movement-image/time-image distinction (examined in chapters 1, 3 and 6 in particular); the Eurocentric positioning of World War Two as the pivot on which the two image categories hinge (especially chapters 2 and 6); and the continued development of the action-image under globalization, that further illustrates the relative, or perhaps, arbitrary nature of the division between the two image categories (chapters 3, 4 and 5). Thus *Deleuze and World Cinemas* does not set out to debunk the *Cinema* books, its very existence being evidence of the contemporary relevance of Deleuze's ideas after all, but to demonstrate the continued usefulness of Deleuze's work on cinema by reconsidering his conclusions through contact with different cinemas from around the world.

As there are a number of books dedicated to explaining and interpreting Deleuze's philosophy in relation to cinema I will not explain the content of Deleuze's *Cinema* books here, instead providing detailed introductions to the relevant concepts discussed in individual chapters. Rather, I will spend the remainder of this introduction clarifying why a reinterpretation of Deleuze's *Cinema* books is necessary. The reasons are complex and intertwined, and primarily relate to the way in which we view the approach, content and conclusions of Deleuze's *Cinema* books. However, they are also informed by the global context we now find ourselves in, in which the ever-increasing availability and circulation of world cinemas can be considered a symptom of the greater move towards globalization of trade since the 1970s (particularly after the end of the Cold War); our enhanced knowledge of different cinema histories; the emergence of a body of scholarship addressing various world cinemas through Deleuze; the manner in which Deleuze's ideas are currently interpreted in the related but very different areas of Deleuze Studies and Film Studies; and the broader issue of Eurocentrism and cinema.

World Cinema or World Cinemas?

Approaching world cinemas, using Deleuze, requires care. To attempt to validate Deleuze's ideas through their application to films from around the world would run the risk of imposing already Eurocentric conclusions onto cinemas that belong to very different, context-specific cultures and aesthetic traditions. This would be directly contrary to the methodology, not to mention the spirit of the study of world cinemas, which acknowledges precisely the aesthetic and cultural differences apparent in films from around the world, even while often exploring their formal and generic similarities and their circulation in the same spheres internationally.

Thus it is not the aim of this book to homogenize world cinemas, grouping together, for example, Argentine films with popular Indian movies as though they were all peas from the same pod. Rather, I combine or, to use a Deleuzian expression, assemble[1] Deleuze's ideas with a deliberately diverse selection of films from different parts of the world, including examples from the nineteenth, twentieth and twenty-first centuries, in order to constructively critique, offer ways to develop upon, rethink and reinterpret Deleuze's conclusions.

A more detailed synopsis concludes this introduction, but a brief overview of the book's content here will help to clarify the different uses these films are put to in critiquing Deleuze's *Cinema* books. Chapter 1 explores cinematic spectacle in order to reconsider how we conceive of the movement-image, and particularly Deleuze's emphasis on montage (over narrative) in his notion of the cinematic whole. Films discussed include early silent movies by French filmmaker Georges Méliès (from the period 1895 to 1906/7 which Deleuze does not discuss in the *Cinema* books) and European "spaghetti" westerns from the 1960s and 1970s. Two chapters on history follow. Chapter 2 refines Deleuze's discussion of the child as seer in the time-image by exploring the construction of history in a contemporary Argentine melodrama. Chapter 3 moves from a reconsideration of specific aspects of the *Cinema* books to the central issue of whether the distinction between movement-image and time-image is always valid, again in relation to the cinematic construction of history, this time as seen in the enfolding of the outside (the outside typically being a feature of the time-image) by the whole (a characteristic of the movement-image) in South Korean science fiction films. Chapters 4 and 5 consider filmic space. Chapter 4 analyses a Jackie Chan action movie from his days in Hong Kong to reconsider Deleuze's concept of the cinematic any-space-whatever in terms of its geopolitical function under globalization. Chapter 5 continues to explore the any-space-whatever, discussing two of Michael Mann's Hollywood blockbusters to uncover the incorporation of the crystal of time (again typically found in the time-image) into the action-image. Finally, chapter 6 returns to the issue of spectacle, discussing the existence of images that do not correspond to either image category, that are found in popular Indian cinema (or Bollywood cinema) from the 1930s to the 1990s. Thus various cinemas from around the world are brought into contact with Deleuze's ideas, the very different assemblages these context-specific case studies enable transforming his philosophy in the process.

Throughout this investigation I deploy the term "world cinemas", rather than "world cinema" to describe the plurality of cinemas that exist globally. This fine distinction requires some explaining. Before we can discuss how to productively analyse the vast entirety of cinemas that exist globally using Deleuze (even leaving aside Deleuze it is questionable whether any single book can do justice to the wealth of cinemas in existence), in what sense should the term world cinemas be understood?

The term world cinema is often considered to have an at best culturally elitist, and at worst almost colonial connotation, due to its potential for constructing an homogeneous Other out of very varied non-Western cinemas. As Stephanie Dennison and Song Hwee Lim note in their introduction to *Remapping World Cinema* (2006), as does Toby Miller in his preface to *Traditions in World Cinema* (2006), the term is often applied like those of "World Music" or "World Literature"[2] to group together the many different cinemas from outside of Europe and the USA as though, due to their divergence or deviance from this artificially constructed norm, they create an "ethnic" Other. Hence its very existence as a category serves to validate the supposedly central presence of Western cinema globally (whether this particular cinema-producing West is constructed as Europe and the USA, or simply Hollywood), and in this sense a "World Cinema" section in a DVD retail or rental outlet might be considered to homogenize different cinemas in an Orientalist manner.

Even so, the complexities of the context in which works of world cinema are produced, distributed and consumed suggest that everything may not be this clear cut. This is an industrial context still dominated by Hollywood, but in which the film industries of Nigeria and India (Nollywood and Bollywood respectively) produce the largest number of films annually, and the widespread and in fact long-standing practice of transnational coproductions increasingly blurs the boundaries between "powerful" and "lesser" national cinemas. Thus, for every argument that acceptance into the pantheon of world cinema is a form of (patronizing) Western exoticizing, or cynical and often extremely selective appropriation, there is always a counter-argument for the benefits of global exposure that filmmakers from smaller film-producing nations enjoy when their works are lauded internationally as works of world cinema. Indeed, many of these filmmakers may consider themselves savvy players in this global market, perhaps deliberately self-exoticizing in order to appeal to (or at least conform to) Western perceptions of Other cinemas (the practice of auto-ethnography not necessarily being considered an entirely negative one from all perspectives[3]) to gain international acknowledgement for their work.

Accordingly, the term world cinema has gained a more positive connotation through a certain usage. For example, Dina Iordanova explores 'the dynamics of world cinema' in a deliberate attempt to focus attention away from Hollywood, and onto the "rest" of cinematic production worldwide; questioning in the process the very nature of global film production's assumed centres and peripheries.[4] Alternatively, Lúcia Nagib attempts to positively redefine world cinema as a means of decentring 'Hollywood and the West' from their assumed role at 'the centre of film history', favouring instead an all-inclusive model of world cinema (including Hollywood) without centre, or indeed, 'single beginning'.[5] Following Nagib, world cinema should not be considered to refer to a minority of film production beyond the Western mainstream. Rather, the Western mainstream needs to be reconsidered as a part of the much broader production that constitutes the overarching totality of the cinemas of the world.

When global cinematic production is viewed in this way, the term world cinemas captures something of its plural nature, and avoids the connotations of a singular entity associated with world cinema. Therefore, for the purposes of this study, despite its problematic widespread economic and, arguably, ideological dominance, Hollywood is considered one more player (albeit a very dominant one) alongside myriad cinemas of varying scale and influence. In this I follow Nagib who advocates the repositioning of Hollywood as 'a cinema among others'.[6] The positioning of my discussion of Mann's films in the penultimate chapter is deliberate, then, in order to avoid granting them a normative position from which to assess the supposed deviation of the Other (or perhaps more accurately, "Othered") cinemas under discussion.

Using Deleuze with World Cinemas

With cinema increasingly considered a transnational or global phenomenon (something it is possible to argue that it has been since the early decades of cinema), so too does Deleuze's work on cinema become both increasingly applicable globally and yet also in need of reconsideration in different contexts. Put in Deleuzian terms, as the global rhizome of world cinemas is increasingly understood in relation to its de/reterritorialized flows, so too must Deleuze's ideas depart on their travels, becoming de/reterritorialized themselves whenever they encounter films in new contexts. Accordingly, while I engage with the transnational dimension of these films (in particular their appeal to international audiences), the book retains a major focus on their context-specific identities in relation to their respective and often very different national cinemas, histories, cultures and aesthetic traditions.

For this reason, my approach is different from the rapidly expanding body of Deleuze-inspired work on modern political or minor cinema, which draws on arguments he outlines in the closing chapters of *Cinema 2*.[7] Minor cinema has the potential to destratify cinema from its national territory and cross national boundaries: for instance, in diasporic or exilic cinemas, as developed in the works of Laura U. Marks and Hamid Naficy on 'intercultural' and 'accented' cinemas respectively.[8] The question raised by minor cinema is how filmmakers attempt to construct a memory of the future for a people yet to come (as Deleuze identified the process) when previously established centre/periphery, major/minor positions no longer hold in quite the same manner under globalization as they did previously. This is the case even if these people yet to come are still engaged with the legacies of recent histories of postcolonialism, neo-colonial regimes, Cold War dictatorships, civil rights movements, etc.

I take a different tack, then, in that I consider films from specific contexts (while retaining a focus on their transnational dimensions), whether or not these are minor cinemas. There are two reasons for this. First, as Dudley Andrew rightly notes as part of a broader discussion of the different ways in which it is possible to map world cinema, 'Deleuze's notions of "smooth nomadic space" founder when one looks at deeply "rooted" cultures.'[9] As Andrew's discussion of Nigerian filmmaking suggests, there is as much to be gained by exploring the location-embedded specifics of certain cinemas as there is from mapping cinema's transnational flows. Put another way, the rhizome of world cinemas should be considered as a gradually spreading forest in which each tree contains its own roots and branches, but which should still be taken as an interconnected multiplicity (forest) rather than a collection of autonomous sovereign nation-states (trees). Secondly, in line with the decentred repositioning of Hollywood that I take from Nagib, I focus on the mainstream and the popular in a way that an emphasis on minor cinema might not necessarily allow. This stresses the continued importance of the dominant forms of the movement-image as they appear differently around the world (European westerns, Argentine melodramas, South Korean science fiction films, Hong Kong action movies, Hollywood blockbusters) for our understanding of the continued relevance of Deleuze's work in a global context.

Therefore, although the title *Deleuze and World Cinemas* may seem suggestive of a book that attempts a Eurocentric exposition of Deleuze's work in Other contexts, in fact, a close reading of these films in their contexts of production shows them resistant to such a reading. When I state that the global nature of world cinemas enables a global application of Deleuze's ideas, then, I mean this in the very specific sense that the global spread of cinemas around the world both facilitates and necessitates a reinterpretation of the *Cinema* books.

In this way I hope to intercede in the ongoing debate as to whether we can legitimately use Deleuze with Other, or Othered cinemas, in particular those absent from the *Cinema* books. In *Deleuze and World Cinemas* I demonstrate that, in fact, this approach is absolutely necessary if Deleuze's theories are to have continued currency in relation to the globally widespread phenomenon of cinema. As I have noted already, I do not think that we should impose Deleuze's ideas on films from other parts of the world, thereby perpetuating the Eurocentric conclusions of the *Cinema* books that it is my aim to constructively critique herein. However, by both exploring the advantages and rethinking the limitations of Deleuze's work through productive assemblages with these Othered cinemas, we can reinvigorate his ideas and broaden their scope for future usage in the field. I would go so far as to contend that perhaps it is only in this manner that we can save Deleuze's work on cinema from a far less productive repetition of the same, in which we may be tempted to follow Deleuze in favouring the time-image with a degree of greater philosophical complexity than the movement-image and weighing our research in its favour accordingly. In its worst excesses this approach can produce questionable acts of homage that perpetually reaffirm Deleuze's conclusions, often by using similar films, drawn from the same geographical areas he himself discussed. Instead, going beyond Deleuze's choice of filmic examples to rethink his conclusions may be seen as the natural extension of his own philosophical project. After all, who is to say how far Deleuze would have gone in his thinking regarding cinema had he had the access to the films we have today?

As no one book can cover the entire output of a world of cinemas I have formulated *Deleuze and World Cinemas* in such a way as to enable me to explore three concepts in relation to Deleuze's work – the cinematic construction of spectacle, history and space, all of which exist in the mainstream of analysis in Film Studies – using the clearest and most dispersive examples from my mental databank of world cinemas. Although personal choices, the films I analyse are not disparate, isolated examples, but different shaped pieces of the same global jigsaw of world cinemas. Undoubtedly scholars with different specialisms and interests would provide alternative mappings of this interlocking territory, yet to my mind this only demonstrates more keenly the need for further work in this manner.

Admittedly I am far from the first to consider various world cinemas fair game for a Deleuzian analysis. For instance, Deleuze's ideas have already been used to examine the films of Senegalese directors Ousmane Sembène and Djibril Diop Mambéty as works of minor cinema (by D. N. Rodowick and Patricia Pisters respectively[10]); of directors from various countries in Asia (as one for instance Wong Kar-wai (Hong Kong))[11] or indeed entire film movements like New Iranian Cinema.[12] There are a growing number of other such examples. This does not mean, however, that I, or these authors, are unaware of the difficulties this potentially throws up. Just as those working on representations of gender in African or Iranian films are those most likely to be aware of both the potential and the difficulties that theories like psychoanalysis pose in different contexts (as seen in the works of Kenneth W. Harrow on African, or Naficy on Iranian films[13]), so too are the scholars working with Deleuze in Other or Othered cinematic contexts usually attuned to the difficulties this raises. In many cases the existing engagement of Deleuze's work with world cinemas has involved an exploration, as opposed to an assumption, of the applicability of Deleuze's ideas to different contexts, while in others it has entailed a more direct reconsideration of Deleuze's conclusions (still perhaps most engagingly in Marks's *The Skin of the Film* (2000)).

The important point this growing body of work demonstrates is that, even if different or Othered films have the potential to challenge theory (be it psychoanalysis, Deleuze's philosophy, etc.), we should not therefore simply give up on such theoretical approaches altogether. Rather, it is precisely because Othered films can "talk back" to existing theories that they are incredibly useful for helping us to understand the strengths and limitations of theoretical works like Deleuze's *Cinema* books. Thus it is worth exploring films that illustrate how, even once the noticeable aesthetic and cultural differences informing many cinemas have been taken into account, Deleuze's ideas offer new and challenging ways of thinking about world cinemas. As this book demonstrates, numerous world cinemas enable us to both reconsider Deleuze's philosophical conclusions and expand our understanding of cinema beyond Eurocentric confines.

Deleuze Studies/Film Studies

In Film Studies, work on Deleuze and cinema has recently begun to gather momentum. In his contribution to François Dosse and Jean-Michel Frodon's edited collection, *Gilles Deleuze et les images* (2008), Andrew recently identified the emergence of three generations of Deleuze-inspired scholars active in the 1990s and 2000s, solely in Anglo-American Film Studies.[14] The attendance at recent conferences of researchers pursuing similar lines of inquiry from various international locations illustrates that this is a global phenomenon.

During this period the experience of many scholars working with Deleuze and Film Studies was often felt to be that of a somewhat marginalized, at times embattled minority position within the discipline. Now things are changing, and the spread of Deleuzian studies of cinema is starting to be seen as somewhat akin to psychoanalysis was previously, if not in that it is threatening to become the dominant theoretical paradigm in the discipline, then at the very least in as much as it is a recognizable framework used by an increasing number of scholars to explore film.

Conversely, within the interdisciplinary field that has rapidly become known as Deleuze Studies, the position taken on Deleuze by some scholars from within Film Studies is at times met with puzzlement. Ironically, while some researchers in Deleuze Studies may wonder what is so wrong with Deleuze's *Cinema* books that they require this degree of critique, scholars in Film Studies will often challenge what is so right about them in the first place.

My position, then, overlaps these two fields. From within Film Studies I apply some of the contextual analysis expected of Film Studies scholarship to Deleuze's work, and opens it up to world cinemas. Simultaneously, however, while working with the other foot in Deleuze Studies, I put Deleuze's ideas into productive assemblages with those of other scholars, albeit working on cinema rather than philosophy, in order to productively transform them. In both instances the aim is to further an understanding of both the theory and the films in question in the hope that it will increase the longevity of Deleuze's ideas regarding cinema. The inevitable consequence of this is the transformation of certain of Deleuze's ideas.

I believe that the major value of this research lies in the constructive critique it can offer of Deleuze's Eurocentric conclusions regarding time that he derives from a selective analysis of cinema. To pursue this direction requires a reconsideration of Deleuze's often ahistorical analysis of films, in which my contextualizing approach is more typical of Film Studies. However, in a way that is perhaps more familiar to those in Deleuze Studies, I also believe that my manner of working with Deleuze's ideas is akin to that which he himself advocated. His books on numerous other philosophers, for example, contain an element of creative re-interpretation that could equally be considered an interpretive critique and development of their works, the example most relevant here being Deleuze's engagement with Henri Bergson in the *Cinema* books. Indeed, by engaging with different or as yet "unknown" cinemas (albeit to many viewers worldwide these are "normal" cinemas), is to engage in, as Deleuze argues in *Difference and Repetition* (1968), the process of writing 'at the frontiers of our knowledge,

at the border which separates our knowledge from our ignorance and transforms the one into the other'.[15] In so doing, underlying assumptions as to
who exactly constitutes this collective "our" are laid bare, as we are forced
to consider just exactly whose borders surround and dissect a world of
cinemas.

Ironically, then, although my approach might in some Nietzschian or
Deleuze and Guattarian respects be considered "anti-Deleuze" (perhaps
even in the sense of, anti-Christ, anti-Oedipus, anti-Deleuze), in this respect
I could equally be considered a Deleuzian disciple of the assemblage. However, I would prefer to describe myself as "a-Deleuzian", a term which can
be interpreted in two ways. First, in the sense of amoral, in that I consider
myself neither pro- or anti-Deleuze exactly, but keen to constructively
critique his ideas in order to increase their applicability and relevance.
Secondly, I deploy the term to mean just another scholar of Deleuze (literally, a Deleuzian) who, acknowledging that they cannot have all the answers,
embarks instead to explore those parts of the labyrinth to which they have
access.

Provincializing Europe – Unthinking Eurocentrism – Deterritorializing Deleuze

Deleuze's *Cinema* books use cinema to map a shift in thinking, or image
of thought, that Deleuze considered to be evident around the time of the
Second World War. This was the dividing line that, for Deleuze, separated
cinema into movement- and time-image. Yet, as Jacques Rancière argues in
Film Fables (2001), while Deleuze's movement- and time-images suggest two
logics of the image in two different ages of cinema, in actual fact these are
two different perspectives, often on the same films, put forward by Deleuze
around a defining rupture that can be argued to only exist as such for
Deleuze. Rancière's analysis of Deleuze's discussions of Robert Bresson's
films across the two volumes of the *Cinema* books goes a long way towards
convincingly demonstrating this position.[16] In *Deleuze and World Cinemas*
I take this line of reasoning a step further, and reveal through various different examples how the distinction between the image categories demonstrates a particularly Eurocentric position on Deleuze's part.

It might immediately be queried as to why Deleuze has been singled out
for critique in this manner? For many scholars, Deleuze's, or at least Deleuze
and Guattari's, thinking is attractive precisely because it offers ways to think
beyond Eurocentrism. A prime example of this approach would be Rosi

Braidotti's work on the potential a Deleuzian approach might offer for understanding what she argues is the 'becoming-minoritarian' of Europe.[17] To be clear, then, I am not arguing that Deleuze's philosophy is Eurocentric. My point, rather, is that the conclusions he draws in the *Cinema* books are Eurocentric. This is due to his ahistorical exploration of films, the geographically limited selection of films he discusses, the apparently universalizing conclusions he extrapolates from them concerning time, and the central positioning of the Second World War as dividing line between movement- and time-image.

It is perhaps ironic that one of the major difficulties with the *Cinema* books in this respect is their positioning of World War Two as the pivotal, divisive moment between the two images. I state that this is ironic because Deleuze's choice of the Second World War may have been intended to have exactly the opposite effect. By pointing to the ruins of Europe as the unstable ground from which new images, and new ways of thinking arose, he may well have been – in line with much post-structuralist thinking – attempting to think beyond the grand narrative of a globally central Europe.[18] The time-image, on this view, emerges from the ruins of Europe to deterritorialize the potential for Eurocentrism of the movement-image. Nevertheless, the effect of this decision to focus on cinema by examining only certain films, primarily from the USA and Europe, and dividing his two major image types around the turning point of World War Two, leads to a Eurocentric overstatement of a perceived shift in "our" understanding of time.

As Dipesh Chakrabarty observes in *Provincialising Europe* (2000), in a manner that can be applied to Deleuze's *Cinema* books, European thinkers are often considered to exist outside of history to the extent to which their ideas are discussed without reference to the very specific historical contexts in which they were formed.[19] It is worth remembering, then, that not only is Deleuze's thought the product of a Western philosophical canon (the *Cinema* books illustrate the informing presence of Henri Bergson, Charles Sanders Peirce, Friedrich Nietzsche and Baruch Spinoza in particular) but so too were his *Cinema* books of the 1980s a product of his position as an intellectual cineaste in post-1968 Paris,[20] with what would now be considered a limited access to world cinemas. Accordingly we should consider his tacit intimation that the cinemas he was discussing were representative of a totality called "cinema", extremely problematic (and this is before we even consider the different philosophical traditions that lie beyond his *Cinema* books, and their interpretations of time, a project beyond the realms of this particular book). As chapters 1, 3 and 6 demonstrate in particular, Deleuze's reliance on predecessors like Bergson, Nietzsche and Franz Kafka often predetermine his conclusions, his findings being thrown into question when his ideas are engaged with world cinemas. Accordingly, any conclusions regarding the nature of time, in any universal or global sense, that are inferred from Deleuze's limited range of cinemas is equally problematic. Although Deleuze draws on a vast knowledge of films, those he discusses really only represent the dominant Western cinemas of the USA and Europe, along with the one or two directors from outside the West (i.e. Yasujiro Ozu, Glauber Rocha, Youssef Chahine and Yilmaz Gűney) who were at that time accepted as world cinema equals to the great Western directors through the questionable Romantic conception of the individual artistic genius, or *auteur*. Accordingly, Deleuze's conclusions regarding our understanding of time from this body of films should be considered equally Eurocentric.

The Eurocentric position that Deleuze takes in his *Cinema* books is not necessarily apparent immediately, especially due to the awesome nature of his philosophical project and the huge range of films and thinkers he discusses. The sheer weight of concentration needed to understand his argument in the *Cinema* books is an ongoing process that, speaking from personal experience, can conceivably last for years, if not decades. However, it can also work to obscure the more obvious limitations of the way the project is framed. Accordingly, Chakrabarty's observations concerning the problematic nature of 'internalist histories'[21] emanating from Europe, which place Europe at the centre of civilized development are particularly applicable to Deleuze's *Cinema* books. This is clearly seen in his isolation of World War Two as the point around which cinema is transformed. While this event did have massive global ramifications, in many contexts outside Europe it is viewed in relation to longer historical processes related to colonization and the spread of modernity, rather than as an abrupt caesura in a (European) nation's historical development. Most obviously, the emphasis on this arbitrary turning point flatly contradicts Deleuze's observation of the invention and development of pure optical and sound situations (time-images) in the pre-war (as well as post-war) films of Japanese director Yasujiro Ozu.[22] After all, this is a process which Deleuze otherwise considers a post-war, and primarily European phenomenon, so it is curious that he does not develop this line of thinking in relation to Japan in any depth.[23] As the chapters that follow demonstrate, such moments of crisis are different in different places at different historical junctures, with popular Indian cinema (the subject of the concluding chapter) most clearly demonstrating not only that the emphasis on this particular moment of historical division is questionable, but that so too is the very distinction between movement- and time-image.

For a film scholar, perhaps the most apparent absence from the *Cinema* books is what most people would consider the world's second largest film industry, India. The inception of *Deleuze and World Cinemas* was an article I published in *Deleuze Studies*, on popular Indian (or Bollywood) cinema. This piece caused me to reconsider my previous interpretation of Deleuze's *Cinema* books in *Deleuze, Cinema and National Identity* (2006), exploring instead the problematic universalizing intent of Deleuze's movement-/ time-image distinction, with popular Indian cinema providing one example of a very different cinematic conception of time and movement altogether. This research confirmed my belief that Deleuze's claim for a global change in image of thought occurring around the time of the Second World War, expressed in the shift from movement- to time-images, must be reconsidered as an universalizing extrapolation from what can be considered a provincial European perspective. This is especially so if we follow Chakrabarty's reasoning, which is formed, noticeably, in relation to a discussion of India.[24] This idea is developed in Chapter 6, the point towards which the preceding chapters aim by demonstrating the transformation of our understanding of various of Deleuze's concepts when they are applied to cinemas from around the world, popular Indian cinema providing the limit case that most thoroughly destabilizes not only Deleuze's conclusions, but potentially also his theoretical ground.

Accordingly, *Deleuze and World Cinemas* does not reiterate the thesis of *Deleuze, Cinema and National Identity*. The previous work's reconsideration of Deleuze's ideas from within the context of the nation (as I formulated it, temporally, drawing on Homi K. Bhabha) remains an informing backdrop to this argument, although it soon begins to transform as the notion of the "whole" is increasingly understood in various transnational ways. Indeed, *Deleuze and World Cinemas* continues to develop certain lines of thought introduced in the former book. For example, considerations of national identity in relation to the movement- and time-image remain, especially in chapters 2 and 3, which explore cinematic constructions of history. I also return to my examination of filmic constructions of different identities in the global city in chapters 4 and 5. However, a major point of departure is that this book does not argue that we should consider contemporary films hybrid movement-/time-images. Rather, here I am concerned to discover the degree to which numerous films from around the world enable us to refine, adapt or reconsider the two categories by looking at films that exist somewhere between, or "instead of" them. Thus, in *Deleuze and World Cinemas*, the movement- and time-image are not considered to constitute the totality of cinema's DNA, as we might consider Deleuze to be arguing in the *Cinema*

books.[25] Rather, cinema is seen to be constructed from many different kinds
of images that can be revealed if we take Deleuze's ideas as a starting point,
rather than as an all-defining taxonomy.

The project of "unthinking" Eurocentrism, both in its numerous cinematic manifestations and in the manner in which we theorize cinema,
has been in progress since the 1980s. It is epitomized by Ella Shohat and
Robert Stam's seminal *Unthinking Eurocentrism* (1994), an influential work
which begins by noting how Western (in its origin, specifically European)
philosophy has been naturalized into the more universalizing position of
"philosophy",[26] precisely as I am arguing is the case with Deleuze's *Cinema*
books. Partly as a result of the intellectual direction epitomized by Shohat
and Stam's work the discipline of Film Studies has increasingly explored
world cinemas as specific cultural and aesthetic products, placing a greater
emphasis on the historically contextualized study of film production, distribution and reception practices. Thus the major problem with Deleuze's
Eurocentric position becomes clearer if we consider that his lack of concern for context leads to conclusions that are no longer viable in relation to
our greater knowledge of the global history of cinema. For this reason,
Deleuze and World Cinemas attempts to variously de- and reterritorialize
Deleuze's conclusions, taking them on their travels via a reconsideration of
his conceptualization of European and US cinemas, to Argentina, South
Korea, Hong Kong and India.

In each case, recognizing and reconsidering the "West and the Rest"
distinction that tacitly structures Deleuze's *Cinema* books is important
because of the specific conditions experienced by different parts of the
world throughout the history of cinema, from colonialism to neoliberal
capitalism. With this in mind the movement-/time-image distinction at the
heart of the *Cinema* books remains key to our understanding of the continued value of (and indeed, the difficulties that arise from), Deleuze's work
on cinema. This is especially the case as various parts of the world negotiate
their own defining moments of historical rupture, their own particular
versions of Deleuze's isolation of the Second World War as key point of
significant change.

The Globalization of Cinema

Many of the films discussed have emerged in recent decades, and as such
can be considered to demonstrate the transformation of cinema under globalization. This is the case even if pinpointing the origins of globalization is

problematic, being for many critics a very recent phenomenon, while for others, such as Walter D. Mignolo, it is part of a larger process dating back several centuries.[27] Indeed, the history of cinema suggests that the contemporary global spread of cinema is not entirely a new phenomenon either, with, for example, international coproduction deals and transnational distribution being a feature of cinema production at various times throughout its history. Yet it is undoubtedly the case that the global reach of film production and distribution has transformed in recent decades, especially since the end of the Cold War. What is essential to this argument, then, is that Deleuze's *Cinema* books of the 1980s do not directly engage with the global spread of world cinemas.

Accordingly, with contemporary globalization of central importance to the understanding of the contemporary films discussed throughout the book, my work is influenced by such writers as David Harvey, Mike Davis and Saskia Sassen. An informing background is also created by the notion of international flows (particularly of people, information, trade, finance and culture) found in the writings of scholars such as Arjun Appadurai, Manuel Castells, Ulf Hannerz, Zygmunt Bauman and Michael Hardt and Antonio Negri.[28] This is because in the early twenty-first century understanding world cinemas is an integral part of the process of understanding the forces – economic, social, historical, geopolitical, cultural – that shape our present existence. The work of these and other writers can therefore assist our comprehension of movies that demonstrate how Deleuze's image categories do not hold for films from many parts of the world.

This need to reconsider Deleuze's ideas due to the changing global context is evident throughout the book, for instance in the transformed nature of the pure optical situation in South American films that explore recent pasts under Cold War dictatorships (Chapter 2); the existence of formal qualities suggesting a cinematic thinking of history – that Deleuze identifies in *Cinema 2* as a characteristic of modern political or minor cinema – now appearing in contemporary South Korean science fiction films that engage with the nation's emergence from a past under military rule (Chapter 3); and the development of small form action-images from locations as diverse as Hong Kong and Los Angeles that negotiate the proliferation of any-space-whatevers under globalization (chapter 4 and 5). In particular, this adjustment to the contemporary geopolitical landscape positions Mann's contemporary Hollywood blockbusters as the necessary contemporary counter-examples to Deleuze's choice of classical Hollywood films, in his discussion of the action-image in *Cinema 1*. Yet once again it is Chapter 6, on popular Indian cinema, that emphasizes most clearly how, as contemporary cinema continues to develop, the Eurocentric division between movement- and time-image must be continually rethought in various contexts worldwide.

Undoubtedly it would be entirely unfair to critique Deleuze, writing in the early 1980s, for not having considered the range of movies from around the world now increasingly available for consumption due to changing historical circumstances. After all, this is a situation that has markedly changed due to the emergence of what Shohini Chaudhuri succinctly describes, in *Contemporary World Cinema* (2005), as 'an enormous multinational system consisting of TV networks, new technologies of production and distribution, and international coproductions'.[29] The global context of distribution alone is now defined by the increased spread of festival and independent cinema circuits, multiplex theatres, cable television channels showing archived movie back catalogues, and technological innovations leading to widespread, cheap availability of films (VHS, DVD, Blu-ray and various forms of online delivery). Moreover, we clearly cannot criticize Deleuze for not exploring films made after he was writing! On the other hand, we cannot simply ignore these films either, or the opportunity they offer us to reinterpret his findings from a broader, more historically, geopolitically, culturally and aesthetically informed perspective.

For this reason I deterritorialize Deleuze's *Cinema* books, visiting historical destinations from nineteenth-century France to twenty-first-century Los Angeles, by way of Cold War Europe, 1980s Hong Kong as it negotiated its transforming encounter with globalization, post-Cold War dictatorship Argentina and South Korea (both suffering economic crises due to a recent legacies of rapidly imposed neoliberal economic policies), and India throughout the twentieth century (from its struggle for independence in the 1930s to its negotiation of economic liberalization and the returning wealth of the diaspora in the 1990s). This process ungrounds Deleuze's ideas, refining, adapting, developing and ultimately critiquing the logic that leads to his division of cinema into movement- and time-image, based on his limited range of examples and a Eurocentric emphasis on the Second World War as defining moment of rupture.

It would, I believe, be fair to note that Deleuze may have considered his own approach to be that of an exploration of a world of cinemas. It would be equally fair to point out that my own archaeology of world cinemas is just one British scholar's point of view on one French scholar's point of view, and equally open to criticism for its Eurocentrism. However, whether this book is considered an extension of Deleuze's project, itself open to critique for similar reasons, a constructive critique of Deleuze's *Cinema* books, or a bit of both, it is surely a line of flight worth pursuing.

Deleuze and World Cinemas

Deleuze and World Cinemas consists of six chapters. Each begins with an introduction to the relevant concepts from the *Cinema* books with which the rest of the chapter engages through analysis of films and the contexts from which they emerged. The order of the chapters enables a progressive build up of Deleuzian concepts, the discussion of the whole in Chapter 1 in particular being integral to the entirety of what follows. The book opens and closes with chapters on two different cinemas of spectacle that Deleuze did not engage with in the *Cinema* books. The four chapters in between are grouped into two on history, and two on space, these three topics, spectacle, history and space all being common currency in Film Studies.

In Chapter 1 I begin by exploring the nature of spectacle in early silent trick films by Georges Méliès, from the late nineteenth and early twentieth centuries. Here a discussion of spectacle entails a broader exploration of the role of historical context in our understanding of different types of popular cinema, and how this approach (which ironically emerged during the 1980s along with the *Cinema* books) can enable a reconsideration of Deleuze's notion of the movement-image. Chapter 1 engages with Deleuze's reliance on the work of Bergson, which resulted in his unfortunate dismissal of early silent cinema. In the films of Méliès I uncover a different type of movement-image to those identified by Deleuze, an "attraction-image" that constructs a non-continuous temporal whole based on spectacle, which is itself suggestive of other potential temporal possibilities available to cinema than solely those Deleuze identified. The chapter then explores the continued existence of the "attraction-image" in different cinemas, using the example of European "spaghetti" westerns from the 1960s and 1970s (*Django* (1966), and *Keoma* (1976)). These films demonstrate how ideally suited "attraction-images" are to the construction of political narratives, in this instance in tales of fantasy tourism or subaltern revolution during the Cold War that appeal to different audiences worldwide.

In the section entitled "History: Deleuze after Dictatorship", two chapters explore the ways in which national histories are negotiated through the aesthetic construction of different types of cinematic image. This process is examined in relation to the Argentine melodrama *Kamchatka* (2002) in Chapter 2, and South Korean science fiction movies (specifically time travel films) in Chapter 3 (*Calla* (1999), *Donggam/Ditto* (2000), and *2009: Lost Memories* (2002)). In both cases the manner in which contemporary films renegotiate national history is considered in relation to a period of military rule during the Cold War that has since given way to more neoliberal economic policy, and the at times socially divisive, if not economic and socially disastrous consequences of national entry into the arena of global free trade. In Chapter 2 I discuss the figure of the child, to demonstrate the complexities of Deleuze's notion of the seer in the time-image when it comes to cinematic constructions of history that take place differently in the present than in the recreated past. Here the time-image is seen to have a different relationship to history in contemporary South American cinema than in the post-war European new waves that Deleuze discusses. Chapter 3 broadens the discussion by examining how mainstream South Korean movement-images about time travel use cinematic devices previously iso-lated by Deleuze in the time-image to "think" history, cinematically, by folding time. Once again the specific negotiation of recent national history evident in these films demonstrates the need to develop our understanding of the manner in which Deleuze's concepts are applicable to various cinemas worldwide, even if this means that his concepts are in need of reconfiguration as a result. As these particular films show, through a com-plex play of folding and unfolding, movement-images are just as capable of thinking history as modern political, or minor cinemas.

In "Space: Geopolitics and the Action-Image", two further chapters examine how globalization has effected the way in which space (specifically the any-space-whatever) functions in action films. The chosen examples are Jackie Chan's stunt-filled *Ging chat goo si/Police Story* (1985) from Hong Kong in Chapter 4, and Michael Mann's big budget Los Angeles-based Hollywood action movies *Heat* (1995) and *Collateral* (2004) in Chapter 5. Both chapters question the way in which the ASA' (or small form) action-image has transformed due to the changing geopolitical landscape of globalization, and the manner in which this has impacted upon the cine-matic construction of any-space-whatevers. In Chapter 4 the focus is on the extended montage that constructs the opening and closing spectacles of *Ging chat goo si*, in which any-space-whatevers are rendered as though affec-tive landscapes that express, in the manner of a facial close-up forming across the city's mutating landscape, the changing aspect of Hong Kong as it transforms from Crown Colony to global city. The global/local negotia-tion of the city's identity is seen to be constructed through the any-space-whatever in a manner that reconsiders the relationship between the ASA' action-image and the national whole found in Deleuze's work, due to the complexities involved in the contemporary context of globalization. Chapter 5 for its part explores Mann's two Los Angeles films, this time examining the way in which the crystal and any-space-whatever structure (which Deleuze identified in post-war European time-image cinemas) now exists in an action-oriented format in the Hollywood ASA' blockbuster, specifically when it takes place in the global gateway city that is Los Angeles in the 1990s/2000s.

Finally, the concluding chapter returns to the issue of spectacle and explores popular Indian (Bollwood) cinema from the silent era to the late 1990s (*Toofani Tarzan* (1936), *Awaara* (1951) and *Dilwale Dulhania Le Jayenge* (1995)). Here the previous chapters' reconsiderations of Deleuze's concepts of the movement- and time-image, in particular Chapter 1's questioning of the influence of Bergson on Deleuze's thought, are taken to their logical extreme. Reconceiving of Deleuze's conclusions regarding the shift in expression of time that occurs with the emergence of the time-image in post-war Europe, in view of the apparent existence of both movement- and time-image in popular Indian cinema from the 1930s onwards a *dharmic* whole is seen to be constructed instead. This *dharmic* whole demonstrates how the specific aesthetic and cultural peculiarities informing popular Indian cinema shed new light on Deleuze's construction of Eurocentric image categories and conclusions. Not merely a temporal anomaly that demonstrates the arbitrary choice of World War Two as dividing moment in the *Cinema* books, the *dharmic* whole actually points to the different models of time that can potentially be found in world cinemas, models which mean that the images on display should not necessarily be considered movement- or time-images, but something else altogether. Thus while the "attraction-image" uncovered in Chapter 1 adds an additional movement-image to Deleuze's existing taxonomy, the popular Indian "*masala*-image" throws into question the very distinction he draws between movement- and time-image.

In summary, with the increased variety of international cinema now in global circulation, and our enhanced knowledge of cinema history worldwide, the image categories that Deleuze conceived of in the 1980s no longer cover all cinematic eventualities. This is primarily due to the limited range of cinemas he explored in developing his concepts, and the Eurocentric conclusions he drew as a result. To demonstrate the continued relevance of Deleuze's *Cinema* books for the current global state of film production and distribution, and the scholarship that accompanies it, dedicated analysis of the applicability of Deleuze's ideas in various other international contexts is necessary. Thus, *Deleuze and World Cinemas* explores six very different archaeological layers of film history from various parts of the world, asking questions of Deleuze's philosophy with regard to films which "talk back" to his conclusions, in a manner that forces them to stutter or stammer in response.

Spectacle I:

Attraction-Image

Chapter 1

The Attraction-Image: From Georges Méliès to the Spaghetti Western

This chapter offers a fresh perspective on the movement-image by exploring the presence of spectacle in popular cinema. The function of cinematic spectacle has produced much critical enquiry since the mid-1970s. Comprehending the role of spectacle in popular films entails a consideration of the aesthetic, industrial and cultural contexts from which they emerge. Yet spectacle (and accordingly, context) is undervalued in Deleuze's conceptualization of the movement-image throughout *Cinema 1*, which primarily focuses on formal qualities, especially montage. For this reason I begin with an introduction to Deleuze's concept of the movement-image, exploring how his thinking regarding montage develops due to his reliance on Henri Bergson's work.

The chapter proceeds by reconsidering Deleuze's stance in relation to early silent cinema from 1895 to 1906/7, a period not discussed by Deleuze. This offers a more nuanced understanding of the role of montage in so-called "primitive" cinema, in light of debates surrounding the spectacular nature of early silent cinema, and in particular its relationship to its context of production and consumption. The 'cinema of attractions'[1] described by Tom Gunning preceded the films of D. W. Griffith with which Deleuze begins his writing on montage in *Cinema 1*, and has a different relationship to movement and time than Deleuze perceived in the movement-images of classical Hollywood. Research into early silent cinema, then, especially the trick films of filmmakers like Georges Méliès, sheds new light on Deleuze's conceptual starting point in *Cinema 1*. In short, I contend, there were movement-images prior to those conceived by Deleuze, which I call "attraction-images".[2]

This is not simply to point to a small omission in the *Cinema* books. Rather, the existence of the attraction-image has a major impact on how we conceive of certain genre films – including several of those not discussed by Deleuze – and their ability to, for example, engage with international politics in a popular format. In short, attraction-images illustrate that there are other ways of conceiving of movement (and time) in cinema than those found in Deleuze's image categories as he theorized them.

To demonstrate this, the remainder of the chapter focuses on the spaghetti westerns *Django* (1966) and *Keoma* (1976). Towards the close of *Cinema 1*, Deleuze uses the US western to discuss a particular type of movement-image, the action-image. Deleuze's position can be critiqued, then, by examining the different aesthetic structure of the European "spaghetti" western, an internationally popular genre that flourished in the 1960s and 1970s with a particular emphasis on spectacle. The spaghetti western is a popular film genre that was only recently reassessed positively by scholars striving to understand its spectacular form in relation to its mode of production and conditions of consumption. Analysing the role of spectacle in the aesthetic construction of these films, then, facilitates a reconsideration of the way the movement-image functions, in particular in terms of the structure of the action-image.

Accordingly, I argue that in early silent cinema and numerous cinemas since, including the spaghetti western, there exist attraction-images (another form of movement-image), which are uncovered only once cinematic spectacle, and the context in which it is produced and consumed, is considered. These movement-images can be used to construct a very particular kind of political cinema that relies upon a non-continuous conception of the whole, which in the spaghetti western is used to meditate (through repetition and spectacle) upon such topics as the global experience of US economic and cultural influence in the post-war era (*Django*) and the cycles of violence experienced by subaltern populations worldwide during the Cold War (*Keoma*).

Image is Everything

In order to understand what is at stake in a reconsideration of the action-image, it is first necessary to understand the thought behind Deleuze's movement-image more generally. In the *Cinema* books, in particular in *Cinema 1*, Deleuze engages with the work of French philosopher Henri Bergson, whose ideas were extremely influential on Deleuze's thinking throughout his career.

There are already several excellent works that examine the influence of Bergson on Deleuze's *Cinema* books, including D. N. Rodowick's *Gilles Deleuze's Time Machine* (1997) and Ronald Bogue's *Deleuze on Cinema* (2003), and indeed on what some consider Deleuze's rather unique interpretation of Berson's comments regarding cinema, such as John Mullarkey's *Refractions of Reality* (2009).[3] A brief summary, then, should suffice. Bergson developed a model of the universe, in particular in *Matter and Memory* (1896) and *Creative Evolution* (1907), which consisted of a vibrational flux of matter in movement that appears as images.[4] People can therefore be considered images among all the others images/things. Moreover, this universe is temporally determined by Bergson as an open and expanding whole, what he refers to as 'duration'.[5] Duration is time considered in the process of transforming, and is not to be mistaken for the spatialized measure of time (space-time) through which we generally experience everyday life. Duration, rather, is a temporality of indivisible becoming that we each experience, uniquely, as it passes. The distinction between these two different ways of conceptualizing time would greatly influence Deleuze's concepts of the movement-image (space-time) and the time-image (a glimpse of duration), as he argued for their existence in different types of cinema.

At the start of *Cinema 1*, Deleuze engages with Bergson's work in order to refute Bergson's conclusion, in *Creative Evolution*, that cinema could not render visible duration, but only false movement, 'immobile sections + abstract time'.[6] This is what Bergson described as the 'cinematographic illusion',[7] cinema's replication of the oldest of beliefs, that movement exists as somehow distinct from the (passing of) the time in which it occurs. For Bergson this erroneous belief is demonstrated once again by film, through the combining of a series of poses (individual frames of film) with an artificially created notion of uniform, abstract time (the machinery of a movie projector). The illusion supposedly further propagated by cinema was the opposite of Bergson's belief that all movement exists within (and is inseparable from) the open and expanding whole of time, duration.

For Deleuze, Bergson's conclusion was considered to be a result of the time at which he writing, when cinema was still in its infancy. Coincidentally, the time span between *Matter and Memory* and *Creative Evolution* corresponds almost exactly with what is now known as the early silent period, from around 1895 to 1906/7. This is the period in which the static shot film dominated until around 1903,[8] when the construction of narrative through montage was beginning to emerge in various forms, especially the initial stage of continuity editing that we now associate with classical Hollywood cinema, including the films of Griffith. For Deleuze, on the other hand, due in particular to the development of movement in the film image – created by, Deleuze believed, the increased mobility of the camera and, more importantly, the development of montage[9] – cinema came to express Bergson's preferred belief that movement is indivisible from the time in which it takes place. As opposed to 'immobile sections + abstract time', cinema actually expresses 'real movement → concrete duration'.[10] For Deleuze, cinema is the perfect expression of Bergson's ideas, as it creates movement-images, 'mobile sections of duration'[11] which express the changing of the whole, of duration, albeit indirectly, as a function of movement. Movement-images, then, express a spatialized version of time (space-time). This indirect image of time is a moving portion of the open and expanding whole, and from this mobile section of duration the existence of the ever-changing whole can be inferred.[12]

Drawing on *Matter and Memory*, Deleuze considers the material universe as a 'plane of immanence', consisting of light, on which movement-images appear as blocs of space-time.[13] These images act and react upon each other, until an interval or gap appears between these two moments, such as that created by a living being perceiving, and subsequently acting upon, the world. The interval presumes an element of selection in which beings determine the impact of what they perceive, and act accordingly. Thus, for Deleuze following Bergson, we exist as ' "centres of indetermination" which are formed in the acentred universe of movement-images',[14] incurring the world around us through the actions we perform based upon the information we perceive. From the universal flux of images we carve out the movement-images through which we understand the world, ensuring that our existence is determined by our sensory-motor interaction with the plane of immanence. What we perceive (sensory input) we act upon (action), the interval between the two containing affection (the internal reaction to sensory stimuli, often expressed through small motor reactions such as facial expressions). Thus, in *Cinema 1*, Deleuze ties the indirect expression of the whole to a sensory-motor regime that he finds in cinema. Deleuze identifies three primary images that appear in film which correlate with our experience as centres of indetermination: perception-image, affection-image and action-image. The majority of *Cinema 1* amplifies the different ways in which these images function in cinema, including additional discussions of the impulse-image, which exists between affect and action, and reflection- and relation-images (I will return to various of these image categories at different points throughout this book).

The important point to note at this stage is the influence of Bergson's thought on Deleuze's work. It shapes the manner in which Deleuze conceives of the role of montage in constructing movement in the movement-image to such an extent that Mullarkey refers to it as the 'script' from which Deleuze works in his *Cinema* books.[15] As I will demonstrate, this is particularly so in his discussion of the action-image, which, due to its emphasis on sensory-motor continuity, seems perfectly akin to Bergson's understanding of the function of the individual as centre of indetermination in a world of images. Accordingly, Deleuze's conclusions regarding the action-image and the US western, which derive from Bergson's worldview, are disturbed by a consideration of cinemas of spectacle like early silent cinema and the spaghetti western.

To summarize this section, the movement-image presents an indirect image of time, of time organized around a sensory-motor regime that moves from perception, through affection, to action. In this respect it is an indirect image of time, of time subordinate to (sensory-motor) movement. This is perhaps most easy to understand in the action-image, where time is edited to suit the movements of a character. Thus in the action-image especially, cinema appears to duplicate the nature of human perception and action. The time-image by contrast expresses a direct image of time, of the aberrant movements of duration that intervene in the interval between perception and action and disrupt the sensory-motor movement from perception to action. This might happen in the wandering of characters without purpose or goal, or the disruptive eruption of the past in the present, for example through a character's exploration of memory. Both of these phenomena, usually illustrated through different forms of discontinuous editing, characterize much post-war European art cinema. Such direct images of time facilitate the exploration of the virtual whole of time, as opposed to the actualized, spatialized and indirect view of duration that is manifest in the movement-image. The key to understanding this distinction more fully, and indeed, the role of spectacle in reappraising Deleuze's thinking on the action-image, is Deleuze's conception of montage.

Deleuze, Montage, US Western (action-image)

For Deleuze, expressions of the whole, whether indirect or direct, are most clearly seen through montage. This is the case whether the whole is perceived through continuous editing that joins together mobile sections of duration (movement-images), or discontinuous edits which express the impossibility of grasping duration's open and infinitely changing nature (time-images).[16] Contrary to the way certain forms of editing are understood, especially classical Hollywood's continuity system, Deleuze does not consider montage to function in the service of narrative construction. Rather, Deleuze believes that narrative is a product of montage.[17] He outlines four schools of montage, American (by which he means US), Soviet, French and German, but, unusually, these are considered four different ways of exploring the whole, rather than four different forms of narration. When Deleuze discusses the Soviet, French and German schools this distinction is particularly clear, as he primarily explores the arrangement of images rather than the development of narrative. In the case of the American school, however, the one most pertinent for this discussion, montage and narrative are at their closest in Deleuze's writing. The development of narrative is seemingly at one with the development of montage. This is at least partly due to the coincidence of the sensory-motor regime of Deleuze's Bergsonian-inspired theories with the centrality of the sensory-motor capabilities of the protagonist in classical Hollywood cinema.

In spite of his emphasis on form (or at least, montage) as opposed to narrative, like many commentators before him who focused on the development of narrative as an indicator of cinema's "maturity", Deleuze considers "cinema" to begin in earnest in the 1910s, in the case of the American school with the work of directors like Griffith. Deleuze describes Griffith's conceptualization of the whole as 'a great organic unity'.[18] For Deleuze, Griffith organizes movement-images accordingly, such that the different parts of this great organism are unified, be they 'men and women, rich and poor, town and country, North and South, interiors and exteriors, etc'.[19] Thus Griffith's use of parallel montage is seen by Deleuze as a way of organizing the diverse elements of the 'ideal community'[20] of the nation. Deleuze notes that the organic unity of the whole is threatened when these binary opposites are brought into conflict, acting and reacting upon one another until a resolution is reached. This format, akin to a duel, produces different rhythms in different films, which are expressed by different alternating or parallel montage forms. Deleuze is thus able to conclude from the presence of Griffith's unified organism that

> The American cinema draws from it [montage] its most solid form; from the general situation to the re-established or transformed situation through the intermediary of a duel, of a convergence of actions. American montage is organico-active. It is wrong to criticise it as being subordinate to the narration; it is the reverse, for the narrativity flows from this conception of montage.[21]

This pattern, in which the organic whole is threatened, and then order restored, appears again in Chapter 9 of *Cinema 1*, in which Deleuze discusses the action-image, and its exemplar, the US western. For Deleuze, the action-image, the dominant form of the movement-image and typified by classical Hollywood cinema, is one in which situation (or milieu) and action are closely intertwined. The milieu impacts upon the character, who finds him or herself forced to act. In so doing, the character's reactions modify the situation. Here we see the sensory-motor continuity of the organism at the centre of montage, as the character is tested in their ability to act upon what they see. As they do so they complete a transformation of the situation by moving from perception, through affect, to decisive action. Deleuze notes of this process that 'The action is itself a duel of forces, a series of duels: duels with the milieu, with the others, with itself.'[22] Deleuze designates this montage one of SAS', the same movement from situation, through action, to changed situation that he found in montage around the time of Griffith.

Although Deleuze discusses other genres as action-images, the US western seems the prime example. This is not only because the duel in the western illustrates the duel at the heart of every action image, but also because in the western it is through physical actions that the individual comes to represent the collective (the sheriff killing the bandits and saving the town, or the cavalry putting the "Red Indians" to flight and saving the settlers, etc.). In the western, then, sensory-motor triumph raises the individual to the equal of the milieu, both the tough country and its inhabitants. The clearest example Deleuze gives of this process is *The Man Who Shot Liberty Valance* (1962), in which the situation (milieu) clearly shifts – from old, lawless west, to new, lawful west – through the actions of the protagonists Ransom Stoddard (James Stewart) and Tom Doniphon (John Wayne) in confronting and killing the outlaw Liberty Valance (Lee Marvin). It is perhaps based on this kind of film that Deleuze – echoing Jacques Rancière, interviewed in *Cahiers du cinéma* in 1976[23] – argues that 'American cinema constantly shoots and reshoots a single fundamental film, which is the birth of a nation-civilization, whose first version was provided by Griffith.'[24]

Yet, although Deleuze is arguing that it is the organic conception of the whole (which, he considers, emerges with Griffith) that causes this repetition of the same myth of origin over and over again (and that any narrative of national identity which might appear in these films is a consequence of this montage and not the other way around), it would appear that this conception of the whole as a unified organism is also an ideological one. A certain degree of ambiguity exists, then, concerning whether Deleuze is purely analysing the formal construction (montage) of cinema, as this does not entirely explain the manner in which the whole is conceived of in the

American montage school (and indeed, the action-image of the US western) as Deleuze describes it.

Implicit in Deleuze's reading is an ideological interpretation of narrative, albeit, for Deleuze, of a narrative that is a product of the manner in which the whole is conceived in the first place. Consider for example his comments regarding the use of montage to construct an 'ideal community', which Deleuze seems to envisage in a manner similar to Benedict Anderson's 'imagined political community'[25] of the nation. This is constituted in the American montage school of elements of the nation, as he states: 'men and women, rich and poor, town and country, North and South'. Add to this Deleuze's specific comments regarding the reiteration of a 'birth of nation-civilization' myth in US cinema, and his conclusion – from his analysis of the Hollywood action-image as demonstrative of the three Nietzschian forms of history outlined in *The Untimely Meditations* (1873–1876) that I explore further in Chapter 3 – that US cinema is very effective in creating a universal form of history.[26] From this evidence it would appear that Deleuze is actually discussing the construction of a historically informed national identity, simultaneously in terms of both montage and narrative content. It is unclear in the case of the American montage school, then, as to whether narrative proceeds entirely from montage (as Deleuze claims), because the two are inextricably linked in his argument, both being a product of the ideological conception of the whole (also, it seems, the nation) from which montage and narrative stem.

As I argued in *Deleuze, Cinema and National Identity* (2006), the ideology underpinning the US construction of the action-image in its SAS' formula is the triumphalism inherent in the belief in Manifest Destiny.[27] Nowhere in classical Hollywood cinema is this clearer than the western, in which the triumphal settler individual (as representative of the collective) in his duel with the milieu is precisely the product, and expression, of westward expansion. In this respect, as exemplar of the US western as action-image I would cite *The Searchers* (1956) as opposed to *The Man Who Shot Liberty Valance*. In *The Searchers*, the revenge narrative ensures that by tracking down and killing the murderous, kidnapping, Comanche Indians, Ethan Edwards (John Wayne) and his nephew Martin (Jeffrey Hunter) are able to rejuvenate the settler community. Thus a new situation arises from their actions. It is possible, then, to consider the unbroken sensory-motor continuity at the heart of the action-image as a product of an ideology that informs the structure of US montage (expression of the whole). Seen in this light the SAS' structure develops as a solution to US cinema's desire to express a narrative of Manifest Destiny. Therefore, to understand the manner in which the movement-image functions in its construction of national identity (the implicit reading inherent in Deleuze's work on the US western as action-image) it is necessary to consider both form and content, both montage and narrative, in ideological terms. As I will discuss further, therefore, understanding the context in which cinema is produced and consumed is extremely important.

To summarize this section, in the case of the US western as action-image, although Deleuze argues that 'narrativity flows from'[28] the conception of montage of the (national) montage school, this should not be understood as a causal relationship, but as an inextricably intertwined interaction between ideology, montage and narrative. It is never entirely clear, in fact, which underpins the other. We might consider this further by remembering the various other contextual factors involved, as cinematic form does not emerge in a vacuum. The parallel editing that Deleuze describes as constitutive of the organic unity of the American (US) montage school existed before Griffith used it to construct a racist image of the national whole in *Birth of a Nation* (1915). It became of great importance around the time of Griffith, however, because it was a moment in cinema history that coincided with the consolidation of continuity editing as an industrial norm in the USA. In fact, the emergence of films like *Birth of a Nation* was the result of a complex interplay of developments in the USA, including: elements related to technological innovations (the multi-reel projector which enabled feature length screenings, and longer narrative formats); industrial structures (the growth of the studio system, a rationalized order of production, and the prominence of the producer); and social and aesthetic considerations (the increased targeting of the lucrative bourgeois viewers, as opposed to the predominantly working-class audiences of the earliest cinema, requiring both a longer narrative format – often the adaptation of a novel or play, as was the case with *Birth of a Nation* – and the upgrading and expansion of Nickelodeons).[29] Therefore it is difficult to consider the development of parallel editing in a film like *Birth of a Nation*, and the racist ends to which it was used in the construction of an image of US national identity, without recourse to a broader consideration of the context in which it developed. This is a more detailed understanding of context than Deleuze's conceptualization of cinema's ability to express the whole (a kind of tacitly assumed ideological critique of national identity) otherwise allows.

With this in mind, I will move to critically examine the assumptions structuring Deleuze's work in light of developments in our understanding of cinematic spectacle, coincidentally from scholarship on early silent cinema

that appeared around the same time as Deleuze's *Cinema* books. This provides the next step towards an enhanced understanding of the way cinemas
of spectacle – like the spaghetti western – engage politically with ideology.

Cinema of Attractions

Cinematic spectacle has received coverage in a number of manifestations,
from pornography to the Hollywood blockbuster, probably the most famous
example being Laura Mulvey's psychoanalytically informed feminist work
on the female body as spectacle from 1975.[30] Perhaps the major development since Mulvey's work in the 1970s has been an increased emphasis on
understanding cinema, including cinemas of spectacle, in specific contexts.
This is often pursued in terms of national contexts of production, and with
reference to industrial and technological concerns; social, cultural and
political considerations that can be seen to influence the aesthetic and/or
narrative; and the nature and conditions of distribution and reception.
In terms of Deleuzian film scholarship and spectacle, in comparison, very
little exists, although Amy Herzog has broken new ground with *Dreams
of Difference, Songs of the Same* (2009) and her contribution to *Afterimages of
Gilles Deleuze's Film Philosophy* (2009), deploying Deleuze's ideas to address
the musical's 'nonlinear deployment of space and time' and thereby exploring 'cinematic spectacles in relation to the notion of a historical image'.[31]
In this chapter I would like to go further still, and discuss how an examination of work on spectacle (and indeed, narrative) in early silent cinema
enables a reconsideration of some of the assumptions underpinning
Deleuze's concept of the movement-image.

  In 'Cinema of Attractions' (1986), Tom Gunning discusses early silent
cinema from approximately 1895–1906, and rethinks previous histories of
cinema that had, until then, been 'written and theorized under the hege-
mony of narrative films'.[32] Prior to Gunning, histories of cinema had positioned early silent films as the "primitive" forerunners of a more "developed"
narrative cinema. By contrast, Gunning argues that early silent films were
not intended as narratives in the classical Hollywood sense. Instead they
were manufactured as attractions to be consumed in contexts like vaude-
ville programmes, cafe concerts, music halls, amusement parks, travelling
fairground theatres and circuses, where a film was simply one more entertainment on a varied bill. At that time just seeing a film (or indeed, seeing
the phenomenon of film) was an attraction in itself. For this reason early
silent films should not be understood as primitive attempts at narrative, but

as deliberately eye-catching spectacles designed for an audience desirous of immediate distraction. To make this point Gunning compares early silent cinemas of attraction with the emergence of amusement parks, like Coney Island in New York, at around the same time. These contextual considerations explain why many early silent films worked hard to solicit the gaze of the spectator, using special effects (slow motion, multiple exposure, etc.), slapstick and other visual gags, direct address to the camera (characters winking at the audience, magicians bowing), close-ups (either for titillation or simply to demonstrate the ability of the new medium to render objects larger than life), and so on.

Gunning's intervention drew together two very different cinematic styles, those of the Lumière brothers and Georges Méliès. These early cinema pioneers had previously been considered the forerunners of two distinct film traditions: the non-narrative (or documentary) and narrative respectively. For Gunning, however, they were both part of the cinema of attractions. The early actuality films of the Lumière brothers (where the attraction was a glimpse of real life captured on film, such as a train arriving in a station, or workers leaving a factory) were repositioned alongside the trick films of Georges Méliès, with their fantastical stories and special effects. For Gunning, in neither instance was there any attempt to create the kind of narrative that would later emerge in the cinema of directors like Griffith. Rather, alongside the quotidian events documented by the Lumières, the narratives that exist in the works of Méliès were reconsidered by Gunning as an excuse for a string of otherwise disconnected spectacles. Thus, in early silent cinema, narrative, if there is one, is of less importance than the spectacles it enables.

Although Marshall Deutelbaum and André Gaudreault have noted the existence of narrative in static shot films like the Lumière's *L'Arroseur arrosé/ The Spinkler Sprinkled* (1895), this is of less import than the spectacle it enables, in this case a visual gag of a mischievous young boy playing a prank on a man busy watering the plants in a garden.[33] As Noël Burch observes, the 'punitive ending' of many such early silent narratives (in this case the young boy is given a smacked bottom) is 'straight from the circus (the clown's closing kick in the behind)',[34] as though marking the conclusion of a discrete comedy routine, again, of one act on a varied bill. Indeed, for theatre magician Méliès the idea for a film would often begin with the culminating spectacle, with a pretence of a narrative then being created to lead up to it as though building towards the headline act of a cabaret bill.[35] For Gunning, then, there is a break in the history of cinema, around 1906, which illustrates the discontinuous nature of the medium when seen in terms of its function within specific historical contexts. Importantly, this can now be considered a shift from a cinema of attractions to a narrative based cinema, due to the kinds of contextual factors outlined previously in relation to *The Birth of a Nation*, rather than an evolutionary transition from "primitive" to "advanced" expressions of narrative.

Gunning's criticism of previous evolutionary histories of cinema illustrates the potential difficulty posed by Deleuze's formally conceived image categories, in particular due to Deleuze's desire to "fit" Bergson's ideas onto cinema. It is perhaps this aim that most influences Deleuze's pinpointing of montage as the starting point for his discussion of the movement-image. It can also be said to structure the particular kind of history of cinema that his taxonomy of images constructs (regardless of Deleuze's statements to the contrary,[36] and a topic I return to in Chapter 6), and undoubtedly influences the question of whether narrative is a consequence of montage or whether (in the case of US cinema at least) the narrative function drives the construction of the ideologically conceived organic whole that is seen in and through the montage. With Gunning's reconsideration of early silent cinema in mind, then, I will begin to unpack these issues.

In *Cinema 1*, Deleuze writes at length about the status of the earliest form of cinema, the single fixed shot film that existed prior to developments in editing, in relation to the movement-image. He states:

> What happened when the camera was fixed? The situation has often been described. In the first place the frame is defined by a unique and frontal point of view which is that of the spectator on an invariable set: there is therefore no communication of mutually referring variable sets. In the second place, the shot is a uniquely spatial determination, indicating a 'slice of space' at a particular distance from the camera, from close-up to long shot (immobile sections): movement is therefore not extracted for itself and remains attached to elements, characters and things which serve as its moving body or vehicle. Finally, the whole is identical to the set in depth, such that the moving body goes through it in passing from one spatial shot/plane [*plan*] to another, from one parallel slice to another, each having its independence or its focus. *There is therefore neither change nor duration properly speaking*, in as much as duration implies a completely different conception of depth, which mixes up and dislocates parallel zones instead of superimposing them. *We can therefore define a primitive state of the cinema where the image is in movement rather than being movement-image*. It was at this primitive state that Bergson's critique was directed.[37] [my italics]

Early silent cinema, for Deleuze, is 'primitive' in that it is not yet move-ment-image. Prior to this he notes the importance of montage (and the mobile camera) in effecting the transition from cinema's 'primitive' state to movement-image, citing Bergson's *Matter and Memory* in the process:

> The evolution of the cinema, the conquest of its own essence or novelty, was to take place through montage, the mobile camera and the emanci-pation of the view point, which became separate from projection. The shot would then stop being a spatial category and become a temporal one, and the section would no longer be immobile, but mobile. The camera would rediscover that very movement-image of the first chapter of *Matter and Memory*.[38]

So far, then, montage is apparently an essential component of the move-ment-image. Even so, for Deleuze there is a certain sense in which the fixed shot of early silent cinema is still considered a movement-image. Deleuze states: 'the spatial and fixed shot tended to produce a pure movement-image, a tendency which imperceptibly came to be acted out by the mobili-sation of the camera in space, or by montage.'[39] Thus he argues that, even in early silent cinema, a small movement within the fixed shot illustrates a qualitative change in the whole:

> Take a fixed shot where the characters move: they modify their respective positions in a framed set; but this modification would be completely arbitrary if it did not also express something in the course of changing, a qualitative alteration, even a minute one, in the whole which passes through the set.[40]

For Deleuze, this potential for expressing the whole, contained even in the fixed shot, is then further formulated in different ways by different styles of montage. Accordingly, the American school is considered the peak of the movement-image's development because its form of montage provides the model closest to Deleuze's Bergsonian worldview, its SAS' organic unity being constructed out of the same sensory-motor images (perception-, affection- and action-images) as those which we deploy in our everyday lives to make sense of the plane of immanence that is our universe. Yet had Deleuze looked more closely at early silent cinema, his thinking with regard to the emergence of the movement-image might have been different.

By referring to early silent cinema as 'primitive', Deleuze is describing its state in relation to the more advanced expression (albeit still indirect) of duration that would appear with montage. While Deleuze's argument may appear similar to the position of the film historians that Gunning is critiquing, Deleuze is not, in fact, recreating the histories of cinema that positioned early silent film as primitive in terms of narrative construction. However, leaving aside Deleuze's decontextualization of the cinema of attractions, what is evident in the above quotes is that his reliance on Bergson's theories means that his 'evolution' of cinema also imposes upon early silent cinema a 'primitive' status, only this time in relation to montage.

In *Cinema 1*, Griffith's unified organic expression of the whole is the first one discussed by Deleuze, and the standard against which the Soviet, French and German schools are explained. The centrality of Griffith to Deleuze's project, then, is a function of the Bergsonian impetus behind Deleuze's thinking. In an attempt to demonstrate that Bergson's condemnation of the 'cinematographic illusion' was due to the 'primitive' state of cinema Bergson might have experienced at the time he was writing, early silent cinema is placed somehow "outside" the functioning of "cinema" in terms of movement- and time-image, with a peculiar status (at least in its earliest form, as fixed shot) as at once 'pure movement-image', and yet at the same time, only a very 'primitive' form of movement-image. For Bergson's work to "fit" Deleuze's model of cinema, Deleuze must prioritize montage (over the seeming lack of editing found in much early silent cinema) as it provides the means for constructing different conceptions of the whole. Due to the sensory-motor nature of Bergson's conceptualization of our position in relation to the universal flux of matter that appear as images, once montage is determined by Deleuze as the means for producing (if not 'pure' or 'primitive' then perhaps we should assume, 'advanced') movement-images, the epitome of the movement-image becomes the action-image (especially genres like the US western), due to its construction through the sensory-motor oriented rules of continuity editing.

Non-Continuous Whole: Early Silent Attraction-Image

Having seen how Bergson's ideas predetermined Deleuze's thinking regarding the primacy of montage in the consideration of the non-'primitive' movement-image, I will now consider how the cinema of attractions is actually suggestive of another type of movement-image altogether, the attraction-image. This will illustrate a major problem with Deleuze's movement- and time-image categories (which recurs throughout the book), which is that they are too neat a reterritorialization of cinema into categories that presuppose the films themselves, often due in large part to Deleuze's heavy reliance on Bergson's ideas.

First, how did early silent cinema construct the attraction-image? Already certain re-interpretations of Deleuze's *Cinema* books could be said to point in the direction of the attraction-image. For example, scholars have noted the existence of time-images in early silent cinema. In *Gilles Deleuze's Time Machine*, Rodowick notes that

> Deleuze's historical understanding of primitive cinema is terribly remiss. By his own criteria one can see elements of the "time-image" emerging through the early period . . . Following a classical film theory paradigm, Deleuze overstresses the importance of montage in this respect. Thus Deleuze's unfamiliarity with the stylistic variety and complexity of early cinema causes him to miss its implications for his own theory.[41]

Furthermore, in *Photography, Cinema, Memory* (2009) Damian Sutton argues for the existence of the time-image in the Lumière film *Barque sortant du port/Boat Leaving the Port* (1895), and the '*ever-present-present*' of its perpetual narrative moment.[42] Indeed, in the preface to the English edition of *Cinema 2*, Deleuze hints that he may have experienced this kind of revelation since the publication of *Cinema 1*, suggesting that pre-war cinema (that previously identified with the movement-image in *Cinema 1*) and even silent cinema contain evidence of 'the workings of a very pure time-image which has always been breaking through, holding back or encompassing the movement-image'.[43] Yet I wish to push this line of reasoning further and consider whether, in addition to identifying the discontinuous temporality of the time-image (its independent 'movement of world'[44]) in early silent cinema, we might also find a non-continuous temporality that signals another form of movement-image.

In 'Non-continuity, Continuity, Discontinuity' (1984), Gunning examines four different types of early silent films, categorizing them in terms of montage. The third of these is continuity editing, and the fourth is the use of parallel editing to construct the illusion of a coherent narrative world that would eventually become synonymous with Griffith. The second, however, which precedes Griffith historically (although dying out by around 1904, at more or less the same time as the single, static shot film), is the non-continuity editing of the trick film often associated with Méliès. In the trick film a disruption in the editing is used to construct a spectacle. For example, stop motion or splicing together of shots might create the illusion of a magical transformation. The splice was initially considered by Méliès to be a substitute for the magician's trapdoor, as in *Escamotage d'une dame au théâtre Robert Houdin/The Vanishing Lady* (1896), in which Houdin's theatre director Méliès, directing events both on and off-screen, causes a lady to vanish from under a sheet, a skeleton to reappear in her place, and then the lady to reappear once again.

In a follow-up article specifically on the trick film, ' "Primitive Cinema" A Frame-up? Or The Trick's on Us' (1989), Gunning argues that, in contrast to the prevailing scholarly view (also apparent in Deleuze's work) that there was very little editing in the early silent period, in actual fact a great deal of work was put into maintaining the illusion of a single point of view from a static position, on a certain space, through editing. This could be considered a form of continuity editing (a continuity of framing), but in the trick film this continuity could be used to foreground the non-continuous spatio-temporal nature of events on screen. As an example, Gunning discusses a Pathé trick film *La Soubrette ingénieuse/Ingenious Soubrette* (1903). Through the use of a constructed set, the viewer is led to believe that they have a continuous view on an unchanging room interior, only for the suddenly unexpected, "impossible" physical actions of the maid cleaning the room (she appears to move up the wall in the process of hanging a picture) to render visible both the trick and the (non-continuous) montage that has enabled it. The splice that has been concealed by the continuity of the viewpoint of the frame is revealed when the audience witnesses the unexpected movement of the maid. It becomes clear that what appeared to be a continuous shot of a room was in actual fact spliced into footage of a purpose built set, enabling the appearance of the maid's impossible vertical movement up the wall.[45]

Thus montage is evident in early silent cinema. At a most basic level, producing the simplest of tricks through stop motion substitutions involved splicing of the film (rather than simply a pause in filming in which to re-arrange objects in the frame) because, due to the hand cranking mechanisms of early cameras, there was a variable speed of film passing through the camera at the point of starting and stopping filming. For the substitution effect of the trick to be successful (the foregrounding of non-continuity), this slowing down and speeding up needed to be edited out so that objects on screen would appear to suddenly disappear and appear.[46] Contrary to Deleuze's understanding of the static shot in early silent cinema, then, and even taking into account the shot's ability to express the changing whole as 'pure movement-image', a type of editing akin to that which Deleuze analyses in later silent movement-images did actually exist at that time. Therefore, the major ramification of non-continuous montage is that, even if we agree with Deleuze that the fixed shot is a 'pure movement-image' in the sense in which he meant it, because it can also potentially consist of montage the fixed shot may also create a different kind of movement-image.

As is illustrated in Méliès's trick films, the fixed shot film is a movement-image in that it has the potential to create an indirect image of time, to express a non-continuous spatio-temporal whole. This may happen without our noticing, as this movement-image may have been constructed so as to conceal its existence as montage, by maintaining continuity of framing. On the other hand, it may choose to reveal its hand through the spectacle of a trick created by editing, even if the fixed viewpoint does not (appear to) change. The trick reveals the non-continuous space-time of this form of the early silent movement-image, the attraction-image. In *Escamotage d'une dame au théâtre Robert Houdin, La Soubrette ingénieuse*, and numerous other such films, non-continuous montage is foregrounded by the sudden jolt of surprise on the part of the spectator when something entirely unexpected happens (the trick, created by montage) in what appears to be an otherwise continuous space constructed by continuity of framing. This surprise felt at this spectacle of incongruity shatters any sense of a unified whole formed through montage, or indeed, of a continuous universe organized around a coherent sensory-motor regime.

Discussing precisely the temporality of the cinema of attractions, Gunning refers to this shock effect as 'a jolt of pure presence, soliciting surprise, astonishment or pure curiosity instead of following the enigmas on which narrative depends'.[47] The ellipsis revealed by the illusion or trick illustrates that non-continuous space-times have been carefully spliced together to create the attraction-image. In some cases, as in *Escamotage d'une dame au théâtre Robert Houdin* the space is continuous (a simple theatrical stage on which to perform the trick of the disappearing lady), although the space-time clearly is not. In others, like *La Soubrette ingénieuse* the jolt of surprise reveals that both space and time are non-continuous. The continuity of framing on the set, however, ensures these different space-times do not become discontinuous, but rather remain non-continuous. There is, then, movement created through montage in early silent cinema, an indirect expression of the whole prior to Griffith's organic conception. This movement does not provide the discontinuity associated with the direct expressions of duration found in the time-image. Instead we are faced with non-continuous montage, and a non-continuous expression of the whole. The attraction-image is therefore not a time-image, but a form of early silent movement-image.

It might be argued that Deleuze's conception of montage does allow for a form of montage without editing, even if chapter three of *Cinema 1* (which is dedicated to the subject) primarily refers to the conjoining of blocs of space-time in the manner I have been discussing. For example, in different places in the *Cinema* books Deleuze suggests that montage can happen within the shot (for example as a result of framing[48] or depth of field[49]). Even so, there are numerous ways in which early filmmakers introduce non-continuous movement into the film, creating this particular form of, as it were, "montage without montage", or indeed, moving camera. In Méliès's oeuvre alone these include in-camera lap dissolves to shift between locales (created without editing, as in a pre-cinematic Magic Lantern); the use of rolling canvas backdrops that suggest vast sea or skyscapes against which to superimpose movement; and the movement of objects in front of the static camera to create an effect equivalent to that of a dolly (or tracking) shot in *L'Homme à la tête en caoutchouc/The Man with the Rubber Head* (1901). This last example again creates a non-continuous view of time, as the impossible inflation of the disembodied head of Méliès is clearly at odds with the seemingly continuous space-time in which it appears to be happening.[50] We might even consider Méliès's trademark use of multiple exposure (running the same film through the camera several times to create the impression that actions filmed in the same space at different times are occurring simultaneously) to produce the illusion of several non-continuous spaces. This is seen, for example, in the line up of multiple Méliès' playing different musical instruments in *L'Homme orchestre/The One Man Band* (1900). We see one Méliès, then another next to him, then another, and so on. These movements are all expressive of the relationship between parts of a set (the relational movement of bodies or objects within the shot) that Deleuze considered one of the two defining facets of the movement-image (the other being its ability to imply movement of the whole).[51] Thus, although for Deleuze cinema reaches maturity with movement/montage, there was non-continuous movement in early silent cinema, whether created by the splice, in-camera, or in front of camera, trickery.

Furthermore, along with Gunning we can extend the notion of the attraction-image to consider the, as it were, "narrative of spectacles" of the trick film as itself non-continuous, even in the cases where a more conventional form of montage is evident. In Méliès's *Voyage à travers l'impossible/Impossible Voyage* (1904) we do not watch a narrative of a (model) train flying to the sun so much as a series of spectacles strung along an excuse for a narrative. They include everything from a train taking off from a mountain peak; flying through a storm, past planets and fiery comets; flying into the sun's yawning mouth; intrepid explorers frozen in an ice box (*glaciere*); a submarine plummet from sun to earth; the submarine under the sea, and so on. For Gunning, such 'attractions do show a sort of temporal structure, but the structure consists more of framing a momentary appearance than an actual development and transformation in time'.[52] Through these various techniques we do not experience a coherent space-time produced by continuous action across discontinuous spaces (an SAS' action-image). Nor is it exactly synonymous with the discontinuous movement of world that we find in the time-image. In *Voyage à travers l'impossible* in particular, spaces do exist before the train arrives in the frame, and persist after it leaves again. Yet this broader movement of world does not function to draw attention to the existence of actions within the encompassing virtual realm of duration as it does in the time-image. Instead, it establishes individual spaces as spectacles in their own right. Thus in the early silent attraction-image, the movement (action) of the machine (train, submarine) becomes equal to the situation (passes through the space) only momentarily, before the next non-continuous shift to a new space, which the machine will eventually catch up with once more. The two movements (movement of machine across space, and autonomous movement of spaces) exist almost in parallel, as a string of fantastic, non-continuous spaces are put on display, tenuously linked only by the foregrounded "narrative" provided by the expedition of the flying train.

In this respect the attraction-image is extremely close to the 'vector' of the ASA' action-image. This is particularly so, as Deleuze argues, of the parade of locations found in the westerns of Howard Hawks, Anthony Mann and Sam Peckinpah, the 'knotted rope' or '*skeleton space*' that draws together disconnected locations that exist without a seemingly identifiable encompassing milieu.[53] However, the attraction-image remains distinct from the ASA' action image (even when the two are closest to touching in the stylistic convergence of Peckinpah's westerns of the late 1960s and early 1970s with the spaghetti western) due to the greater degree of decontextualization or disconnection of character from location that exists in the attraction-image. This degree of disconnection is typical of the attraction-image, as is seen in both Méliès films and the spaghetti western, movies that very often position characters as fantasy tourists in spectacular settings. Elizabeth Ezra has argued, for example, that the ability of Méliès's films to transport the spectator to fantastic, "Other" worlds correlates with the 'transportation revolution' of the time, thematizing the new opportunities to encounter previously unknown locations and peoples that were opened to tourists by automobile and aeroplane travel.[54] Thus, for Ezra, *Le Voyage dans la lune/A Trip to the Moon* (1902) can be interpreted as a parody of colonial conflict, *Voyage à travers l'impossible* as a satire on the irresponsibility of upper class tourists, *Le Raid Paris-Monte Carlo en deux heures/An Adventurous Automobile Trip* (1905) as an exposition of the emergence of the popular as a political and cultural force, and so on.[55] As I will demonstrate momentarily, it is precisely this use of fantasy to explore 'social possibilities'[56] that is deployed by the attraction-image spaghetti western, also through its disconnection of character and fantasy locale, to provide the potential for political critique in a genre that may otherwise appear remarkably politically unengaged.

To summarize, in the attraction-image montage is not used to construct the continuous view of time that characterizes the movement-image. Yet nor does this structure correspond to the discontinuous linkages found in the time-image. Rather, montage is motivated primarily by the construction of non-continuous spectacles, for a viewpoint situated to facilitate appreciation of the 'display'[57] of events taking place on screen. The attraction-image, then, takes the form of a series of spectacles through which a non-continuous movement of the whole can be perceived, even in the fixed shot, through non-continuous montage. Therefore, in contrast to Deleuze's decision to interpret Bergson's pronouncement on the 'cinematographic illusion' as a statement pertaining to the lack of montage in early silent cinema, it is possible to consider the cinema of attractions as producing a certain kind of early silent movement-image. It is an indirect expression of duration after all (as are all movement-images), only of a non-continuous experience of time, not pre-determined by the sensory-motor emphasis Deleuze draws from Bergson's philosophy when defining the action-image.

What these early silent examples show is that a more enhanced understanding of the movement-image is possible if we consider the context in which it emerged. Such an approach impacts not only on the formal emphasis, but also the historical nature of Deleuze's *Cinema* books. Although in the preface to both the English and the French editions of *Cinema 1* Deleuze is at pains to deny that his *Cinema* books construct a history of cinema, it is clear from the above analysis that in terms of montage Deleuze considers cinema an evolutionary form. As it is montage that reveals the whole (either directly or indirectly), then Deleuze's concepts of movement- and time-image can be considered to mark evolutionary shifts in this history of cinema. The shift which Deleuze perceives in *Cinema 1*, from primitive cinema to movement-image – itself a product of his engagement with Bergson as opposed to a conclusion reached by examining early silent cinema – looks rather different when examined archeologically, and contextually, rather than as an apparently linear, evolutionary development of film form. Thus, when the cinema of attractions is seen as a historically, industrially and socially specific phenomenon produced with an audience and mode of consumption in mind (as opposed to a primitive stage in the development of cinema towards montage), then both its status as movement-image and, indeed, the totalizing conclusions of Deleuze's taxonomy are called into question.

Early silent cinema, however, is only the tip of the iceberg. Gunning concludes his piece on the cinema of attractions by noting how, even though narrative cinema comes to replace early silent spectacle once continuity editing progresses towards the norm (roughly speaking in the period 1907–1913), nevertheless, 'the system of attraction remains an essential part of popular film-making'[58] which reappears at different times throughout film history. This is evident in research that notes the continued presence of spectacle throughout cinema history, everything from classical Hollywood musicals through Japanese Godzilla movies to contemporary digital effects-driven blockbusters. For the remainder of the chapter, then, I will explore one such example, from another archaeological layer in which the attraction-image resurfaces (albeit in a slightly different form), that of the spaghetti western in the 1960s and 1970s.

Attraction-Image not Action-Image: Spaghetti Westerns

Although usually associated with Italy, the spaghetti western was an international coproduction genre formula that flourished in Europe during the 1960s and into the mid-1970s.[59] The rise of the spaghetti western coincided with the decline in production of the Hollywood western in the early 1960s.[60] Spaghetti westerns were not only popular in Europe and the USA, but also in various parts of Latin America, Africa, the Middle East and Asia.[61] For many years the spaghetti western was misunderstood as a "primitive" or "derivative" take on the US western, hence the derogatory nickname. Serious study of the spaghetti western only began to grow with the turn to European popular genre cinema in the early 1990s.[62] In particular, moving beyond initial attempts by Christopher Frayling to recuperate certain Italian westerns (such as those of Sergio Leone), as 'critical' westerns that formally responded to the ideology of the US form,[63] Christopher Wagstaff and Dimitris Eleftheriotis turned their attention to the cheaper, and often more widespread serial films, like the Django and Ringo movies, studying them as products of specific contexts. These lower budget serial films outnumber the classical narratives of Leone's westerns. They are also distinctive in their narrative structure. Typically this style eschews the psychological motivation and linear development of both US westerns and Leone's films (and consequently their interaction between individuals and milieu so typical of the SAS' form of the action-image), being marked instead by a repetitious series of spectacles typically involving gunfights, horseback riding, barroom brawls and other action sequences.

The contextualizing factors foregrounded by these critics demonstrate why spaghetti westerns can be viewed as attraction-images rather than action-images. That is, the spaghetti western can be considered not as a derivative take on the classical Hollywood western, but altogether different from the US action-image western. Like early silent cinema, understanding the spaghetti western as an attraction-image relies as much on the extent to which it can be seen to be "fit for purpose" (in the sense of an image constructed specifically for a certain type of audience and viewing experience), as it does on formal comparison with a dominant, apparently normative US action-image western. Such an approach enables an appreciation of the degree to which the spaghetti western both engages with, and departs from, the editing format (and narrative structure) of the US action-image western, both formally and ideologically.

When viewed as products of the context in which they were produced, and the target market they courted, the episodic nature of spaghetti westerns appear deliberately formulated. In the spaghetti western, the disconnected episodic pattern avoids the construction of an indirect expression of the whole (as in the SAS' action-image), replacing the action and reaction of milieu and individual with a string of spectacles in which these two forces meet periodically. These spectacles construct a series of duels that do not ultimately function to change the situation, but rather to display the non-continuous nature of the whole as spectacle. Even so, this pattern can be considered to function slightly differently depending on the contextual filter through which we choose to view it. To begin with, then, I examine how Wagstaff and Eleftheriotis provide different perspectives to assist us in understanding the distinction between spaghetti westerns when viewed as products of national or transnational contexts of production and distribution.

National/International Genre: *Django* (1966)

Analysing the spaghetti western within the Italian national context, Wagstaff provides an account of the industrial factors relating to their production context and of the manner in which they were consumed. Industrially the spaghetti western was the result of a number of conditions, including: a fragmented production sector made up of numerous small companies;

limited possibilities for distribution and the consequently conservative approach of distributors; and available state subsidies and tax rebates favouring international coproductions. Together these factors were conducive to the production of serial low budget genre films that, due to the specifics of this situation, guaranteed producers a return on their money.[64] Thus spaghetti westerns flourished alongside a number of other popular genres, including the *peplum* (epic hero-fantasy films), *giallo* (detective stories), comedies, melodramas, horror films, etc.

Wagstaff focuses on the reception of the cheaply made '*terza visione*' (third run) spaghetti westerns, which played in outlying areas of Italy and were more numerous than the urban based '*prima*' and '*seconda visione*' (first and second run) westerns.

> The audience of the *terza visione* cinema was more like the television audience than like a *prima visione* cinema audience. The viewer (generally he) went to the cinema nearest to his house (or in rural areas, the only cinema there was) after dinner, at around ten o'clock in the evening. The programme changed daily or every other day. He would not bother to find out what was showing, nor would he make any particular effort to arrive at the beginning of the film. He would talk to his friends during the showing whenever he felt like it, except during the bits of the film that grabs his (or his friends') attention.[65]

In such viewing conditions (akin to that of the early Nickelodeons where silent films were played,[66] common throughout the world for much of the twentieth century and continuing in some places today), the episodic narrative of spaghetti westerns makes perfect sense. A series of spectacles, offering either 'laughter, thrills [or] titillation'[67] acted rather like a cinema of attractions to hail or court the constantly wandering attention of its viewers. For this reason the psychological realism of the US western, or of a *prima visione* western like those of Leone, is missing from the spaghetti western. Its episodic structure is a radical dismantling of the SAS' narrative of the classical Hollywood western into a series of markers of the genre (gun fights, bar-room punch-ups, horseback rides, abductions of prostitutes, massacring of settlers, etc.). These markers are then reconstructed into a string of spectacles designed to target a specific audience's viewing patterns. As a result, in these attraction-images there is far less connection between situation and action than in the action-image. Characters do not become equal to their situation through action in a manner that influences the whole (as in the SAS' action-image western), rather, actions take place

in situations which – to use the old western maxim – just "happen along".
In this respect spaghetti westerns formally veer towards the pole of the time-
image (in that the sensory-motor regime no longer has the same power to
make a change to the milieu) in order to meet their audience's needs. Even
so, they still do not produce the discontinuous wandering of the protagonist of the time-image. Instead, the attraction-image displays the whole in
a non-continuous manner, through a string of spectacles in which the protagonist momentarily becomes equal to the situation, only for the process
to begin again interminably. An examination of one of the most famous
spaghetti westerns, Sergio Corbucci's *Django* helps to illustrate this point.

The narrative structure of *Django* is, as Frayling notes, straight off the
'Cinecittà assembly line'.[68] Django (Franco Nero) arrives in a town dominated by two warring factions, looking for revenge. He kills practically
everyone. The end. Like Méliès's trick films, then, the narrative is not the
point of the film, but the spectacles it enables.[69] Accordingly, Django happens across a number of scenes that serve no real narrative purpose, including: the prolonged whipping of a prostitute; Django machine-gunning
Major Jackson's (Eduardo Fajardo) men; General Hugo (José Bódalo) and
his bandits cutting off the ear of a corrupt priest and feeding it to him; the
crippling of Django's hands by rifle butt and horses' hooves; an ambush in
which Major Jackson's men kill General Hugo and his men; and a final
shoot out in a cemetery in which Django kills Major Jackson.

Through these various spectacles Django walks, dragging the coffin containing his machine gun. His actions in these situations do not change them
for the better. Rather, the spaghetti western's narrative facilitates a series of
attractions, focusing on Django's superhuman ability to act, especially to
shoot. As in early silent cinema, in the spaghetti western's non-continuous
pattern there appears to be an equivalence between character movement
(the unifying drive of the action-image) and the movement of world we
usually find in the discontinuous editing of the time-image. In the series of
spectacles offered by the spaghetti western, character action is equal to
each new situation (as in the action-image), but action cannot drive the
non-continuous montage alone. Simultaneously, a parallel movement of
world takes place, shifting the milieu independently of character, from
(spectacular) location to location. The classical narrative drive of the US
genre is thus destabilized. Its exploration of character motivation and the
interaction between character and milieu of the SAS' format are reconsti-
tuted as disconnected spectacles. Yet this reconfiguration provides a
viewing format that suits the context-specific ends to which these films were
designed. Thus Wagstaff's nationally contextualizing position on spaghetti

westerns illustrates that their restructuring of the US genre format is much clearer in intent than a purely formal comparison with the US western might suggest. Viewed in this light, like early silent trick films, spaghetti westerns are attraction-images.

Even so, Wagstaff's position is not the only available context within which to consider the spaghetti western as an attraction-image. In *Popular Cinemas of Europe* (2001) Eleftheriotis develops the debate surrounding the spaghetti western in a broader international arena. Although popular with Italian audiences, spaghetti westerns were constructed to appeal beyond national boundaries, often produced with finance from some combination of Italy, Spain, France and Germany and then dubbed and exported not only to the US drive-in market[70] but also to various destinations across Europe, the Middle East, South America, Africa and Asia. From this broader contextual position, Eleftheriotis argues that spaghetti westerns should be understood as providing international viewers in the 1960s and 1970s with a form of 'fantasy tourism' or 'pauper's travelling'[71] in which they journeyed into a fantastic version of the old west, and took part in a series of spectacles recognizable from US westerns. In a Cold War context of increased US global dominance, the spaghetti western provided audiences worldwide with a chance to reciprocate the movements of the various flows of people and money (from tourism to commerce to military intervention) emanating from the US.

The role of spectacle is again integral to this process. Formally contrasting the US and the spaghetti western in terms of cinematography and editing, Eleftheriotis comments on how Django's individualism detaches him from the contexts in which he acts, contexts which are reduced to mere backgrounds to his actions, and the spectacular functioning of the absurd sight of Django slowly lugging his coffin through the mud.[72] This spectacular recreation of the old west ensures the international accessibility of the spaghetti western as a fantastical travel genre, by deliberately erasing the normally defining national identity of characters in the US genre.[73] Aiming at an international market, spaghetti westerns

take the mythical aspect of the West as well as the legacy and the conventions of the American western as raw material that they process and transform. This process . . . shatters the particular relationship between historical events, ideological operations, cultural meanings and aesthetic forms that defines the American genre. . . . [T]his involves first a weakening of the historical referent by structuring the film around the presence of unique heroes who transcend historical and cultural specificity;

second, a disengagement of the *mise-en-scène* from the ideological and
iconographic values of the American western; and finally, a detachment
of the heroes from a point of view system that could place them in an
interactive relationship with other characters.[74]

In contrast to Wagstaff's nationally contextualizing direction, viewing
the spaghetti western from a perspective informed by Eleftheriotis's work
illustrates how its international aim led to the deliberate construction of an
identity-less arrangement of spectacles that would appeal transnationally.
In this respect, the isolation of individuals from milieu typical of the attraction-image makes complete sense, as this is very often the experience of the
tourist, virtual or otherwise. Thus the only common factor for all viewers,
be they Italian or in any other country peripheral to the USA but subject
to its influence, is the fantasy tourism (and corresponding pleasure of a
virtual invasion of the US genre) enabled by the detaching of the hero from
his milieu. Following Eleftheriotis's argument, then, we can see how, in
Deleuzian terms, the spaghetti western ensures the replacement of the SAS'
pattern (in which the active protagonist's role is vital to narrative progression) with the parallel movements of character actions and various situations. Appealing to a larger audience worldwide, the spaghetti western
deliberately de-linked the relationship between protagonist and milieu that
Deleuze observed in the organically structured (national) whole of the US
western.
     By this point the distinction between the (SAS') action-image and
attraction-image westerns should be clear. Furthermore, the genre's need
to appeal to international audiences also clarifies why the European
spaghetti western is different from the ASA' westerns Deleuze discusses in
Cinema 1. In the ASA' action-image, especially in the Hawks, Mann and
Peckinpah westerns Deleuze cites, it is as though the viewer has been
dropped into the middle of the action of an SAS' western, and must follow
the clues to understand why characters are acting as they are. Actions thus
reveal the situation. In many cases, especially in Peckinpah's late career
westerns (certain of which appear to have been in dialogue with the spaghetti western), the small form action-image could almost be described as
having an attraction-image's episodic structure. Deleuze describes certain
of these films precisely as a parade of spectacles, as 'no longer a milieu, a
West, but Wests: including Wests with camels, Wests with Chinamen, that is
totalities [*ensembles*] of locations, men and manners which "change and are
eliminated" in the same film'.[75] The crucial distinction remains, however,
that in the US western there is a far greater link between action and milieu

('totalities of locations, men and manners') necessitated of the movement-image's sensory-motor regime, no matter how discontinuous that milieu becomes in the ASA' form ('Wests with camels, Wests with Chinamen', etc.).

To clarify this distinction, consider the ASA' Mann westerns. In *Winchester '73* (1950) Lin McAdam (James Stewart) arrives in Dodge City seeking revenge on his brother for murdering their father, and clears the unstable countryside of outlaws in the process. Again, in *The Man From Laramie* (1955) Will Lockhart (James Stewart) uncovers the identity of the man who sold the guns to the Indians that were used to massacre his brother's cavalry troop, and in so doing unites the ageing, feuding landowning classes. In a spaghetti western like *Django*, by contrast, although the viewer also lands in the midst of the action the situation is not revealed (or cleansed) in the same manner. Although Django arrives in the old west seeking revenge, this is not for some identifiable personal injury. This is a revenge that can never be satisfied, and neither can it help repair a community or establish a new situation. Rather, Django's thirst for revenge is a universally understandable drive, ensuring that he only exists in the old west (like the virtual tourist posing for a souvenir photo) to be seen, and to be seen to be, "acting" there. His actions are divorced from any interactive relationship with the milieu that we would expect from the US western, in either its all-encompassed large form (SAS') or its small form totality of 'locations, men and manners' (ASA').

Eleftheriotis's commentary on the deliberately decontextualized representation of Ringo's (Mark Damon) golden pistol in Corbucci's previous western, *Johnny Oro/Ringo and His Golden Pistol* (1966) is helpful here.

> The significance of the golden pistol is that it links looks and actions: to be pretty is to shoot well and vice versa. The gun, then, becomes relatively independent of narrative function and of moral or ideological codes: its function is to shoot, and if this looks good everything is fine.[76]

Ringo's pistol, then, exists in relation to Ringo, rather than in the service of the collective, the situation or milieu. This is very much in contrast to the way in which, as Bogue has shown drawing on Philippe Demonsablon, in *Winchester '73* the eponymous rifle links the otherwise discontinuous spaces of the frontier's outlaw and Indian country in the ASA' western.[77] Instead, the golden pistol solely relates to the character, whose actions it enables for the individual's benefit alone. Similarly, in *Django*, Django's actions are not there to reveal the broader issues at stake in the interaction between individual and milieu, but as ends in themselves. *Django* does not end, after all, because Django has changed the situation for the better (SAS'), or because his actions have revealed a bigger situation (ASA'). The film simply ends because there is nobody left for Django to shoot! Like *Ringo*, then, Django's simply looks good killing, a fact that is reiterated in a series of non-continuous spectacles to which the viewer is exposed.

As this decontextualization of character from situation is a result of the construction of the viewpoint on the old west for the fantasy tourist, we no longer see a unified organic whole in which characters change the milieu for the better. The SAS' western, after all, epitomizes the ideology of the American dream of Manifest Destiny, and not that of the spaghetti western's international audience who were increasingly subject to the imperialist aspect of this ideology during the Cold War. Instead, the globally peripheral subaltern viewer gets a chance to visit the US on an unidentifiable quest for revenge that has no intention of rejuvenating the fantasy US milieu. Here the parallel lives of individuals (tourists) and milieu (virtual fantasy locations, or film sets) are shown to intersect in a series of non-continuous standout moments, a series of attraction-image spectacles.

Cold War Revolutions: *Keoma* (1976)

While *Django* is typical of the industrial production line spaghetti western (as is notable in the numerous sequels it spawned), certain spaghetti westerns provide further useful material for our understanding of the attraction-image. One standout example is Enzo G. Castellari's *Keoma*, one of the last spaghetti westerns that, on first viewing, seems to contain time-images. On closer inspection, however, these images are not evidence of the discontinuous temporality of the time-image, but further clarify the functioning of the non-continuous temporality of the attraction-image. Through these temporal anomalies *Keoma* also provides further evidence of the attraction-image's ability to provide a political critique in a spectacular form.

The argument surrounding the manner in which politically engaged spaghetti westerns negotiate historical conditions is often made with reference to those that deal with the Mexican revolution. These include Damiano Damiani's *Quién Sabe?/A Bullet for the General* (1966) and Sergio Leone's *Giù la testa/A Fistful of Dynamite* (1971). *Quién Sabe?* for example, was scripted by Franco Solinas (who also wrote the extremely well-known political film about the Algerian struggle for independence from French rule, Gillo Pontecorvo's *La battaglia di Algeri/Battle of Algiers* (1966)), and director

Damiani (who previously wrote neorealist scripts for Cesare Zavattini) specifically described the film as 'not a western' but 'a political film'.[78] *Quién
Sabe?* depicts a fantastical journey through the Mexican revolution. As it
emerged at a time of social and cultural upheaval and revolution in many
parts of the world it is often considered an allegory for that period, hence
its international appeal. After all, the years immediately prior to *Quién Sabe?*
saw the Cold War spread to various parts of the world, not least in the USA's
involvement in attempting to halt the spread of communism, including
their entry into Vietnam and the increasing use of US counterinsurgency
experts in post-Cuban revolution Latin America, as well as involvement
in the overthrow of democratically elected governments in such places as
Guyana, Brazil, Bolivia and the Dominican Republic. Thus Frayling,
approaching the film through Franz Fanon's work, interprets it as an exploration of first and third world relations in the context of political struggles
in South America, Vietnam, and indeed, within the USA.[79] Similarly, for
Howard Hughes, *Quién Sabe?* is understood as a critique of US imperialism.[80]
In both instances the historical context of the Mexican revolution is considered a location in which to set a discussion of politics that would be considered relevant, and in many cases directly applicable, to circumstances
experienced by spaghetti western audiences in various parts of the world.
If we explore the context from which *Keoma* emerged it can be interpreted
in much the same way.

The spaghetti western was at the height of its popularity in the mid- to
late 1960s. By the mid-1970s, when *Keoma* appeared, it had practically run
its course. This was due to such factors as the cyclical rise and fall of different genres, rising ticket prices and the gradual closing of many rural and
provincial cinemas, but also the general decline in cinema production
worldwide due to the rise of television. Yet in the intervening years between
Django and *Quién Sabe?* (both 1966) and *Keoma* (1976) the expansion of the
Cold War into third world countries had proliferated. This period saw the
US escalation of, and ultimate defeat in, the war in Vietnam; revolution and
genocide in Cambodia; the establishing of military governments in several
Latin American countries (including Uruguay, Chile and Argentina) and
the high-profile death of the left wing president of Chile, Salvador Allende
in the CIA-backed military coup of 1973; the Arab-Israeli wars of 1967 and
1973 with the two sides backed by the USSR and the US respectively; the
ensuing OPEC oil crisis of 1973 and the inflation and recession it caused
internationally; and the US support for dictatorships in countries like
South Korea, including the levels of popular unrest they caused among

civilian populations (especially from the rapidly industrialized working classes) experiencing a compressed form of modernization under police and military repression. *Keoma* also coincides with civil war in Lebanon, and closely precedes the Iranian revolution of 1979 and the Soviet-Afghan and Iran-Iraq wars that would shortly follow, thereby emerging during a period of increasing social unrest brought on by the widening gap between wealthy and poor, and Western influence, in the oil rich Middle East.[81] Thus, although the US and USSR were formally involved in *détente* at this time, in terms of the struggle between capitalist imperialism and various forms of opposition throughout the third world (not to mention the often related post-colonial independence movements throughout Africa, again including US involvement in conflicts in places like Angola, Ethiopia, and Rhodesia (now Zimbabwe)),[82] this period of the Cold War was a volatile and violent one, which is reflected in the popularity of the similarly confrontational spaghetti western at that time.

Like *Django*, *Keoma* is another attraction-image constituted of a string of spectacles that revises the US action-image western both ideologically and formally. However, emerging in this volatile era, *Keoma*'s reconfiguration of the western as an attraction-image with a political message that appeals internationally is more foregrounded than in *Django*. In this it is also partly a product of the spaghetti westerns of the intervening years – not least of which was *C'era una volta il West/Once Upon a Time in the West* (1969) – which had made the spaghetti western's engagement with politics, especially the revision of US history, far more evident.

For this reason *Keoma* shifts its register from fantasy tourism in the old west to a reimagining of the old west as a third world subaltern nightmare that exists at one with the wealth of the developed capitalist world, in which repetitious cycles of violence, suffering and death are the only constants. The non-continuous time of the attraction-image is here used to recreate the (if I may suggest this without a pejorative meaning) non-continuous history of the third world during this particular phase of the Cold War. By this I do not mean to suggest that history in these countries "stalled" during this period, but rather to evoke the cyclical rise and fall of governments, revolutions, and civil wars that occurred, and the "episodic" development of these areas under these conditions. In this my thinking correlates with that of Greg Grandin in *The Last Colonial Massacre* (2004), who, arguing precisely against the stereotyping of Latin America as a homogenous region somehow ahistorically determined, or "fated", to experience perpetual cycles of revolutionary, nevertheless notes that:

[T]he Latin American Cold War as a whole represented a protracted revolution, dispersed through time and space yet entailing a coherent and legible logic of insurgency, violence and transformation. Not only did each of Latin America's twentieth century revolutions take place in domestic and international arenas simultaneously, each contributed to an accrual of experience and perception that challenged in increasingly focused terms the authority of the United States as an ascendant world power. Starting in Mexico and continuing to Nicaragua, successive revolutions functioned as radicalizing transit points where itinerant activists sought sanctuary, applied theory, gained knowledge and carried the message elsewhere, throughout not just the Americas but the world.[83]

Thus an ideological examination of the potentially devastating effects of the Cold War on various parts of the world, made manifest in a non-continuous but connected series of context-specific revolutions, is contained within the episodic form of the spaghetti western. *Keoma*, then, illustrates Marcia Landy's contention that the spaghetti western 'reveals that "the West" is no longer the United States; rather, Americanism is a phenomenon that is larger than the geographic and cultural boundaries of the United States and its Cold War domination, coming to represent worldwide transformations and conflicts'.[84]

Global Wilderness

Keoma's narrative concerns the return of Keoma (Franco Nero) to the town of his upbringing. He has been away fighting in what is probably the US Civil War, but, as in *Django*, exactly which war is left unspecified, thereby providing more points of entry for different viewers internationally. Keoma is of dual heritage, or, according to the conventions of the genre, is a 'half-breed'. When a baby he was the only survivor of a massacre of a Native American encampment. He was saved that day by an old woman (Gabriella Giacobbe). Keoma's father (William Berger), a rancher, took him in after the massacre. We discover through flashbacks that Keoma had a difficult upbringing due to the perpetual conflict he endured with his three half-brothers. He was helped by his father, however, and George (Woody Strode), who between them taught him to fight with guns and bow and arrow. Through the mannered conversations between Keoma and the old woman it becomes evident that she performs a similar role to the character of Death in Ingmar Bergman's *The Seventh Seal* (1957), making the film's barest essential reading a dialogue between death (the old woman), freedom (represented by Keoma) and life (represented by a pregnant woman that Keoma saves early on in the film).

On his return from the war at the film's opening, Keoma finds that the town is enslaved by the Skidoo Mining Company. Its greedy owner, Caldwell (Daniel O'Brien), an ex-soldier still in command of his men during peacetime, is buying up the town. He also employs Keoma's three half-brothers. Caldwell and his men have divided the people of the town into two sections, the healthy, and those who have 'the plague'. The infected are kept in isolation and doomed to die as Caldwell blocks the arrival of medicine into the town and advances his claims to empty land. Helped by his father, the rejuvenated George (who has become the town drunk in Keoma's absence), the pregnant woman and the recurring supernatural reappearances of the old woman, Keoma battles Caldwell, his men and his three half-brothers. Eventually he cleans up the town. The film ends with Keoma riding away, leaving the old woman to care for the newly born child of the pregnant woman. The child is Keoma's double, the new representative of freedom, its survival of the town's destruction mirroring Keoma's survival of the encampment massacre when an infant.

Despite this narrative's greater depth when compared to most spaghetti westerns, actually a result of the backstory afforded by the flashback structure, *Keoma* is, typically, constructed as a series of spectacles. This is apparent almost immediately when the first shootings are elaborately depicted in Peckinpah-inspired slow-motion, not to mention all the knife throwing, trick shooting, fist fights and occasional horse riding stunts that follow. The point of the narrative of *Keoma*, then, is to ultimately come full circle after first passing through a number of spectacles. In fact, Castellari filmed the opening and closing scenes first, and gradually built the narrative of spectacles in between, improvising script and shooting on a day-to-day basis, making it precisely an excuse of a narrative along which spectacles are strung. Thus the film's circular motion back to the start provides a correspondence between beginning and end that is quite different from the linearity of the classical Hollywood action-image, its string of spectacles providing a reconfiguration of the ideological conservatism of the US action-image western, in both form and content.

The opening of *Keoma* is key to this understanding of the film. As was the case with Corbucci's *Django*, *Keoma* is the work of another veteran director of spaghetti westerns, Castellari, who paid homage to several US directors in his film. The distinctive opening scene is a direct reworking of the start of *The Searchers.* At the start of *Keoma,* before we even see any titles, a striking image appears. The screen is almost entirely black, apart from a small vertical rectangle of light to the far right of the screen. This chink is a window, its ruined, empty frame banging open and closed in the wind. Aside from the noise of the wind, we can see the ruins of the dust-blown town through the window, and a rider approaching. This is Keoma, returning from the Civil War. The shot then cuts to the hands of the old woman, scrabbling in the dirt outside for anything of value, then back to the view of Keoma approaching seen through the window, and finally back to the old woman outside. The camera then cuts outside the house, providing various internal and externally situated points of view of Keoma's approach from different parts of the town, as though he is seen from the perspective of frightened people hiding in and amidst the locked and ruined buildings. Finally, Keoma's path leads him to the old woman. A conversation ensues, and when she asks him why he has returned, Keoma replies that 'The world keeps going around and around so you always end up in the same place.'

In the opening of *The Searchers,* I would argue the epitome of Deleuze's SAS' action-image, the camera is initially positioned in complete darkness inside a homestead. As Aunt Martha (Dorothy Jordan) opens the door, the centre of the screen fills with light. It becomes a frame within a frame, through which we see the brightly lit desert exterior. The camera tracks outside, following Aunt Martha, and then a conventional shot/reverse shot pattern positions us alongside her point of view as she gazes anxiously into the desert wilderness, and spies a lone rider approaching. This is Ethan (John Wayne) returning from the US Civil War. On his arrival he is welcomed into the homestead by Martha and her family. As Eleftheriotis has shown, the opening of *The Searchers* aptly demonstrates the construction, through editing and *mise-en-scène,* of the ideologically defining binaries that 'exist in tension and in mutual capture'[85] in the US western. These binaries, such as civilization and wilderness, inside and outside, community and individual, were first identified by Jim Kitses of the US western in *Horizons West* (1969). In Deleuzian terms, the opening illustrates precisely the interconnectivity of characters and milieu of the US action-image, and indeed, the binary oppositions that construct the unified organic whole of the American montage school.

In *Keoma* the initial alignment of the audience with the civilized side of the equation of *The Searchers* is eradicated. Any clear division between interior and exterior, or civilization and wilderness is destroyed, again through the use of editing and *mise-en-scène.* In *The Searchers* the camera establishes the audience as inhabiting the same civilized space as the homesteaders, looking out (albeit with anxiety) into the surrounding wilderness. In *Keoma*, the camera positions suggest that civilization has gone into hiding amidst the ruins of the town, the inhabitants peeking out in fear, powerless as the wilderness-individual rides into the middle of town. Thus, although riding away from a war zone, rather than arriving home (no matter how fragile or under threat this home is in the opening of *The Searchers*) Keoma simply finds himself in another space of conflict.

Accordingly, in *Keoma* the line of sight between the two realms is offered by a broken window that has been left open, banging in the wind. This is in stark contrast to the image of a sturdy brick wall across which the credits of *The Searchers* play, our first introduction to the fortified homestead of the settler family with which civilization protected itself from wilderness during its westward expansion in the USA. In *Keoma* there is no one "inside" with whom the viewer can be aligned, as there is with Aunt Martha in *The Searchers*. Everywhere is now "outside". Many inhabitants of the town have been killed, and those who might be left are hiding, afraid to identify themselves. The role of Aunt Martha has passed to the old woman, a representative of death who is scavenging among the ruins. Thus, with no protective distinction between inside and outside, civilization and wilderness, collective and individual, and indeed, milieu and character, the centrality of the civilized gaze in the positioning of the door in *The Searchers* has been pushed to the edge of the frame in the broken, open window. The traumatized town is unable to control the space it overlooks, and is powerless to avert the massacre that comes not from the "Red Indians" who inhabit the wilderness in *The Searchers*, but the commercial interests of one of their own, the mine owner, Caldwell. In *Keoma*, then, civilization has collapsed into wilderness. They are no longer binary opposites that exist as part of a unified organic whole in this transnational take on a US cinematic myth.

Most noticeably, *Keoma* has dropped the historically and nationally defining intertitle with which *The Searchers* is introduced, 'Texas, 1868', leaving the place and time non-specific, and therefore applicable to international audiences. This marks the major difference between *Keoma* and a similar revisionist replaying of *The Searchers* in *C'era una volta il West*. In Leone's film the slaughter of the settlers by Native Americans seen in *The Searchers* (itself a colonialist reversal of US history as it is typically constructed in Hollywood westerns[86]), is replayed as the ruthless murder of a family in the name of profit as the railroad expands westward. In Leone's film the engagement remains with US history, then, as opposed to the more open sense of applicability that comes with Keoma's non-nationally or non-historically specific opening. Thus in *Keoma*, *The Searchers* is revised in a manner that, as Frayling shows, is typical of the spaghetti western.[87] However, unlike *C'era una volta il*

West, with its SAS' structure, and instead in line with *Django* and other spaghetti westerns of the attraction-image format, *Keoma*'s revision of the US
western can equally be interpreted as depicting the damage done to the third
world during the Cold War by the triumphalist ideology underpinning
the US western. It is for this reason that in *Keoma* there is no longer a distinction between civilization and wilderness, as the global reach of the Cold
War has extended worldwide to create an international frontier, a global
wilderness.

Transnational Subaltern Warrior

In this respect, Keoma's status as a 'half-breed' ensures that he functions
as a globally representative everyman figure. Most obviously he gestures
towards the internal divisions within the USA that, Ken Nolley notes in
Hollywood's Indian (1998), were due to such factors as 'the decay of an
initially generous postwar optimism into Cold War pessimism' and the 'context of a growing general awareness of an American tradition of racism – an
awareness that was engendered by the developing civil-rights movement'.[88]
The actions of 'half-breed' freedom fighter Keoma, then, hint at the US's
internal third world that was increasingly evident to public consciousness
during the Cold War. The heroic Keoma is evocative of the high profile
achieved by the Native American population during this period, both in the
occupation of Alcatraz in 1969 and the activities of the American Indian
Movement in the early 1970s.[89] However, his role in critiquing US society
is most apparent when he teams up with George, an African-American ex-
slave, who taught him to fight with bow and arrow when he was a boy. Woody
Strode's presence as George continues the revisionism of his own celluloid
past as a subservient African-American sidekick, in films like *The Man Who
Shot Liberty Valance*, that was previously seen in his brief appearance as hired
assassin in *C'era una volta il West*. In the context of the increased visibility of
the Native-American and the growth of the civil rights movement (particularly after the Watts riots, the assassination of Martin Luther King, the revelation of the disproportionate number of African-American servicemen dying
in Vietnam and the growth of such organizations as the Black Panthers),
George and Keoma fight together as two US subaltern underdogs.

Yet the appeal of *Keoma* as the subaltern 'half-breed' again goes beyond
its specific resonance in the US context. For Eleftheriotis, the hero of the
spaghetti western is usually a man from outside the community (often 'with
no name, no place and no nation'[90]), and as such exists 'in a relationship
of mutual exteriority in terms of cinematic codes and ideological values'.[91]

As I have shown above, this perfectly describes the manner in which the arrival of Keoma in the ruined town is presented cinematically. Indeed, the remainder of the film sees Keoma fight injustice on behalf of the oppressed, stirring up popular support from among the community, and taking on Caldwell single-handedly when that fails. Keoma, then, can also be understood as a stand in for Grandin's Cold War 'itinerant activist', representing any number of post-colonial, Cold War freedom fighters, from South East Asia to South America, experiencing a never-ending cycle of (non-continuous) revolutionary violence.

When interpreted in this way *Keoma* can be considered a correlative to US westerns that allegorically deal with the Cold War, in particular *The Magnificent Seven* (1960). This story of poor villagers fighting for their rights under the benevolent guidance of US mercenaries can be viewed as an upbeat image of US military and CIA intervention in the third world, one to which Keoma responds with its dark vision of revolutionary struggle. Yet there is another way of assessing the film, alongside several (third) "world cinema" classics of the 1960s and 1970s. These films, although very different in aesthetic, narrative and generic format, also deal with the perpetual nature of revolution, struggle and violence.

Glauber Rocha's classic work from the Brazilian Cinema Novo movement, *Deus e o Diabo na Terra do Sol/Black God, White Devil* (1964), contains a similar preoccupation with the perpetual cycles of violence endured by an indigenous rural people. It also takes place within a bleak desert wasteland setting in which outlaws become 'symbols of popular resistance to the merciless social and economic institutions that had marginalized them'.[92] We could again compare *Keoma* with the Mexican film, *Reed, México insurgente/Reed: Insurgent Mexico* (1973), a film about the American journalist John Reed and his coverage of the Mexican Revolution, whose narrative cycles through seemingly interminable periods of waiting and fighting, advancing and retreating, during the prolonged revolutionary struggle. It also has similarities with the popular Indian film *Sholay/Flames* (1975), sometimes dubbed a "curry western", that uses its two criminal angry young male protagonists to explore the impact on the Indian countryside of the recent war with Pakistan in 1971; the mass unemployment, social unrest and lawlessness that appeared in its wake; and the state of emergency and government crack down on civil liberties in 1975. In each instance the aesthetic is extremely different, but the consequences for the people and the countryside caused by constant warring is very similar across the four films, as, crucially, is the sense of an unending narrative of unrest, uprising, revolution and suppression.

In *Keoma*'s string of spectacles, then, we experience the unremitting cycling of violence that was then being enacted upon the subaltern during the Cold War, as a series of non-continuous attractions. This ideological narrative is as impossible to extricate from the formal structure of the spaghetti western as is that of the US action-image western in its portrayal of Manifest Destiny. This is the case even if here it takes on a broader, trans-nationally applicable form. In *C'era una volta il West*, the replaying of the opening of *The Searchers* is integrated into a classical narrative format. In *Keoma* by contrast, it becomes a moment of spectacle with which to open a string of other spectacles. Its purpose is solely to return the film, in its conclusion, to its opening. In this way it demonstrates the impossibility of the SAS' narrative of Manifest Destiny in the post-Vietnam era. Any sense of a unified organic national whole, in which the characters and milieu enter into a progressive relationship, is denied. It is replaced by a series of spectacles that demonstrate the devastating non-continuous cyclicality of destruction during the Cold War when numerous uprisings or revolutions were brought back to degree zero by the ideological war being fought on other territories by the USA and USSR.

Keoma, the representative of freedom, must fight a perpetual revolution that is renewed each time the attraction-image's non-continuous movement of world takes him to a new situation. Each shift he experiences, however, only takes him to a new situation that is effectively the same as the previous one. As Keoma has it: 'The world keeps going round and round so you always end up in the same place.' Thus *Keoma* demonstrates the temporary nature of any becoming-equal of character and situation, only this time, unlike the fantasy tourists of Méliès voyages or spaghetti westerns like *Django*, Keoma represents those who cannot move through the world as they would like. He exists at the opposite end of the geopolitical spectrum, representing those who, as Zygmunt Bauman notes in his work on global-ization, are subject to, or moved by, the world.[93] Although clearly not a pas-sive character, Keoma the 'itinerant activist' is thus caught in the cyclical history of the period. In its episodic structure, then, the attraction-image facilitates as ideological a narrative as any of the classical Hollywood SAS' westerns.

Non-continuous Temporal Attractions (not time-images)

While sharing its basic episodic structure with other spaghetti westerns, *Keoma* is different in one important respect, the presence of what initially appear to be time-images. However, as distinct from Deleuze's time-images, these moments of temporal convergence of past and present function as spectacles in their own right, thereby maintaining the indirect, non-continuous expression of time of the attraction-image. They provide further evidence of the way in which the attraction-image constructs a cyclical view of history out of its string of spectacles, as opposed to the time-image's direct view of the whole of time. Accordingly, *Keoma* reveals the ambiguous border territory between the non-continuous (indirect) expression of time found in the attraction-image and the direct expression of the movement of the whole found in the time-image.

If we were to follow the logic of Deleuze's progression from the pre-war development of the movement-image to the post-war emergence of the time-image, *Keoma* (released in 1976) could be seen as further evidence of this shift in trajectory. However, due to the uneasy relationship between individual and milieu of the attraction-image (in which individuals do become equal to situations, but only temporarily, until the next situation "happens along") it would be difficult to see these moments as illustrating the drifting, sensory-motor discontinuity of the time-image. Rather, *Keoma*, a post-war attraction-image, demonstrates the premature fixity of Deleuze's categories of movement- and time-image, that is revealed when they encounter films that do not quite fit either model as they are currently defined.

When Keoma and the old woman meet in the film's opening the first such image appears. Recounting the story of Keoma's survival of the massacre of his tribe, the old woman looks off-screen to her right. The camera pans in that direction to reveal the devastated encampment in which the young Keoma is plaintively calling for his murdered mother. After revealing his dead mother and the arrival of his father in the past, it pans back once again to the old woman's face in the present. The continuous movement through space that we expect of a panning shot here creates instead a movement in time, suggesting the interconnected nature of the virtual layers of the past that Deleuze discussed in *Cinema 2* (drawing once again on Bergson), as illustrative of the time-image. After all, such a reading of the pan as facilitator of the time-image has been convincingly made by Neil Campbell in relation to the western, *Lone Star* (1996).[94]

This is only the first of several such instances that are interspersed throughout the film, as the past invades the present during moments of sensory-motor discontinuity, just as we would expect of the time-image. The fluid interplay between sheets of the past and the present is clearly evident when Keoma returns home to visit his father, and finds himself witness to an event from this childhood. The adult Keoma stands in the left-hand side of the image. His childhood self then runs past him, pursued by his three half-brothers, as he remembers his conflict with them as a boy. Keoma remains a doubled presence in the shot, simultaneously both adult present and child past, until his father appears, to call him into the house. Here the shot/reverse shot between father and son in the past, and father and son in the present, is cleverly intercut such that the different layers of time in which the adult and child Keoma, and young and old father exist, become indiscernible. Past and present seem to be communicating with each other precisely as we might expect of the time-image.

There are two other such occasions. First when Keoma is reunited with his three half-brothers, and the shot/reverse shot pattern between Keoma riding towards his half-brothers in the present is crosscut with the same point of view shots seen in the boy Keoma's arrival at the family ranch in the past. Secondly, when Keoma is confronted by his three half-brothers in the present, their encircling presence on horses creating a shift in time to a similar moment of childhood bullying, again seen from Keoma's point of view. In these instances the editing and cinematography suggest a blurring of temporal layers typical of the time-image, and an image that we might normally consider directly expressive of the open and changing whole of time.

So why consider these anything but time-images? In an interview about *Keoma* Castellari notes that the appearance of these unusual flashback devices was an idea he took from an Elia Kazan film he had seen sometime previously.[95] This is most likely *The Arrangement* (1969), a time-image film about US bourgeois ennui, in which advertising executive Eddie Anderson (Kirk Douglas) experiences a mid-life crisis, causing past and present to commingle confusingly in the image. As his sensory-motor incapacity (he is recuperating after a car accident) enables him to slip between layers of time, Anderson brings forth memories of the past, and his lover, in a way that makes them seem to exist in the present. This is very much like the coexistence of characters from the past and the present in the same image that is seen in *Keoma*. However, there is a subtle difference which has a large bearing on how we understand the past and present to coincide in *Keoma*. In the Castellari western these images of the past do not function in quite the same way as they do in *The Arrangement*. Although they demonstrate the existence of characters in the giant virtual memory of Bergsonian time, the slippage between sheets of the past that characterize the time-image, and even the coexistence of child and man that Deleuze observes in Fellini's films,[96] even so the potential confusion created by temporarily overlapping layers of time in the time-image is avoided in *Keoma*.

Most obviously there is the use of children who are made-up to resemble Keoma and his three half-brothers, and the contrasting of the youthful face of Keoma's father from the past, with his aged face in the present. In this way *Keoma* creates images in which past and present characters coexist in order to draw a direct equivalence between the two moments in time. There is far less to be confused about here than there is in *The Arrangement*, as child and adult (and indeed, young and old father) are visually very different in age. What is of interest in *Keoma*, then, is not the indiscernibility of past and present in the image, as it is in the time-image, but the equivalence of past and present in the image. It is as though we witness Keoma remembering his childhood as a film within the film, a mini version of present-day events being enacted by children. The sense of temporal equivalence this creates is most clearly seen in the match created between the adult Keoma's distinctive headband, and the same headband (and indeed, long hairstyle) worn by his childhood self. This has a humorous impact, as well as serving an important purpose in maintaining clarity of character identity when these potentially disorienting flashbacks first begin to appear. Yet it also points to the non-continuous nature of history in *Keoma*, as past and present, although younger and older versions of each other, are effectively defined by the same conflicts. In short, past and present are shown to be equivalent moments in a perpetually cycling narrative.

Crucially, the flashbacks in *Keoma*, although formally constructed like those in *Lone Star*, do not have the same revelatory function in terms of narrative progression. Nothing new is learned from them. There is no Nietzschian powers of the false with which to inform the future as Deleuze argued in *Cinema 2* (in the case of *Lone Star* the realization of a non-triumphalist origin with which to destabilize US national identity, or 'forget the Alamo'), only affirmation that the present must repeat the past as though they were non-continuous episodes strung out across time. These are not time-images, then, but attraction-images, non-continuous rather than discontinuous expressions of time, indirect rather than direct images of time.

Furthermore, the flashbacks in *Keoma* are less revealing about the role of the past in present events than the flashbacks in the Leone revenge westerns *Per qualche dollaro in più/For a Few Dollars More* (1965) and *C'era una volta il West*. In the Leone films the flashbacks are recollection-images that provide clues as to character motivation. In both instances, character actions are motivated by revenge, the resolution of which is found in present-day actions. In *Keoma* the flashbacks do not function to progress the narrative to a new, resolved situation as in these linearly determined SAS' action-images (which reaffirm the "correctness" of one single timeline), but only to return it to the next, non-continuous episode after demonstrating how events will play out once more. Not time-images, then, but not the recollection-images we expect of action-images either. Rather, they are attraction-image flashbacks, non-continuous rather than continuous expressions of time, although in this instance they remain indirect images of time, or movement-images.

The attraction-image flashbacks in *Keoma* create a closed circuit between past and present that defines them as neither time-images nor recollection-images, but non-continuous movement-images. They provide an indirect expression of duration in that, while they demonstrate the gigantic Bergsonian memory of which we are all a part (and a more disruptive manner than the recollection-image), ultimately each of these flashbacks functions to emphasize the non-continuous nature of time that marks the violently repetitive cycles of *Keoma*. These are indirect images of time even though they do not depict an entirely linear, spatialized form of time determined by a continuous sensory-motor regime, as, for instance, the action-image does. After all, they do not provide the direct expression of the discontinuous movements of duration found in the time-image either. Most noticeably, there is no falsifying narrative to emerge from the powers of the false.

In fact these images provide non-continuous spectacles of past and present in which the only certainty is that a movement of world, although it can be temporarily matched by character movement, will inevitably lead to a further such non-continuous movement. The present, then, repeats the past in a non-continuous form, and these images remain indirect expressions of Bergson's duration, the past being in many ways even less informing of the present than in the recollection-image that characterizes the linear form of time of the action-image. These images provide just one more episodic movement of world to which Keoma must become equal through action. They remain attraction-image spectacles of the non-continuous movements of world and characters. No permanent change is possible in this non-continuous whole. Rather, these images function to further demonstrate both the non-continuous nature of the attraction-image, and of a transnational whole marked by a repetitious form of temporality typical of the political and social upheaval experienced, globally, by many societies during the Cold War.

The best that the protagonist can hope for under such circumstances is that they can become equal to their situation once again. As things were in the past, so must they be in the present. The image of adult Keoma in the same shot as his childhood self, again fighting his three half-brothers, is thus an image of his realization that he is reliving the repetitious past in the present. To make the present equal to the past Keoma must therefore ferment popular resistance and confront his half-brothers once again. Having done so, however, the cycle merely begins again. It is this inevitability of cyclical, violent revolution that explains the distinctive, prophetic soundtrack to the film, which comments on events even before they happen. It is also this inevitability of conflict that is seen most clearly as Keoma rides out of the devastated town at the close, leaving behind a child who will share his own fate, left in the hands of the old woman just as Keoma was as a child. Once more, past and present match, creating a non-continuous whole, the old woman (death) holding the baby (freedom) in her arms. In this way the film's narrative creates a match between past and present not through a linear progression in the classical narrative sense, but in the equivalence of the temporal cycle.

In the film's conclusion, *Keoma*'s temporally disruptive attraction-images demonstrate that the US past and the global present are one and the same. Just as US civilization, propelled by the myth of Manifest Destiny was built on the burned ruins of the Native American encampment, so too is the present a time of perpetual battles over the land that the subaltern inhabits.

Conclusion: Does Deleuze Need Spectacles?

In this chapter I have explored the emergence of the attraction-image in early silent cinema, and considered one example of its re-emergence several decades later in the spaghetti western. Historically, this particular type of movement-image pre-exists the categories that Deleuze outlines in *Cinema 1*, and forces us to reconsider his definition of the movement-image due to its over-reliance on Bergson's philosophy. Although it is true that, for the Deleuzian scholar, understanding Bergson's model of time enables a greater comprehension of when an image is or is not a time-image, in actual fact focusing on the films themselves illustrates that it is often useful to depart from the Bergsonian underpinnings of Deleuze's project. Adhering to these theories can potentially squeeze films into predetermined categories that the films themselves resist, as seen if we consider their nuanced play with non-continuous forms of time.

As I have shown, the attraction-image is far from unique to early silent trick films, and recurs throughout cinema history. Spaghetti westerns from the 1960s and 1970s use the distinctive, non-continuous consideration of the whole of the attraction-image to appeal to audiences worldwide.

Here the episodic form of the attraction-image specifically enables these films to comment on issues of relevance to inhabitants of countries experiencing the influence of US ideology during the Cold War.

I have also shown how important it is to analyse the context-specific ends to which different types of cinema have been produced, especially if the more spectacular genres and modes (like the attraction-image) are to be seen as fit-for-purpose products, as opposed to "primitive", or poorly constructed derivatives of supposedly more mature cinemas. This context-specific understanding of cinema enables a reconsideration of Deleuze's highlighting of the role of montage in the construction of the sensory-motor oriented movement-image, and the larger ramifications of this for considerations of ideology and narrative that are disavowed in Deleuze's accounts of the movement-image. The attraction-image, then, provides a first example of the relative nature of Deleuze's image categories.

History:

Deleuze After Dictatorship

Chapter 2

The Child seer *in* and *as* History: Argentine Melodrama

The next two chapters focus on Deleuze's engagement with history in cinema, examining depictions of the past from national cinemas that have rejuvenated, both domestically and internationally, after periods of military rule during the Cold War. In each case – Argentina in this chapter, and South Korea in the next – the way that the national past is depicted provides scope for detailed analysis, critique and advancement of the way Deleuze conceived of history in the *Cinema* books. While the chapter that follows explores how certain South Korean films "think" history by folding time (specifically, by enfolding certain formal aspects of the time-image within a movement-image format), this chapter interrogates the specific issue of the seer in the time-image that is so crucial to Deleuze's argument in *Cinema 2*, and its relationship to history in films set in the past.

The chapter begins with an introduction to the role of the seer in the time-image, to locate the importance of both the child, and historical context, in Deleuze's formulation of the time-image. While Deleuze's examples focus on films from post-war Europe in which children are witness to the emergence of history in the present (for example, *Germania anno zero/ Germany Year Zero* (1948)), the impact and immediacy of the situation to which the seer must react is very different when the events are recreated in retrospect. Accordingly, the child's relationship to history is different in the Argentine melodrama, *Kamchatka* (2002), which is set during the 1970s.

In *Kamchatka* the child appears as a conduit through which the viewer encounters a reconstructed national history of military rule, requiring a more sophisticated understanding of the way the child seer functions to record, or witness, history in recreated historical moments. Rather than asking the question of "what *is* happening?" what is taking place at a certain moment in history as in *Germania anno zero*, *Kamchatka* uses the child's point of view to reconsider "what *has* happened?" in the past.[1] Thus the child seer (or, as it will be seen, the "adult-child seer") functions differently when situated *in* history as it is being made (*Germania anno zero*), and *as* a part of history (the recreated past) in *Kamchatka*. In this respect *Kamchatka* exemplifies a trend in South American films that has recently emerged – including *Machuca* (Chile/Spain/UK/France, 2004), *O Ano em Que Meus Pais Saíram de Férias/The Year My Parents Went on Vacation* (Brazil, 2006), and *Paisito* (Uruguay/Spain/Argentina, 2008) – that locates child protagonists in a recreated past under military rule to meditate on those who disappeared, and the manner in which such lost pasts can be reconstructed by the generation who were children at that time.

There is not room to discuss all these films here, but *Kamchatka* is extremely similar to its contemporaries from Chile, Brazil and Uruguay for two reasons. First, in its self-conscious construction of a virtual layer of the past, which is designed specifically to oscillate with and inform the national present. In this reconstructed past the child seer thus functions to construct history, if we follow Bergson's notion of duration, as a child that *is* (a child able to tap the potential of the virtual whole of the past for the benefit of the present) rather than a child that *was* (an actualized recollection).[2] Secondly, like its neighbours, *Kamchatka* delves into the recreated past to find the layer of time in which the origins of the contemporary present can be found, in this instance the economic policies introduced under military rule in the 1970s being evoked to suggest that the economic crisis of the 2000s clearly resonates with events in this historical period. The child seer represents someone at once politically powerless, and yet with a remarkable capacity for historical (hind)sight. They are a figure who illustrates how film can fill in the gaps in our collective pasts, reconstructing events which we cannot have experienced personally, in a manner often referred to in discourses surrounding 'postmemory' (especially in the South American context) or, more generally, 'prosthetic memory'.[3]

The point of this chapter, then, is not simply to note the different function of the child seer in contemporary South American films, but to use one such example to reveal the arbitrary, Eurocentric pinpointing of World War Two by Deleuze (who considers the child seer to emerge from the ruins of post-war Europe) in the development of his two image categories. As *Kamchatka* shows, in various parts of the world this moment of defining rupture can take a number of different forms, and can appear at diverse moments in history.

The Child seer in the Time-Image

The seer is a vital part of Deleuze's formulation of the time-image. It appears on the first page of the preface to the English edition of *Cinema 2*, and the child as seer on page three of Chapter 1. However, the concept really emerges out of the interstice between *Cinema 1* and *Cinema 2*. In the concluding chapter of *Cinema 1*, Deleuze begins to address the conditions that facilitated the emergence of the time-image, the 'crisis of the action-image'.[4] Deleuze identifies five aspects that mark the crisis of the action-image, all of which pertain to the disintegration of the movement-image's totalizing sensory-motor regime. First the calling into question of the notion of a 'globalising situation'[5] that characters are able to influence through action, as in the SAS' form action-image. This is replaced by a more dispersive situation, with multiple characters whose lives interact but who are unaware of the mutually intertwining situation they all inhabit. Secondly, in the ASA' form of the action-image, the connections through which situations come to be revealed by actions is weakened, with chance taking a stronger hand in creating connections. Thirdly, the decisive action of the sensory-motor regime has been loosened, the movement of narrative towards a foreseeable resolution (in classical Hollywood, usually a deadline) being replaced by a 'stroll',[6] a meandering journey or voyage, often through the city, without clear destination. Fourthly, the proliferation of clichés in a world without the totalizing rationale of an encompassing situation. Fifth and finally, the recognition, and condemnation of a giant conspiracy that keeps the clichés circulating. This may be associated with state enforced surveillance, for example, often in relation to the interests of an increasingly global form of capitalism.[7]

As examples of these five points of weakening of the sensory-motor regime of the movement-image, Deleuze chooses predominantly US independent films. He discusses the dispersive situation in John Cassavetes' *The Killing of a Chinese Bookie* (1976); the stroll in Martin Scorsese's *Taxi Driver* (1976); and the proliferation of clichés and recognition of the conspiracy to propagate them in Robert Altman's *Nashville* (1975). As all these films are from the 1970s, it is perhaps no surprise that – immediately after listing the five characteristics – Deleuze states that he is discussing 'the crisis of both the action-image and the American Dream',[8] suggesting further that the whole (the globalizing situation) in which we can no longer believe is conceived by Deleuze to be a national whole. Thus Deleuze chooses as exemplars films that emerge during a certain moment in US history, after the social turmoil of the 1960s, the loss in Vietnam and the Watergate scandal, as well as (we might add, considering the impact of this time of change on cinema) the drop-off in attendance experienced by classical Hollywood films and the rise of the new breed of *auteurs*.

Despite the fact that *Cinema 1* contains discussion of many European films as illustrative of different types of movement-images, by its conclusion

Deleuze establishes the action-image as the dominant form of the movement-image, and equates the movement-image with classical Hollywood cinema. In these final pages, then, classical Hollywood functions as a tacitly understood norm against which post-war European art films are seen to differ in *Cinema 2*. Deleuze's phrasing is very revealing in this respect. For example, consider his use of the words 'cinema' and 'American tradition' in the following sentence from the final chapter of *Cinema 1*: 'the cinema had to begin again from zero, questioning afresh all the accepted facts of the American tradition.'[9] Here we see the normative position Deleuze attributes to classical Hollywood, in relation to all other 'cinema', as the dominant form of the movement-image. By positing the action-image as norm, the 'pure optical situation'[10] (or 'opsign'[11]) in which the seer is first encountered in *Cinema 2* – in particular in Italian neorealism and the European new waves – can then be said to emerge due to a slackening of the sensory-motor regime (and indeed, continuity) of the action-image. Accordingly, the seer inhabits the interval between perception and action that is prolonged when they become uncertain as to how to act in relation to their milieu, and emerges precisely from the uncertainty of ruined post-war Europe.

Subsequently, at the start of *Cinema 2* Deleuze argues that the pure optical situation, arising in films like Roberto Rossellini's *Germania anno zero*, creates a 'cinema of the seer and no longer of the agent'.[12] The pure optical situation is one in which perception struggles to progress to action. The sensory-motor link of the action-image has been loosened by the emergence of situations to which the character does not know how to respond physically, and they become instead a witness to time passing. This is the evolution that Deleuze charts from the crisis of the action-image to the emergence of the pure optical situation, the time-image thus beginning to become visible along with the seer. From the opsign the rest of Deleuze's work on the time-image follows: from the appearance of time in the image (crystal images, peaks of present, sheets of the past, the labyrinthine powers of the false), to the thinking-image that I discuss in Chapter 3. In this process the role of the child becomes extremely important. Deleuze notes that:

> The role of the child in neorealism has been pointed out, notably in De Sica (and later in France with Truffaut); this is because, in the adult world, the child is affected by a certain motor helplessness, but one which makes him all the more capable of seeing and hearing.[13]

The child is very often confronted by situations to which he or she does not know how to respond, be they at either end of the spectrum that Deleuze

identifies: banal, everyday situations, or indeed, 'exceptional or limit circumstances'.[14] In either case, the child seer encounters something 'intolerable and unbearable', something 'too powerful, or too unjust' and therefore
beyond their power to act upon.[15] Instead they are only able to gaze upon,
to witness or contemplate the pure optical situation, a direct image of time.
As such an unbearable situation, encountered in an any-space-whatever,
is 'invested by the senses, before action takes shape in it'.[16] The child
seer, in other words, is formed in a two-way sensory relationship with the
pure optical situation, even if they are not necessarily able to decisively
overcome it with action, as their predecessors might have done in the
movement-image.

The intolerable situations that shape the lives of these child seers are
directly linked to historical circumstances, around the break Deleuze
perceives as occurring after World War Two. In the preface to the English
edition of *Cinema 2*, Deleuze asks:

> Why is the Second World War taken as a break? The fact is that, in Europe,
> the post-war period has greatly increased the situations which we no
> longer know how to react to, in spaces which we no longer know how
> to describe. These were 'any spaces whatever', deserted but inhabited,
> disused warehouses, waste ground, cities in the course of demolition or
> reconstruction. And in these any-spaces-whatever a new race of charac-
> ters was stirring, kind of mutant: they saw rather than acted, they were
> seers. Hence Rossellini's great trilogy, *Europe 51, Stromboli, Germany Year 0*:
> a child in a destroyed city . . . [17]

Whether we consider this shift to the wandering seer to be solely due to
the world of immediate post-war reconstruction (as in Italian neorealism)
or the expansion of modernity (as in films like Federico Fellini's *La Dolce
Vita* (1960)), the seer is, for Deleuze, a specific product of the post-war
world. Deleuze is emphatic on this point only a few pages later (after examining an isolated example from Asia, finding the pure optical situation in
the films of Japanese director Yasujiro Ozu that, incongruously if we follow
Deleuze's argument, appeared prior to the war), when he discusses the
state of transformation encountered by the seemingly passive but, Deleuze
argues, actually mutating characters of the time-image:

> In the west as in Japan, they are in the grip of a mutation, they are them-
> selves mutants. On the subject of *Two or Three Things* . . . Godard says that
> *to describe* is to observe mutations. Mutation of Europe after the war, muta-
> tion of an Americanized Japan, mutation of France in '68: it is not the

cinema that turns away from politics, it becomes completely political, but in another way.[18]

A clear sense comes through in Deleuze's argument, then, that the seer (including the child seer) encounters history in the making, and this is very often a national history. These are characters directly encountering contemporary social and political mutations, and who are mutating along with these historically shifting contexts. This is seen specifically in the immediate post-war films, for example as we follow Rossellini's child seer through the rubble of immediate post-war Berlin in *Germania anno zero*, or when we consider the child observing his father's meandering voyage around a rapidly redeveloping post-war Rome in search for his stolen bicycle in Vittorio De Sica's *Ladri di biciclette/Bicycle Thieves* (1948). In both these instances, the child seer invests these situations with their gaze, taking stock of the event as it takes stock of them, in preparation for the mutually informing action (or perhaps rather, mutation) that is to follow.

Thus it becomes clear that the pure optical situation that is experienced by the child seer provides a way of showing the sudden loss of a coherent whole (encompassing situation) that occurs during a time of national mutation. This despite the fact that Deleuze's *Cinema* books seemingly chart the change from movement- to time-image as though it were illustrative of a globally informing shift in conception of time that emerged after World War Two. As is evident once we apply this logic to an Argentine film, made in the 2000s but set in the 1970s, the manner in which Deleuze establishes this binary between certain types of US and European cinemas towards the end of *Cinema 1* and into *Cinema 2* is one of the most difficult aspects of his work. Indeed, Deleuze's positioning of the Second World War as a pivotal moment that marked the emergence of the time-image does not make sense of this contemporary South American film's evocation of a pure optical situation, or its locating of a child seer in the national past, in the 1970s.

Neorealism/Neo-history

A brief plot synopsis will assist in this discussion of the distinction between the child seer in neorealism and in recent South American films like *Kamchatka*. *Kamchatka* opens in Argentina in 1976 just after the junta has taken power through military coup, establishing a period of military rule that will last until 1983. A middle-class family (research scientist mother

(Cecilia Roth), lawyer father (Ricardo Darín) and two sons) flee Buenos Aires in their Citroen family car for a secluded house in the suburbs. They are wanted by the state, which is rounding up left-wing students, revolutionaries, militants, subversives, those connected to them, and anyone potentially in opposition to the right-wing military regime. The protagonist, the little boy Harry (Matías Del Pozo) struggles to understand what is happening, and why, from the snippets of conversations he overhears, and the reports he sees on television. He comes to terms with his internal exile by associating himself with Harry Houdini, playing out in miniature the acts of the military regime on the populace as he tries to emulate Houdini's greatest escapes. As the overriding sense of oppression and terror gathers force (the military remains a primarily unseen but omnipresent threat to the family dwelling), the parents leave Harry and his younger brother with their grandparents, and flee. Like many opponents of the regime who disappeared at the time, they are never heard of again.

In *Kamchatka*, the intolerable situation is the nation's mutation under military rule. This manifests itself through the experiences of a child who inhabits a kind of sensory-motor limbo while his family is on the run from the military government of the nation-state. Harry experiences a prolonged temporal interval between perception and action, an extended hiatus with little hope of an end through decisive action upon the now militarized milieu. Once abandoned and hunted by the state, and with no further redress to influence the whole, the seer encounters the pure optical situation. The loosening of the sensory-motor regime he encounters creates a situation in which time is experienced in its full force, this direct image of duration replicating at once the conditions of internal exile (perpetual and fearful watching and waiting), and indeed, the indefinite sense of temporality that exists in the realm of the child. Here, then, the sensory-motor regime is brought into crisis by a national event. This time, however, rather than post-war rebuilding (whether across Europe or in Japan); May '68 in France; or Vietnam, Watergate or a more general crisis of the American Dream; in Argentina the whole no longer functions as a globalizing situation because the onset of military rule has broken the previously defining link between the people and their milieu.

What marks *Kamchatka* as different from the films Deleuze discusses is that the pure optical situation of military rule is here recreated in retrospect, as though reconstructing the immediacy of this experience in a cinematically manufactured virtual layer of the past. Under military rule, censorship, along with the detention, murder and disappearance of filmmakers, ensured that this transforming moment in history was not captured in the same way as is found in Italian neorealism. Although the conditions for transition featured previously in documentaries like *Hora de los hornos/ The Hour of the Furnaces* (Argentina, 1968) in the main depictions of this transformation were censored until the end of military rule. From the 1980s onwards numerous films addressed subjects such as the disappearances of political opponents, not least the Oscar winning *La historia oficial/The Official Story* (1985). Even so, unlike, say, Rossellini in post-war Italy, Ozu in post-war Japan, Godard in post-May '68 France, or Altman in post-Vietnam USA, Argentine filmmakers were unable to make such directly political films at the time, to film with any degree of freedom the pure optical situations that emerged in these historically determined any-space-whatevers at the point of violent historical mutation.

Accordingly, something very different happens to the role of the child seer when they are depicted witnessing recreated events in the past. Rather than the child seer observing a mutation of (or a breaking with) the national past in the present, as in neorealism, the child seer in *Kamchatka* provides a pathway into the past for the film's audience. Harry grants the (often adult) audience access to the pure optical situation of a country mutating under military rule that was censored or banned from cinema screens at that time. Instead of a film made and set in the present commenting on the mutating present (*Germania anno zero*), *Kamchatka* is a film set in the past which comments on the interaction between past and present, and thereby reconsiders this moment of transformation in national history in a virtually reconstructed form, that may yet inform the actual present. In Italian neorealism the intolerable event can be witnessed by the child at first hand, in films that position characters within the spaces of their mutating post-war milieu and ask the question of "what is happening" in the pure optical situation? In a post-dictatorship film like *Kamchatka*, by contrast, events are recreated from a historical distance of over 30 years, and the question asked becomes instead "what has happened" in the pure optical situation? In each case the role of the child seer is different depending on whether they are witnessing history in the making, or its retrospective recreation: whether they are situated *in* history as it happens, or are figured *as* history as it is recreated.

The key to this difference lies in the function of the interval between perception and action, and its relationship to the time-image. In the pure optical situation the seer catches a glimpse of duration, of time passing in its own right. Into this interval the past may often intercede, interacting with the present, for instance, in the mingling of virtual layers of time in the works of directors like Federico Fellini and Alain Resnais. The interval which the seer inhabits, then, has a particular relationship with the past, due to the crisis of the action-image that occurs when the whole (encompassing, or globalizing situation) begins to mutate.

In the films in which Deleuze observes the child seer, the past remains quiet, and fails to disturb or inform the child seer in the interval between perception and action. In neorealism in particular, in the interval between perception and action there is a lack of informing past for the child seer to draw upon. The present stretches ahead of the child seer into an uncertain future. The past, for its part, is absent, as is emphasized by the fact that the child is also new to the world, the equivalent blank slate with which to explore such a past-less place as a city in ruins. In *Kamchatka*, by contrast, the child seer inhabits a recreated virtual layer of the past that exists in a circuit with the actual present. In the interval between perception and action we see not the hope for the future found in neorealism, but the foundations of the present in which we watch the film. In neither instance do we see an informing past intervene in the child's present in the sense of, say, a flashback. However, what we do see in *Kamchatka*, which we did not in neorealism, is, precisely, the past. We see on screen, as though (like a child) witnessing a situation to which we do not know how to react, the emergence of the virtual and informing past that appeared during the national mutation to military rule. The fact that this is a cinematically recreated past, and that the difficulties of cinematically recreating this link to the past under military rule is the subject of self-conscious exploration, is therefore entirely appropriate. This is, after all, a reconstruction on film of the previously censored mutation that occurred at that time.

If we remain with Bergson's model of time, in *Kamchatka* history is constructed for the viewer in a similar manner to our processing of memory, the major difference being that the national history we see is constructed, as opposed to remembered. Accordingly, the film creates a fulfilling layer of the past to enable a form of historical attentive recollection, but because this layer of the past was officially censored, its construction is self-consciously foregrounded by the film. In this way, a virtual layer of the national past is provided that can be inhabited by a present generation, once rendered childlike, in search of the lost past. Hence history is created in these particular time-images rather like a nationally informing memory.

In *Kamchatka* the child seer observes a pure optical situation which, unbeknown to them – but known to the virtual, time travelling filmmakers and audience – is teeming with the past. This moment of mutation is brim full of the history of the nation since the 1970s. For the child seer, then, overcoming this situation, learning to extend perception into action, is also to overcome history, to provide a new direction for the (national) whole, for the present, from the past. We are witnessing the virtual double of a national mutation in the present, the virtual or shadow past of the actual present (a virtual layer of the past that is offered as a potential labyrinthine past that may make sense of events in the present) the oscillation of which with the present creates history. The pure optical situation of the past thereby extends itself through virtual/actual conjunction with the present, in order to construct history without the linear sensory-motor continuity of the movement-image.

(Adult)-child seer/Adult-child seer

There is a double address in *Kamchatka*, of a child's point of view that is informed by an adult's recreation of childhood. The child seer functions in retrospect with a sort of double vision, their perspective informed by the years since this (national) childhood in the 1970s, such that the filmmakers portray the child seer encountering events that they cannot understand but about which the filmmakers (and the audience) are informed. Various critics have noted how this double address, which I think of as the "adult-child seer", typically exists in some form in child-centred films made by adult filmmakers.[19] For example, Karen Lury notes in *The Child in Film* (2010) how the apparent innocence of the child character is often 'framed by the adult's knowingness and retrospective understanding'.[20] This is especially so in autobiographical films like Truffaut's *Les quatre cents coups/The 400 Blows* (1959). Even so there is a subtle difference between the way this happens in existing limit situations that capture a historical moment as it changes (*Germania anno zero, Ladri di biciclette*) and in films where these situations are recreated in order to observe them mutate once more. This effect has already been observed in another context. Paul Sutton, discussing the Italian film *Io non ho paura/I'm Not Scared* (2003) by director Gabriele Salvatores (also set during the 1970s), argues for a reconsideration and development of Deleuze's position on the child:

> [F]or Deleuze, the child remains ultimately passive, despite the active spectatorial affects that his or her optical witness might provoke. Salvatores's film revisits this specific cinematic heritage but, as a contemporary film set in the 1970s, it allows the spectator to share in Michele's [the child protagonist's] innocent and immediate witness of events while also enabling the active critical reflection that accrues from the adult spectator's historical knowledge of events during this period.[21]

In child films set in the past, then, the child seer has a different degree of agency due to the more informed relationship that the adult filmmaker has to history.

This is not to say that child films set in the present are somehow "objective" renderings of the moment in time during which they are set. It would be a fallacy to consider that any film was able to objectively capture history as it is being made. There are political agendas structuring the revisionism of films which address even the most recent past, such as Rossellini's *Roma, città aperta/Rome Open City* (1945) which deploys child seers as witnesses to the activities and sacrifices of the Italian resistance only just prior to its making. Even films shot in the immediate post-war present like *Germania anno zero* (made in 1947, set in 1947) clearly manipulate the manner in which "reality" and "history" are depicted. Thus, although Rossellini may have shot parts of his immediate post-war films on location in the ruins of Italy and Germany, his use of constructed sets and the generic elements and stereotypes that he deploys (in particular drawing on the melodramatic tradition for his sexually perverse Nazi villains and his embattled Italian families) demonstrate the carefully constructed, real*ist* nature of these films.[22] As Rosalind Galt argues in *The New European Cinema* (2006), concerning the problematic history created by films shot in the post-war ruins of Germany:

> The ruin image proposes a fictional break, which preempts any need to engage with the recent past. It enables the reassuring idea that Nazism is firmly consigned to the past, producing a discourse of new beginnings, at once optimistic and self-indulgent. For any claim on German subjectivity, it is a sign of guilt and a sign of penance. It implies a new "we" – the we who regret – and this new subject cancels out the old Nazi one, articulating a non-Nazi German subject that precludes any possibility of Nazis remaining in the rubble.[23]

Thus, regardless of the "real" (ruins shot on location) or "fake" (recreated 1970s locations) nature of the any-space-whatevers captured on film – or indeed, the manner in which they are used to create pure optical situations inhabited by child seers – there is as much recreation of history in a neorealist film made and set in the present of 1947 as there is in a South American film made in the 2000s but set in the 1970s. Both are cinematically (re)constructed virtual layers of history. Even so, the relationship between the child characters and the adult filmmakers remains noticeably different.

As the work of Galt, and others writing on rubble films demonstrate, movies like *Germania anno zero* often attempt to construct a break with the historical past[24] which echoes Deleuze's thinking regarding post-war films set in urban ruins. The child is depicted by an adult filmmaker, both of whom exist in a present which has been cut off from its past by the 'fictional break' of which Galt speaks. In neorealism, whatever the agenda of the filmmaker, the adult and the child are equally uninformed by the past. In addition, for both the future that will emerge from the rubble is unknown. Thus there is a greater degree of autonomy for the, as it were, "(adult)-child seer" shown casting about in the interval between perception and action in search of a way to inform their actions in the present. The adult filmmaker cannot foresee the future any more than the child actor can. In *Kamchatka*, by contrast, the adult filmmaker is entirely aware of what has happened in the decades in between, and depicts instead an "adult-child seer" searching in an interval that occurs in the pure optical situation (the cinematically recreated past) for a way to inform the present. Herein lies the major difference, then, that in the South American film the filmmakers and their audiences know what lies in store for the children depicted (because the child's future is the filmmaker's/audience's past), whereas those watching *Germania anno zero* could not foresee the future of the child protagonist. In the later films the absent past that characterized neorealism's break with history is supplanted by a past-present temporal circuit that reconstructs history. This reconstructed history is created through an adult-child relationship which enables the audience to perceive the (national) past again, as it were, like a child, caught in the interval between perception and action.

Unlike the neorealist directors, the South American filmmakers – by reconstructing their national childhood past through the eyes of the child seer – create a different relationship between viewer, film and history. Here Emma Wilson's argument is helpful, that a child's response to events in a film can have a remarkable impact upon an adult spectator, creating involuntary emotions and a 'lack of mastery' akin to that of the 'motor helplessness' Deleuze observed in the child seer. Wilson writes:

Emotions felt, remembered by an adult temporarily dispossessed, also recall a child's (more extensive) lack of control over its circumstances, its environment, even at times over its own body. The adult, overwhelmed by experience, by emotions of intensity of either negative or positive affect, in the very experience of being overwhelmed involuntarily returns to the child's state of helplessness (motor, emotional or political).[25]

This coexistence of the adult and the child in the viewing experience, 'where adults suddenly *feel* like children',[26] correlates precisely with the emotional identification of the adult viewer with the past via the "adult-child seer". In *Kamchatka*, then, the visit to the pure optical situation of a childhood lived under military rule viscerally transports the viewer into this virtual layer of the past, rendering them childlike in the face of history. The "adult-child seer" experiences the helplessness of a child when the whole, whose operations they cannot comprehend, ceases to function in the manner they are used to, ceases even to respond to the legitimate actions of their parents. This is precisely the power of the "adult-child seer" in these films, to at once be overwhelmed (to paraphrase Wilson, in motor, emotional and political terms) by the limit situation, and yet (through the critical reflection noted by Sutton) to be aware of its historical resonances, even if the child character is not.

For this reason, the child's point of view on the moment of historical mutation is different in neorealism and the South American films. In neorealism the "(adult)-child seer" provides a fresh pair of eyes through which to see a present that has suddenly lost its past. In *Kamchatka* the "adult-child seer" provides a way to observe again a layer of the past that resonates with the present. Thus *Kamchatka* uses childhood in a manner that is often deployed in cinema, as a metaphor for the national past.[27] Military rule becomes a moment of "national childhood" in the 1970s, a period of watching and waiting, and sensory-motor inaction, from which the post-dictatorship present day stems. This explains the coincidence of *Kamchatka* alongside the child-centred films from Chile, Brazil and Uruguay in the early mid-2000s (all countries under military rule in the 1970s when their narratives are set) that use the child to address the national past in a way that is pertinent for the filmmakers and audiences who have reached a point in their adult lives when such a re-examination of their, and their national past, is of interest.

I should make it clear, however, that I do not consider all child films set in the past to necessarily function in precisely this way. Nevertheless, examining issues pertinent to national history, child films are increasingly found in various world cinemas, circulating, as Thomas Elsaesser observes,[28] on the art cinema circuit (international film festivals, independent cinema chains and specialist DVD distributors). There is, then, a recognizable international child film format to which these South American examples belong, even if *Kamchatka* is most accurately considered a mainstream melodrama (typically it focuses on a family in peril that represents the nation in microcosm, and at various points uses the film's formal features to construct an emotionally affective drama), than an art film. Although there are numerous examples of this trend from around the world, the paradigmatic case is undoubtedly the Spanish film *El espíritu de la colmena/Spirit of the Beehive* (1973), which, Rob Stone argues, uses the analogy of a beehive dulled by smoke to stand in for the suppressed state of post-war Spanish society, a situation which only the child, Ana (Ana Torrent) is able to challenge into potentially reawakening with her vital life force.[29] As various critics noted at the time of its release, the film subtly redraws Spain's national history through its focus on an isolated rural community in the 1940s, in a manner that provided, Paul Julian Smith observes, a 'political and social challenge to the Francoism which still clung to power on its release'.[30]

Similarly, national past and present are put into dialogue by these South American films. In *Kamchatka*, the child left "orphaned" by historical events is a representative of a generation reaching middle age (including the filmmakers and the audience) when the film is produced over 30 years later. Rather than observing a child in a ruined city as the origins of the next, future generation (as in neorealism), the child under military rule is figured in an informing layer of the past that is of relevance for the present generation. The mutation of the national whole is thereby explored by this recreation of the past. The search for informed action that will influence the future of the whole is no longer focused exclusively on the question of "what is happening?" as we mutate, but on "what happened?" when we mutated. In both instances the events are manipulated (this is a film after all), as is the child seer's reaction to the pure optical situations they encounter. Even so, the difference remains between a child *in* and a child *as* history, an "(adult)-child seer" situated so as to react to events as they are happening (*Germania anno zero*) and an "adult-child seer" placed (by filmmakers who have lived this period of history as a child) to witness events as they happened in *Kamchatka*.

Therefore, although for Deleuze the child seer emerged in the post-war era as a way of considering a changing post-war situation (or more accurately, national crises of various sorts which negotiated this changing global situation), in *Kamchatka* and other South American films of the 2000s the "adult-child seer" is a tool for exploring and (re)creating history. The function is still the same, to observe a mutating national history, but the manner in which this occurs is slightly different when this occurs in a constructed present (neorealism) or a recreated past that oscillates with the present (*Kamchatka*).

Kamchatka (2002)

Kamchatka is a self-conscious meditation on how the Argentine past under military rule has been, like the many opponents of the military regime still unaccounted for, "disappeared". The film recreates this period of national history by focussing on the family in exile, in the secluded moment before the disappearance of the parents, who function as a metaphor for a generation's "disappeared" past. The house they inhabit in the suburbs becomes the limit situation to which Harry must learn how to react if this history is to be overcome. Because, historically, this family will eventually disappear (the parents captured and murdered, the children orphaned), *Kamchatka* self-consciously foregrounds its reconstruction of this virtual layer of the past, stressing its informing nature for the present generation and its cinematic absence from national history. Through children's games learned in this self-consciously magical cinematic visit to a reconstructed past, *Kamchatka* explores the pure optical situation, at once an escape into the past and an escape from the past. It also enables international audiences to understand Argentina's history of military rule in a way that potentially impacts on contemporary middle-class society, both nationally and internationally.

As noted above, in *Kamchatka* the wandering route through the mutating city of neorealism is replaced by a more secluded story of life in hiding, or internal exile. There is still, however, a sense of a journey without a goal, and therefore a limit situation in response to which characters are incapable of acting. The house in the suburbs in which the family hides is a temporary refuge in which to experience the mercilessly slow passing of time, because there is nowhere else to escape to. In this sense the intolerable situation which the "adult-child seer" witnesses is as much this moment of familial crisis as it is the national silence and secrecy that surrounded the disappearances themselves. Even before the parents are captured the family is in exile, their original names are deliberately forgotten as they try to establish new, fictional identities after the state has ceased to recognize them, ceased to enable them to act in a manner that might influence the whole.

One standout moment towards the end of the film sums up its self-conscious reconstruction of this cinematically disappeared moment of national history. The family risks a visit to Harry's grandfather in the country, on his birthday. While there, Harry asks his grandmother why she has kept his father's room as it was when he was a child. She replies that 'It's my time machine. Whenever I come to dust I sit here and look around, and remember things.' Within this context of one generation evoking the childhood of their offspring through observation of the pure optical situation (a room preserved in its past state, in a sense akin to a film set, through the toys, posters, clothes, and other remnants of Harry's father's youth in which to sit and contemplate the past) Harry and his father have a symbolic exchange by the lake. Harry's father is depicted through the viewfinder of Harry's camera, the screen being suddenly reduced in size by a large black frame and a light meter, to suggest a point of view seen through a camera. In this self-reflexive moment Harry's father is initially playful, stressing his dislike of having his photograph taken in a jovial manner, until, directly addressing the audience who are positioned along with Harry, his tone turns serious.

Harry: What are you thinking?
Father: That we should have come here more often.
Harry: And why don't we stay?
Father: Because we can't. . . . We can't son, we can't. Do you understand?

At this point Harry's father, overcome with sadness, moves out of shot, and Harry snaps the photo too late (the shutter is clearly heard on the sound-track) taking only a shot of the empty lake.

In terms of the diegetic world, when Harry's father says that they cannot stay at his father's he is discussing the danger they would all be in if they were found there. Yet, coming as it does at this moment of cinematic self-reflexivity, in which the film meditates on its own existence as a device for framing the past, his words can also be interpreted as referring to the impossibility of prolonging cinematically this visit to the disappeared past.

Kamchatka shows that cinema is the time machine that can temporarily transport the adult-seer to a nostalgic world recreated in the manner of a preserved little boy's bedroom. However, while it is possible to visit this disappeared layer of the past, we cannot stay indefinitely. Rather, the return to a fully unified familial origin in this virtually reconstructed pure optical situation can only be sustained long enough for a lesson to be learned from the past. After all, this is a past that cannot be captured permanently (exactly as Harry cannot capture his father's image in a photograph), because it has already disappeared.

This sequence has resonances with many other cinematic depictions of the disappeared, whose representation, whether in literature, theatre or

cinema, has always been a difficult issue.[31] Catherine Grant discusses precisely this problem in relation to *La noche de los lápices/The Night of the Pencils*
(1986), an Argentine film that appeared in the immediate wake of military
rule and dealt with the disappearance of six high school students guilty of
demanding reduced rates on public transport (only one of who was ever
released from prison). As Grant notes of the use of photographs in the film,
because of the status of the young students as "disappeared", the film 'cannot
explicitly memorialise them as *dead*, because what happened to them . . .
was not known'.[32] Accordingly, 'the film's "story", in particular its ambiva-
lence about the conventional association of testimonial photography
with death, was always already circumscribed by that particular History'.[33]
Similarly, in *Kamchatka* Harry's failure to snap his father's picture suggests
that the past cannot be recaptured on film, only revisited. After all, the pure
optical and sound situation that confronts the "adult-child seer" can only
last as long as the film does.

   In this respect, then, the film functions as a virtual layer of memory in
the manner conceived of by Deleuze's Bergsonian perspective in *Cinema 2*,
as an informing past that *is*, as opposed to an actualized past that *was* (the
latter being a recollection-image).[34] It refuses actualization as memorial,
refuses to create an actualized image (a photographic snapshot of one of
the disappeared) that might correspond to the present, as, for example, a
recollection-image flashback does when it fills the gap between perception
and action in an informing manner.[35] Instead, it creates a virtual past that
can oscillate with the actual present. As the past has been disappeared,
Kamchatka stresses the virtual and transitory nature of the past that it creates.
This is a layer of history that can never be actualized because it has been
disappeared from our cinematic history banks. Instead, in *Kamchatka*, the
virtual past can be visited by the time travelling viewer only long enough for
the past to be recreated, and a lesson learned from this process.

Houdini Escapes the Past

Kamchatka begins with a science class in which Harry is being taught the
origins of life. Harry and his friend are distracted, and play hangman. The
word they are searching for is 'ABRACADABRA'. Then, when the family
initially arrives in the house in the suburbs, Harry finds a children's book
about Houdini, hidden away in a wardrobe. From this magical entry point
into the film, until Harry "signs out" at the end (he writes his name and the
date in the Houdini book and replaces it in the wardrobe), the time travelling

"adult-child seer" is magically transported into the past to explore, through child's play, the recreated pure optical situation of 1976.

In this self-consciously recreated past the lesson that *Kamchatka* offers, the tool with which to overcome the prolonged moment of history found in the pure optical situation, is contained in the children's games that Harry plays during his time in limbo. These micro-movements replay in miniature the actual historical events that the film cannot capture, replacing the actual limit conditions (not the city in ruins of neorealism in this instance, but the military crackdown on the population) with lessons for the "adult-child seer" on how to "escape" from the past under military rule.

When a junta news broadcast appears on the television, noticeably the only one seen in the film, Harry's father becomes absorbed in the denial voiced by the Minister of the Economy, José Alfredo Martínez de Hoz, of the taking of political prisoners. Harry's father describes this as a 'white-washing' of the disappearances. Simultaneously, Harry gets his little brother to tie him up so that he can practice escaping like Houdini. His little brother, however, taking his father's words literally, begins to paint the captive Harry's face white, claiming that he is 'whitewashing' the prisoner. Again, after Harry's father has shown Harry and his brother where to hide if there is an emergency, and the way to the local village (presumably in case of his and their mother's arrest), Harry similarly devises an escape route for the toads in the swimming pool. When Lucas (Tomás Fonzi), the young militant who comes to stay with the family first arrives, Harry "interrogates" Lucas as to his origins and identity, questions which Lucas refuses to answer. In the course of this interrogation, Harry learns that there are other reasons for leaving home than either a fight with parents or marriage, such as wanting to save the world. Later, Harry persuades Lucas to tie him up, again so he can practice escaping like Houdini. The too-tight knots inadvertently become torturous, causing Harry pain. Noticeably, once Lucas has freed him, Harry immediately questions what might happen to him and his brother should his parents not return to the house one day.

What is played out in miniature through Harry's games is inferred to be taking place in the larger mutation of the whole. Although the encompassing situation is absent from the screen the power of the nation-state is still evidently controlling the family's life. Accordingly, after learning about the threatening situation through childhood games of torture and escape, when Harry visits his grandfather (Héctor Alterio) he gives him a full, frank and detailed picture of the dangerous situation they face. This moment is a revelation for his grandfather who, living in the countryside, has not understood the dangers to his son's family imposed by the military crackdown.

It is also an indication of the knowledge that has been acquired through children's games, by the "adult-child seer" in the pure optical situation. In this moment Harry appears at his most adult, as he puts the recent histori-cal events – that he has processed through absorbing events that he sees and playing out their consequences – into perspective for this grandfather. Thus these games replay in microcosm the major political events overshad-owing the family, which are not seen in the film, and although they cannot enable the "adult-child seer" to overcome the situation, they can point towards a possible future escape from the past.

The most evident lesson in this respect is that provided by the board game, *T.E.G* (*Plan Táctico y Estratégico de la Guerra/Plan for War Tactics and Strategy*). When Lucas leaves the family, Harry risks a bus journey to Buenos Aires to visit his school friend, only to be turned away at the door by his friend's mother, even though Harry knows his friend is in. When she sug-gests that in future he call first before visiting, Harry (having been warned many times by his mother of the dangers of making phone calls) puts events together and realizes that should he call, his life, and that of his family, would be in danger. On his return he plays a final game of *T.E.G* with his father. *T.E.G* is a board game about armies conquering the world, very similar to *Risk*. Previously Harry's father had always beaten him, but on this night Harry holds the entire board/world, except for the far-flung Russian province of Kamchatka. Try as he might, he cannot breach his father's last-ditch stronghold. The film ends soon afterwards when Harry and his brother are left with their grandfather, Harry's father's parting advice to him being the whispered word, 'Kamchatka'. In Harry's final voiceover he states that 'Kamchatka is the place to be when you want to resist'.

The film's ending further illustrates that this disappeared moment in the national past, even though a virtual limbo that cannot connect to the present by becoming actual again, can still form a temporary circuit that will inform the present. It is a "place" – at once a peninsula of Eastern Russia, a part of a children's game about military domination, and even a film – that can provide an escape into, and from the legacy of, the past. The origin of this conflation of the past with Kamchatka lies with the script-writer Marcelo Figueras who used Herman Melville's *Moby Dick* (1851) as inspiration for the film's name, citing Melville's description of the char-acter Queequeg's island of origin in particular.[36] According to Melville, Queequeg originated on 'Kokovoko, an island far away to the West and South. It is not down in any map; true places never are.'[37] Thus the place, Kamchatka, from which Harry will draw strength in the future, is also the film *Kamchatka*, both of which are a non-existent place – a place of exile and a disappeared past – but also a place from and in which to resist. Noticeably, Figueras had previously collaborated with director Marcelo Piñeyro on *Plata quemada/Burnt Money* (2000), another story about a closely knit outlaw grouping in a liminal location, as were other films by Piñeyro, such as *Caballos salvajes/Wild Horses* (1995). In *Kamchatka*, then, Figueras and Piñeyro out-law the family to a recreated past, in which they temporarily reside as internal exiles. While there, by confronting the disappeared nature of the past as a pure optical situation, resistance is made possible. Hence the reali-zation that the past has been disappeared is the motivation that *Kamchatka* offers for overcoming history and escaping this historical legacy.

At the time the film was made, Figueras felt that the then contemporary search for identity in Argentina found its origins in the 1970s.[38] The 1970s was the period of Figueras's childhood, who, born in 1963, would only have been slightly older than Harry at the time of military rule. Like many of his generation, then, his investigation of this time requires an investigation of the disappeared. In this Figueras is far from alone, with similar examples existing in a range of different media. The films *Los pasos perdidos/The Lost Steps* (2001) and *Cautiva/Captive* (2003), for instance, both concern teenagers uncovering forgotten pasts as children of the disappeared. There are also documentaries which address the relationship between the chil-dren of the disappeared and the past, such as *Los Rubios/The Blonds* (2003); along with literary works like Laura Alcoba's novel *The Rabbit House* (2008) exploring autobiographically the period of the coup through the eyes of a child in hiding (and thereby distinct from adult accounts of captivity to appear immediately after military rule, like Alicia Partnoy's *The Little School* (1986)); and the street graffiti and murals (*Escrache*) of H.i.j.o.s (Hijos por la Identidad y la Justicia contra el Olvido y el Silencio/Sons and Daughters for Identity and Justice Against Forgetting and Silence), the organization of the sons and daughters of the disappeared, founded in 1995, who work to perpetuate both the memories of their parents and the public exposure of their killers.[39]

This output is in addition to the recent films set during military rule itself, such as *Garage Olimpo* (1999) and *Buenos Aires 1977/Chronicle of an Escape* (2006), that began to emerge in the 1990s after a period of relative silence on the topic in Argentine cinema[40] (following the amnesty laws of the late 1980s, and the *Indulto* (Pardon) of the military granted by Carlos Menem in 1990).[41] In this sense, *Kamchatka* appears rather like a younger generation's updating of María Luisa Bemberg's costume drama *Camila* (1984), that appeared in the immediate aftermath of military rule, allegorically critiqu-ing the regime's repressive nature by focusing on a young couple in hiding who are ultimately executed.[42] The couple are replaced in *Kamchatka* by a young family in hiding, thereby giving the next generation's perspective on the years under military rule. As Constanza Burucúa argues in *Confronting the 'Dirty War' in Argentine Cinema, 1983–1993* (2009), the family is often a recurring element of post-dictatorship Argentine cinema because it bears testament to 'the family unit as the primary victim of a fascist and repressive policy of state'.[43] Thus in *Kamchatka* the family experiences this national mutation in miniature, in the pure optical situation.

1976/2002

Despite the subject matter, *Kamchatka* is not entirely pessimistic, as it attempts to offer viewers in the 2000s a way to learn from the past. For example, although the family is forced to erase their previous identity, this is also a chance to choose a new identity. Harry Houdini enables the "adult-child seer" to observe, relive in miniature through children's games, under-stand, and finally, escape the past. Yet the question remains of how this self-conscious past engages with the actual present of early twenty-first-century Argentina. How is the recreated virtual past put into contact with the present by the "adult-child seer"? The answer lies in the economic mutation of the nation that is alluded to in the film. In 1976 the mutation occurring in Buenos Aires was not one that was as visible as post-war Germany in ruins in *Germania anno zero*. Rather, in Argentina this was an economic transformation that would cause social mutation during the years of military rule and the decades afterwards, as Argentina's formerly protectionist and nationalized economy was increasingly opened up to privatization and free trade with the outside world.

Across South America, in line with the commercial and ideological interests of the USA – and backed by the austerity measures imposed on indebted countries in return for financial aid from the International Monetary Fund (IMF)[44] – the eradication of left-wing opposition (be it communist, socialist or simply opposition to military rule) coincided with the USA's broader Cold War aims of expanding the capitalist free market across the third world.[45] This was most clearly seen in the influence of neoliberal economic policy in Chile after the 1973 coup, which preceded Argentina's swing to military rule by only a few years. The cities in "ruin" that were to follow under the junta were due not only to the military crackdown on the population (seen in Argentina in the presence of the Triple A death squads raiding homes, interring, torturing and disappearing the population), but also to the monetary policy of the junta, which set the stage for the decades that followed. In particular, these policies saw cities "ruined" by the dismantling of the welfare state, rising unemployment, elimination of trade unions, the widening gap between rich and poor, homelessness, bankruptcies, sale of public utilities, inflation, increased cost of living, sudden influx of cheap foreign imports due to the removal of trade barriers, closed factories and shops, etc.[46]

In *Kamchatka*, then, as the city cannot be shown undergoing its mutation, these historical changes are alluded to instead. On the one television news broadcast seen by Harry and his father it is Martínez de Hoz, the Minister of the Economy, who is shown, and not, noticeably, President Jorge Rafael Videla. This is worth stressing because, of all the footage available of the junta, this is the specific snippet chosen. Why? The two events reported by Martínez de Hoz are a state denial of the violent rounding up of Argentine citizens in the wake of the coup, and an announcement regarding the opening up of the domestic market to the flows of international free trade. *Kamchatka*, then, focuses on the effect of these pronouncements on a middle-class family. Harry's father is a lawyer, not a terrorist or guerrilla fighter, and there is very little to indicate that he holds any particularly strong political views (for instance, socialist of communist). Thus, although the junta emphasized the centrality of the middle-class family in their social order, in *Kamchatka* it is precisely the middle-class family that is in peril, perhaps due to Harry's father having conducted legal services on behalf of opponents of the regime. In order to open up the country to international trade it was vital to present a humanitarian front to the new regime, as we see Martínez de Hoz do in his television broadcast. The price that the nation pays for this economic manoeuvre, however, is that experienced by the middle-class family in *Kamchatka*, the disappearance of a generation of potential opposition to an increasingly neoliberal economic policy.

Their fate was not by any means that of a minority of the population, as around a third of the 30,000 who disappeared in Argentina were middle-class professionals,[47] the working classes constituting a further third, with students being the next largest group. Accordingly, when forced into conflict with the state, Harry's father does not take up arms but attempts to protect his family using military tactics to out-manoeuvre the junta (effectively going underground with his family, the guerrilla-like nature of which is emphasized by the arrival of Lucas, who is also on the run), a skill that, facing inevitable defeat, he then passes on to his son through *T.E.G.* He fights a tactical war using the tools of his middle-class education and professional training as a lawyer. In the *T.E.G.* inspired finale, then, the stronghold of

Kamchatka illustrates the need for continued resistance, even if the forces threatening the family (which are shown in the junta television broadcast to be at once military and economic) are as nationally pervasive as the Argentine military, or even as globally aggressive as neoliberalism. The effects of this would not have been lost on Argentine audiences in the wake of the economic crisis of 1999–2002.

Even though it was not until the post-dictatorship era, especially during the 1990s under Menem, that neoliberalism really took hold of the Argentine economy, as Luis Alberto Romero notes in *Argentina in the Twentieth Century* (2002):

> The year 1976 was a turning point in Argentine history. The changes that have taken place since then, whose significance in some ways remained hidden during the first years of the democratic transition, were demonstrated during the 1990s.[48]

Indeed, Romero sees Menem's monetarist Minister of the Economy Domingo Cavallo as a direct inheritor of the legacy of Martínez de Hoz, the Minister of the Economy from 1976 to 1981[49] who David Pion-Berlin describes in *The Ideology of State Terror* (1989) as being, like his advisers and associates, 'loyal to the monetarist cause'.[50] In *Democracy in Argentina* (1999), Laura Tedesco similarly draws comparisons between the authoritarian state of the 1970s and the neoliberal state of the 1990s,[51] noting both that unemployment grew along with the gap between rich and poor in the wake of military rule,[52] and the subsequent impossibility of reversing the 'bloody partial restructuring of social relations in Argentina'[53] (including the diminishing of the power of the middle classes), that took place under military rule. Both Pion-Berlin and Romero argue that the military was able to implement this shift in policy – effectively a reversal of conditions that had existed, in terms of 'state planning, regulation and control of the economy'[54] since the 1930s – because it had the power to forcibly eliminate those sections of the population likely to mount a significant opposition to it. This included students, the working classes and perhaps most dangerous of all, the politicized middle classes like Harry's parents.[55] As Carlos H. Waisman observes: 'the new regime's central goal was . . . the destruction of the guerrilla organizations and what the armed forces considered to be their social base, that is, the political left and considerable segments of the intelligentsia.'[56] The 2002 economic crisis, then, can be considered the long-term outcome of the reforms begun under military rule that are alluded to in *Kamchatka*. Although a straightforward linear historical development is not suggested, the film's construction of a virtual past to inform the present creates an oscillation between the two historical moments, which crystallizes the present as a reflection of this past. It is clearly not a coincidence that as Martínez de Hoz makes his pronouncement on television, Harry's father is restarting a grandfather clock, suggesting both that there is a clear historical link between the two moments, and indeed, the need to "restart the clock" in order to rethink the nation's past economic legacy after the most recent economic crisis.

By following the larger trends within globalization, towards a weakened state, the exposure of the domestic market to international trade and (as a consequence) a marked unequal division of wealth, *Kamchatka* suggests that Argentina's adherence to the Washington Consensus[57] left not only the country in ruins but also – with the majority of the 30,000 disappeared aged between fifteen and thirty-five[58] – a generation without its (parental) link to the past. For this generation, in both 1976 and 2002, like the armies in *T.E.G.*, neoliberalism is taking over the world. The only place left in which to resist it, Harry learns, is an imagined land, be it 'Kamchatka' or, by extension, *Kamchatka*.

Thus, due to its focus on the family, *Kamchatka* can be placed alongside several other contemporary Argentine films, including *La ciénaga/The Swamp* (2001) and *La niña santa/The Holy Girl* (2004), that similarly address the impact of neoliberalism on the domestic sphere. This is so despite *Kamchatka*'s more conventional melodramatic aesthetic. After all, in *Crisis and Capitalism in Contemporary Argentine Cinema* (2009), Joanna Page argues that Argentine cinema's recent retreat into the family is not necessarily evidence of a lack of engagement with politics, as is sometimes thought, but an acknowledgement of the changing impact of politics on public and private spheres. Specifically this inward turn can be interpreted as a commentary on the failure of the state to provide the Argentine population with protection from the global forces of neoliberalism,[59] which are seen to be directly impacting upon the family instead. *Kamchatka*, then, exists within a broader trend of Argentine films to explore the state of the nation through the threatened bourgeois home and family, the difference being that it uses the child seer to do so. Accordingly, although it might seem the antithesis of a film like *Hora de los hornos*, which explicitly targets the Argentine bourgeoisie for their neo-colonial rule of the nation at the expense of the majority of the people, it is nevertheless politically engaged with the often intangible spectre of neoliberalism. This holds true in spite of its seeming lack of oppositional "political" engagement, and its emphasis on the family in peril, rather than the larger contextual (particularly economic) factors surrounding military rule and the disappearances.

International Middle-Class Audience

Exactly how internationally understandable is this historical use of the "adult-child seer"? *Kamchatka*'s nostalgic recreation of 1976 – complete with emotive shots of Harry's parents dancing by the lake at sunset, and the family looking for shooting stars outlined against a fantastically clear, entirely artificial, night sky – could understandably be accused of a degree of historical gentrification. This is, after all, a world where state brutality is never actually seen, the disappeared are represented by a middle-class nuclear family at a time when many in the middle classes benefited economically under military rule, and the Catholic Church (at times an ally of the regime) provides a safe haven and education for Harry and his brother. Not surprisingly, then, David William Foster argues that this 'Hollywoodish' film 'undercuts its own effectiveness by the appeal to bourgeois norms and a universal idealization of human experience'.[60] However, this manner of reconstructing history is a result of the deployment of the gaze of the "adult-child seer" to address both national and the international audiences, the latter demographic in particular being a major concern since the "(adult)-child seer" films of neorealism.

Like many contemporary South American films, *Kamchatka* is an international coproduction that aims to recuperate its budget through international sales. This is an important factor if such films are to compete in the global market,[61] and explains why *Kamchatka* is at once a family melodrama with two international stars (Ricardo Darín and Cecilia Roth) in its lead roles (facilitating a mainstream market appeal across Spanish speaking territories), and yet is similar in many ways to child-centred art films, in the style of *El espíritu de la colmena*, that circulate on the festival circuit.

Kamchatka was produced by Argentine independent production company Patagonik, which was co-owned at that time by Argentina's Grupo Clarín (a multimedia conglomerate) and Disney's Buena Vista International.[62] As Tamara L. Falicov notes in *The Cinematic Tango* (2007), Disney's investment in Patagonik can be attributed to various factors, including the profit achieved by previous "foreign language films" that crossed international borders in the 1990s, *Como agua para chocolate/Like Water for Chocolate* (Mexico, 1992), and *Il Postino/The Postman* (France/Italy/Belgium, 1994).[63]

For example, Patagonik had previously coproduced several films that had been successful internationally, including *Evita* (1996). *Kamchatka* also received funding from Ibermedia, the Spanish-based fund for filmmakers in Spain, Portugal and Latin America, and TVE (Televisión Española, Spanish state television). In terms of box office receipts it made over US$565,000 in Argentina, and US$107,000 in Mexico, but a far greater US$2.9m in Spain, where it was distributed by Twentieth Century Fox.[64] It also received a distribution deal with Menemsha Films in the US, and was Argentina's entry for the Best Foreign Language Film category to the Academy Awards. The value of the international market for *Kamchatka*, then, is clear.

In terms of selling overseas, *Kamchatka*'s courting of the middle-class audience makes perfect sense economically. The family focus targets the predominantly middle-class demographic for a child-centred melodrama released internationally. Admittedly, Harry the "adult-child seer", functioning as witness for the disappeared, observes the break up of a middle-class family rather than the assault on a Peronist political opposition movement that had its strongest roots in the working classes. As Foster rightly observes, the danger of this approach is that it gives a false impression, that the junta's violence predominantly affected the middle classes.[65] However, Foster may not be absolutely correct when he states that 'Piñeyro's film monumentalises a section of society that is not the one that suffered most under the generals.'[66] It was the working classes who were previously protected by the state's nationalization and protectionist practices that were most undermined by the regime's free market policies, with the size of the industrial working class decreasing by 26 per cent from 1976 to 1981.[67] However, the middle classes also suffered in different ways, experiencing the adverse effect of the free trade policies of the junta, for example, with small- and medium-sized businesses unable to compete with the influx of cheap foreign imports, laying off staff (including managerial positions), or going bankrupt.[68] Moreover, as Tedesco notes, the military targeted the link between the working classes and the bourgeoisie that was the basis of the broad-based support of the Peronist movement.[69] Therefore, although the social restructuring of Argentina impoverished the working class, as is seen in *Kamchatka* the middle class were also threatened by the junta, both economically and in some cases physically.

Foster's argument also betrays a negative bias against the 'Hollywoodish' nature of *Kamchatka*. He compares it unfavourably with the politically engaged 'imperfect cinema' that emerged in Latin America during the 1960s and 1970s[70], which at times seems to position the film as though it were depicting Argentine history in a manner that should only be expected of Hollywood.[71] However, keeping in mind Page's stance, as Burucúa argues, since military rule, genre films have enabled a complex exploration of the period.[72] Rather than view the film as Foster does, then, it is worth remembering that this international coproduction uses its focus on the family and "adult-child seer" to make Argentine history visible to a broad international market. It thereby offers a story of importance for this demographic in a more universal way, due to its critique of the historical period during which neoliberalism began to take hold globally, starting with South America in the 1970s.

In *Kamchatka*, then, the reconstructed image of Argentina under military rule shifts to one of violence against a political opposition that includes the middle class, thereby broadening its applicability internationally. Due to this shift in emphasis, the danger to the family that we see on screen alludes to a struggle that seems applicable to the film's international target audience. *Kamchatka*'s "adult-child seer", then, uses its recreated virtual layer of history to render universal the struggle over neoliberal economic values that many in the international audience may consider an unquestioned part of their daily lives precisely because they belong to the middle classes. After all, David Harvey notes in *A Brief History of Neoliberalism* (2005), increased social inequality is the aim rather than the side effect of neoliberalism, in spite of its claims to the contrary.[73] Indeed, in *Local Histories/Global Designs* (2000), Walter D. Mignolo goes so far as to argue that neoliberalism is not just an economic formation, but a 'new civilising design', the latest in a five-hundred-year history of colonization in South America.[74] What *Kamchatka* shows is that universal global conformity to this economic model, which continues to effect middle-class families to this day, was not inevitable, but enforced. Its continued global dominance, therefore, is open to question, and was an extremely pertinent issue at the time of the film's release both in economic crisis-ridden Argentina, and beyond.

Neoliberal Invaders

Finally, this reading of *Kamchatka* is greatly informed by the integrated presence of a certain US television show in the film. Harry and little brother come to understand the difference between themselves and the state that pursues them through reference to *The Invaders* (1967). As Harry's mother removes her children from school at the start of the film she is waved through a military roadblock, at which the car behind is stopped, and its inhabitants arrested by soldiers. Immediately following this, Harry – last seen watching the arrest from the departing car – is pictured watching *The Invaders* on television. Harry learns that the invaders who are taking over the earth, are: 'Aliens from a dying planet. Destination: earth. Purpose: to dominate the world.' Using a device typical of continuity editing, this voiceover begins as Harry watches the military arresting people at the road-block in the previous scene, thereby linking the two scenes in a conventional way. In so doing, however, it provides an allegorical reference to the manner in which the junta (in line with the spread of neoliberalism across South America during the Cold War) acted at the expense of many of the Argentine people. The military, then, are figured as the human hosts for alien invaders from another planet, hosts, as it were, for neoliberal economic policy. Significantly, immediately after watching *The Invaders*, Harry overhears his mother talking about how the military has arrested his father's partner in their law firm, establishing in his mind a link between the Argentine military and the body snatched minions of the alien invaders in the television show.

The presence of this particular US import has somewhat ambivalent connotations. It enables a new identity for the family (Harry's father chooses to rename himself David Vincent, after the show's main character), and for Harry and his brother, a way of making sense of the events shaping their lives. However, it is also another example of the spread of US culture abroad during the Cold War, especially because, due to the censorship imposed upon filmmakers under military rule, young Argentine children grew up on a diet of inoffensive home-grown comedies and musicals and Hollywood imports.[75] Thus, although *Kamchatka* provides the virtual archive with a way of considering the unrepresentable, or disappeared past, even so there is an ambiguity raised by its evocation of a US television show to comment on US intervention (both physical, in the form of CIA training in torture and financial aid, and ideological, especially in terms of monetarist policy) across South America at this time.[76]

On the one hand, *The Invaders* could be understood as an allegory for the potential threat of communism spreading to the US through "alien" impostors, as seen in films like *Invasion of the Body Snatchers* (1956). According to such a view, the presence of *The Invaders* in the film encapsulates the experience of many people internationally, of the spread of US culture during the Cold War, propagating fear of the red menace through film and television. We might argue that the show's ideological promotion of democracy against communist invaders attempts to naturalize the detrimental economic changes being enforced by military means in various countries worldwide. Yet this is clearly not what is happening in *Kamchatka*. Rather, Harry does not know who the invaders are, or where they originate from, only that someone has taken over the Argentine military machine and is using it to capture various members of the population. Accordingly, then, we can consider the film's reference to *The Invaders* in line with the argument put forward by Mark Jancovich in *Rational Fears* (1996) who reads a range of US films from the 1950s (including *Invasion of the Body Snatchers*), as far less concerned with a potentially invasive "alien" red menace emanating from the USSR as they are with negotiating the struggles of modernization, rationalization and conformity that beset the USA during the Cold War.[77] On this view *Kamchatka* shows how *The Invaders* may have meant different things to audiences in various countries, in this instance appearing as a narrative of internal "alienation", as a section of the population are forced to conform to the ideology of "alien" masters like a military regime imposing US-approved economic policies through force. To Harry, then, the TV show provides a way of understanding the military take over of Argentina by its own armed forces, whether or not he realizes that the economic ideology is US in origin.

For this reason, *Kamchatka*, while 'Hollywoodish' in its appearance, may also operate on different registers internationally, offering the opportunity for audiences to read the film as a critique of US "alien" involvement in South America, albeit packaged as an emotionally engaging Hollywood-style melodrama for consumption by a broad, international middle-class audience. As this analysis of the film's deployment of the "adult-child seer" demonstrates, *Kamchatka*'s emphasis on the middle-class family, its "Hollywood" aesthetic, and attempt to appeal to a wide international audience may be less of a detriment to the film's historical integrity than Foster considers.

As Phil Powrie has shown, in spite of their specific regional and historical specificity, child films have the capability to provide a nostalgia that is open to all viewers. They grant access to a specific realm of the past, at once extremely unfamiliar and yet universally familiar as well. For Powrie, viewers associate with such films, relocating themselves within the nostalgically recreated past as though thinking: ' "I wish to be that boy in that place, because I was once (like) that boy in that place. I once also inhabited a very specific place." '[78] This spectatorial appreciation of a strange yet familiar historical past explains the appeal of the child film internationally, even of films about a subject as difficult as military rule. It also goes some way towards clarifying the attraction of the period detail, including a retro appeal to 1970s fashion and motorcars that appears in *Kamchatka*. Once viewers have been transported back in time to a 'very specific place' akin to that of their own childhood, they can be taught the strategies needed not only to escape the (disappeared) past, but also a similar future. After all, if the struggles of the 1970s were not a battle between democracy and communism, but rather, a military imposition of free market economics that threatened anyone who stood in its way, including the middle classes (those now watching the film), who is to say who is safe under democracy?

Thus *Kamchatka* reflects upon the extent to which the economic crisis that Argentina faced at the time of its release was located under military rule in the 1970s. Although the past has been disappeared, a past-present circuit is enabled by the film which offers a way of overcoming the history of the intervening years, and of reconsidering the continued impact of the Argentine national mutation of the 1970s, both nationally and globally. Accordingly, we should not necessarily consider the film's focus on the middle classes, its recourse to melodrama, its "Hollywood" aesthetic or its attempts to appeal internationally as negative attributes,[79] but as deliberate attempts to consider the links between the Argentine past and the present in a manner that global audiences can understand, through the eyes of the "adult-child seer" of neoliberalism.

Conclusion: Child seer *as* History

In contemporary South American films set during military rule, the role of the child seer is slightly different than in the post-war neorealist films that Deleuze discussed in *Cinema 2*. The "adult-child seer" has a specific relationship to the manner in which history can be recreated cinematically, in nations where military rule has left a layer of the past unrecorded, that is equally as momentous as that of the cities in ruins of post-war Europe. In the disappeared past of *Kamchatka* the "adult-child seer" is witness to the recreated pure optical situation in order to overcome the several decades of history which it represents for the fractured (national) whole. This past-present historical circuit is different to the present-without-a-past offered by the child seer in neorealism. Thus the child *as* history (as opposed to the child *in* history) illustrates how the pure optical situation is specific to the nation whose national and historical whole it interrupts. Even so, this child seer film has the potential to speak to audiences worldwide whose present could easily reflect this same story.

In the chapter that follows, South Korean cinema of the 1990s/2000s offers another example of how the national whole reconstructs itself through cinema, in the wake of military rule, in order to "think" history through film. Again, as with *Kamchatka*, what is at stake is not one national cinema's take on the time- or movement-image, but the very manner in which we conceive of these image categories in a global arena, especially once we move beyond Deleuze's isolation of the Second World War as defining moment in their division, as he conceived of this split in relation to US and European cinemas.

Chapter 3

Folding and Unfolding History: South Korean Time Travel Movies

This chapter analyses three South Korean time travel movies, *Calla* (1999), *Donggam/Ditto* (2000) and *2009: Lost Memories* (2002), to examine the manner in which movement- and time-images "think" history by folding time. On different occasions in the *Cinema* books Deleuze examines how movement- and time-images engage with history. However, the conclusions he draws are not applicable to many films, including those under discussion. Instead I expand the applicability of Deleuze's ideas to cinematic constructions of history by drawing on his conception of the fold, derived from Gottfried Wilhelm von Leibniz. I examine how these particular science fiction films fold time cinematically, bringing into contact the past and the present in a manner that enables a rethinking of national history. As such they offer a different Deleuzian way of considering the cinematic thinking of history than those found in the *Cinema* books.

Calla, Donggam and *2009* appear to be movement-images, but also explore the temporal whole in a way that toys with the labyrinthine powers of the false found in the time-image. Thus their examination of the whole is self-consciously rendered through the subtle foregrounding of their status as cinematic works capable of folding the whole of time, and, accordingly, of thinking history in new ways. Examining the consequences of recent history (in this instance, South Korea's experience of compressed modernity) by unfolding and enfolding time, these films can be understood to be actualizing the virtual potential for considering history that Deleuze conceived of in the time-image. These apparent movement-images, then, while displaying the virtual potential that the concept of the outside (derived from Maurice Blanchot) offers the time-image, ultimately contain it within their conception of a unified (national, historical) whole. In other words, we see a process in which the whole (movement-image) enfolds the outside (time-image) in order to think history. As the analyses of the three films demonstrate, this process occurs differently when this national whole, and national history, are conceived for different national and international markets. What is at stake here is the distinction between movement- and time-image as it is constructed in the *Cinema* books, which is thrown into question by an encounter with South Korean films.

History in the *Cinema* Books

On several occasions in the *Cinema* books Deleuze deploys an implicit reading of national history that is key to our understanding (and critiquing) of his concepts. As discussed in Chapter 1, the manner in which he conceives of the organic whole in the US western is a case in point, as is the way historical context shapes Deleuze's conception of the mutation of cinema from movement-image to time-image after World War Two, discussed in Chapter 2. For the majority of the *Cinema* books, however, history is a factor that is pushed into the background in favour of formal analysis and broader philosophical argument. Thus, although his initial discussion of the pre-war montage schools in *Cinema 1* ensures that his formations of the movement-image are to some degree nationally informed, this is not a practice sustained throughout the two books, in which the figure of the more ahistorically determined *auteur* becomes the prominent structuring device.

Two moments in which Deleuze directly addresses history stand out, however, one each in *Cinema 1* and *Cinema 2*. First, in *Cinema 1* Deleuze discusses 'Hollywood's historical conceptions'[1] as bringing together the three categories of history put forward by Friedrich Nietzsche at the close of the nineteenth century in *Untimely Meditations* (1873–1876). Rounding off his opening discussion of the relationship between situation and action in the action-image, Deleuze discusses how Nietzsche's monumental, antiquarian and critical or ethical forms of histories can be seen to exist in the work of great Hollywood directors like D. W. Griffith and Cecil B. DeMille (in particular in epics like *Intolerance* (1916), *Samson and Delilah* (1949) and *The Ten Commandments* (1956)). Put briefly, monumental history is created in films that draw analogous parallels between the great monuments of history. These are moments of optimum importance, which, for Nietzsche, are understood by monumental history to exist as the peaks in a giant historical mountain range of human achievements.[2] Hollywood epics are understood by Deleuze to function thus, while also displaying the same reverential attitude towards the milieu of the past of Nietzsche's antiquarian history. To this blend of the first two types of history a critical, or rather, ethical dimension is provided by the duel between good and evil at the heart of the action-image.

In this way Deleuze considers Hollywood to construct a universal, but ultimately nationally representative history that focuses on effects rather than interrogating causes. Thus, from the epic's ethical judgement regarding the rights and wrongs of the past the Hollywood historical film is able, Deleuze argues, to 'constantly rediscover America'.[3]

This section of *Cinema 1* has been taken up by Film Studies scholars working on the historical film, including Marcia Landy in *The Historical Film* (2001) and Robert Burgoyne in *Hollywood's Historical Film* (2008). In both instances it is an excellent resource for facilitating their respective discussions of the historical film. However, Deleuze's recourse to Nietzsche's categories to describe the construction of history in US cinema demonstrates the same difficulties I explored in the first chapter in relation to Deleuze's use of Bergson to conceive of separate movement- and time-images. Here again the theoretical position feels rather imposed upon the films. In terms of Nietzsche's ideas regarding history (themselves a product of, and meditations upon, nineteenth century Germany), there will always be occasions in which it seems very difficult to squeeze the film to fit the theory. This might be in relation to films from a different national or historical tradition, or simply individual films that buck the trend. Indeed, Deleuze tacitly acknowledges this in a footnote that concludes the section of the chapter on the action-image in which Nietzsche's historical categories are applied to US cinema. He states:

> We would need to ask the same question for each great current of the historical cinema – what is the implicit conception of history? . . . [T]he problem raised is more fundamental than that which we have indicated here, and concerns the relationship between historical utterances and statements on the one hand, and cinematographic utterances and images on the other. Our question would only be a part of this latter problem.[4]

Thus, while Landy's and Burgoyne's work demonstrates that Deleuze's argument for the universal history constructed by Hollywood is still applicable to the historical film, it is not universally applicable to all movement-image cinemas. As Deleuze notes, we need to 'ask the same question' for other historical cinemas, in order to understand how they conceive of history.

The second standout instance of direct engagement with the question of history comes in chapter eight of *Cinema 2*, in the section on 'modern political cinema'[5]. As such it relates to Deleuze's conceptualization of cinema as a form of thinking. Modern political, or 'minor cinema'[6] is a mode of potentially revolutionary cinema that facilitates the emergence, or equally the conceptualization or "thinking" of, a new people. This might be necessary, for example, due to conditions created by colonialism, neo- or post-colonialism, military occupation, dictatorship, civil repression, minority status (and so on) in which there is a perceived need, at the very least on the part of the filmmakers, to effect political change in difficult and potentially dangerous circumstances. As examples, Deleuze discusses filmmakers such as Yilmaz Güney, Glauber Rocha and Ousmane Sembene. We can conclude from these choices that, although Deleuze does not delve into the national contexts of production which shaped these filmmakers and their output, he is implicitly acknowledging that minor cinema has the ability to intercede in history during times of political turbulence. For example, the Senegal depicted in Sembene's films was at that time newly postcolonial, and engaged in the construction of an independent identity, while both Rocha's Brazil and Güney's Turkey were experiencing political turmoil and military rule. Thus, for Deleuze, in contrast to the conceptualization of a people found in the different unified wholes of the various national movement-images, minor cinema is involved in the thinking of a new people, in the planting of 'the seeds of the people to come'.[7]

Importantly for this discussion the concept of minor cinema appears at the close of the chapter, as though the culmination of the argument Deleuze has been developing in the final chapters of *Cinema 2*. This argument pertains to the manner in which cinema is able to think. In chapter seven, 'Thought and Cinema', Deleuze argues that there 'is a new status of the Whole in modern cinema',[8] which no longer expresses the open and changing whole of time. Rather than the whole becoming apparent through the linking of images (as in the sensory motor logic of the movement-image, which links images through the progression from perception to action), the whole now emerges in the interval between discontinuous images. Drawing on Blanchot, Deleuze argues that the whole is now the 'Outside'.[9] Thus, rather than a unified whole we see the whole at work in aberrant movement between images, emerging in the interval between images as a thought from the outside.

Just prior to the section on minor cinema, Deleuze summarizes his findings up to that point concerning the manner in which cinema thinks, noting that, 'the three cerebral components are the point cut, relinkage and the black or white screen'.[10] That is to say: the point cut, or irrational interval that joins together discontinuous images or spaces; their relinkage in such a way as to affect a new form of thought that reconnects us to the world; and finally, the black or white screen in which the rejuvenative power of the outside becomes visible in its own right. In short, for Deleuze, modern cinema is characterized by the aberrant movement of montage once freed from a sensory-motor rationale, which may, for example, explore linkages between discontinuous times – such as different periods in a country's history – without the monumentalizing/universalizing emphasis of the Hollywood epic. Hence it is possible to find connections between the images of the otherwise discontinuous world in which people (seers) find themselves confronted by situations to which they do not know how to react, these connections being made by the appearance in the irrational cut or interval of the thought from the outside. The new people that can emerge out of minor cinema, then, are a product of cinema's ability to reconnect us to the world in potentially overpowering, but nonetheless real historical situations, where the possibility of sensory-motor actions are limited, damaged or impossible.

In both instances when Deleuze discusses history in the *Cinema* books what is emphasized is the need for further consideration of the manner in which film can think history. Yet with each position there is a difficulty of transposition to other cinemas, due to the fact that Deleuze approaches films from a preconceived theoretical direction, rather than vice versa. In the case of minor cinema, the structuring presence of Nietzsche found in Deleuze's discussion of the universal history of the Hollywood epic is replaced by that of Franz Kafka from whose literature Deleuze develops his three-part model of minor cinema. This is a cinema engaged in the creation of a people yet to come; emphasizing the dissolution of the boundary between public and private which ensures that all personal actions become political; and foregrounding the process of storytelling that constructs new collective utterances of identity.[11] Again not many films are capable of matching the requirements predetermined by the theory, even though they may have the same aims or impact. In this instance, then, it is Deleuze's desire to consider certain films in the same manner as he and Félix Guattari did for literature in *Kafka* (1975), which creates this situation. Hence, as was the case with his reliance on Bergson and Nietzsche, so too does Deleuze's recourse to Kafka, although providing an innovative new way of considering cinema, also construct a potentially unwieldy framework that is limiting in the range of films that can be said to fit within it.

One alternative way of considering how cinema thinks history is through the concept of the fold. This approach does not take us very far from Deleuze's *Cinema* books, and provides a way of broadening his ideas. It also enables an engagement with recent South Korean time travel movies which, while they fit neither of the two categories listed above, are nevertheless

engaged in a sophisticated process of thinking history that can be understood as an enfolding within the whole of the rejuvenative potentiality
contained in the virtual outside. This approach does not provide any definitive answer as to how films "think" history, but it does illuminate one way in
which this can happen.

Folding Time/Folding History: The Whole enfolds the Outside

In *The Fold* (1988), which appeared quite soon after the *Cinema* books,
Deleuze draws his concept of the fold from the work of Leibniz. Deleuze
considers existence as a process of folding matter. This can apply to our
personal experience of the world, our subjectivity as a process of folding
the self in history (as seen in Deleuze's *Foucault* (1986)), but also to different ways of understanding the fold, such as the folding of time. The opening to chapter one, entitled, 'The Pleats of Matter', discusses the labyrinthine
model of time that was found, in *Cinema 2*, to enable the time-image's
powers of the false. Deleuze states: 'A labyrinth is said, etymologically, to be
multiple because it contains many folds. The multiple is not only what has
many parts but also what is folded in many ways.'[12] In chapter five of *The
Fold*, Deleuze again has recourse to this labyrinthine model, making the
same progression from Leibniz to the work of Argentine writer Jorge
Luis Borges that he previously followed in *Cinema 2* when developing his
argument through the powers of the false (chapter six) to the relationship
between thought and image (seven).[13] Thus, the labyrinth of time when it
appears in time-image cinema – with its potential to offer multiple (falsifying) pasts, numerous incompossible worlds – is a process of folding and
unfolding of both matter and time. After all, as Deleuze considers cinema
to be matter appearing as light, then so too is cinema a manner of folding
matter, which, in the time-image at least, entails the potential for folding
time. In this respect we can consider cinema capable of thinking history
through its temporal foldings.

Several commentators have noted the usefulness of the concept of the
fold for interpreting both the *Cinema* books, and indeed, cinema itself.
Both D. N. Rodowick and Tom Conley observe the trajectory of thinking
that leads Deleuze through the *Cinema* books to *The Fold*;[14] Michael Goddard
discusses editing in the movement-image as 'an operation of folding';[15]
Timothy Murray uses Deleuze to help him examine the 'temporal folds
of time's cinematic image' in new media art;[16] Giuliana Bruno explores 'the

texture of cinematic time-space' through the fold;[17] and Ronald Bogue analyses the *Cinema* books using the terminology of folding and unfolding, rereading them as though through the filter of the latter work. Not only is the movement-image described by Bogue as 'an expressive enfolding and unfolding of the open whole through individual images',[18] but so too are the temporal foldings of the thought from the outside (which characterizes the time-image by appearing in the irrational cut) discussed in terms of 'relinkages . . . that allow leaps from present to present or slidings from sheet to folding sheet'.[19] The importance of the fold is thus evident in relation to both montage in the movement-image (enfolding and unfolding the whole), and indeed, in the folding of time found in the time-image. In terms of cinema thinking history through the fold, however, Laura U. Marks provides the most sustained engagement, demonstrating in various publications how cinema enfolds information, and indeed, history.[20] This includes a piece on unfolding in Arab cinema in *Cinema at the Periphery* (2010), in which Marks observes that 'images, perceptible representations of history, come into the world and retreat back . . . in a ceaseless flow of unfolding and enfolding'.[21]

Yet perhaps of most importance for the discussion that follows is Scott Nygren's *Time Frames* (2007), in which he considers Japanese film history in the light of the fold created by the post-war acceptance of Japanese cinema into Western markets with the international success of *Rashomon* (1950). Arguing that film history can be conceived of as a process of folding like that of origami, Nygren argues that *Rashomon* marks a point at which the Western outside is folded into Japanese cinema, facilitating not only a new kind of Japanese cinema, but also a new way of thinking of Japanese film history (a new lineage and chronology founded in retrospect after *Rashomon*) around the rupture or break that is created by this particular fold in time.[22] Nygren's innovative use of the fold to investigate the historiography of Japanese national cinema can also be applied to the folding of national history as it appears aesthetically in the three South Korean films under discussion (the famously divided nature of Korea as a nation notwithstanding). The possibility of this intellectual transposition is evident in the following quotation:

> History changes shape, by a process of folding and refolding, so that moments previously disregarded as insignificant and unrelated suddenly come to the foreground and seem linked and determining.[23]

Accordingly, in *Calla*, *Donggam* and *2009*, cinematic foldings of history are used to explore recent South Korean national history, bringing previously unlinked events in the past and present into contact (a form of irrational cut) to suggest new histories and new chronologies after military rule.

In *Calla, Donggam* and *2009* a Bergsonian conception of time is evident, characterized by a labyrinthine shifting of history between constructed layers of the past. Yet the overarching logic that determines the construction of the whole is sensory-motor in its orientation. It is, therefore, extremely difficult to say whether these are clear-cut cases of movement- or time-images, of indirect or direct expressions of the whole. Instead these movement-/time-image films can be considered different ways of folding history, that construct more or less direct or indirect expressions of the national whole.

Accordingly, instead of considering movement- and time-images indirect and direct images of time we can equally consider them as different ways of folding time. As Bogue's words suggest (and keeping in mind Deleuze's *Cinema* books equate film with matter and time), direct and indirect images and direct and indirect folds of time effectively amount to much the same thing. Admittedly, D. N. Rodowick notes towards the end of *Gilles Deleuze's Time Machine* (1997) that 'only the movement-image pretends that thought can be presented directly, in or by the image. Alternatively, time always divides thought from the signs that express or represent it'.[24] Nevertheless, even the movement-image's pretence at thinking still creates an image of thought[25] in which an actualized version of the virtual powers of thought (their ability to invade the image through the interstice) is rendered visible in the thinking of national history. In the films in question, then, we can see how the movement-image's whole enfolds the time-image's outside, actualizing its conception of time (virtual, aberrant in movement, labyrinthine, falsifying), and uses it to think history. As is typical of the movement-image, movement enfolds time (it remains an indirect image of time after all), but even so this is a process through which history is thought by cinema.

Through the enfolding and unfolding of the image/matter/time, *Calla, Donggam* and *2009* self-consciously express the thinking of history, using techniques reminiscent of the 'cerebral components' Deleuze identifies in the time-image (the irrational cut, relinkage and black or white screen). They use these components to fold history, but do so in a manner that renders them "coherent" within a unified whole (typical of the movement-image), rather than to make a connection with the outside (time-image). Each movie is marked by a standout moment or moments in which the folding of history is foregrounded as part of their time travel narratives. In *Calla* a visual interplay between shots of a black screen and the otherwise persistent diegetic world marks the point at which national history is seen to stop and be restarted once more. Here the fold in the narrative's time renders visible the splice in the montage that reconstructs the whole by momentarily allowing the outside to infiltrate the diegesis. In *Donggam* this folding process is even more clearly seen in a recurring split screen shot that shows characters from two different historical moments communicating across time. Here narrative world, history and image are all seen to be folded such that two different points in time (past and present) are brought into contact. In *2009* at the point of travel between different dimensions (different incompossible worlds) the screen whites-out, an over-exposed shot suggesting once again the power of the outside to offer an alternative history, but with this cerebral power safely constrained by the diegetic conceit of time travel. In all three cases, then, the folding of history is represented in a manner evocative of the 'cerebral components' of the time-image (a black or white screen, or a split screen linking discontinuous temporal layers), but these effects are "explained by" and thereby contained within the conventions of the science fiction narrative world. Self-consciously they evoke a "faulty splice", or perhaps a "forgetful splice" in both cinema and national history. However, rather than drawing too much attention to this metacinematic consciousness (the outside) they reaffirm the unity of the whole by coding the irrational cut, relinkage and black or white screen as conventions through which time travel is illustrated in the diegesis. In this way the movement-image's image of thought appropriates the temporal dimension of the time-image, actualizing it in order to explore the different possibilities offered by the enfolding of history.

In *Calla* and *Donggam*, in line with Deleuze's implicit alignment of the whole with the nation in *Cinema 1*, the whole that enfolds the outside is the unified organic whole of national history. These South Korean movement-images, then, provide another way of considering the temporal whole as an expression of national history (as in Griffith, Sergei Eisenstein, etc.) but one that is not reducible to a model of universal history drawn from Nietzsche, or to minor cinema's desire to think a people yet to come. Indeed, as the final discussion of *2009* will demonstrate, as was the case in the previous two chapters, national history is not the only form that this whole can take, a transnational whole being constructed in this particular film in order to appeal internationally.

South Korean Cinema: Unfolding/Enfolding Compressed Modernity

With the national and international success of the South Korean blockbuster *Swiri/Shiri* (1999), a new era of South Korean cinema burst onto the international stage. South Korea was transformed in the eyes of the world from a relatively small, nationally oriented industry which occasionally produced art cinema gems like Im Kwon-taek's *Seopyeonje/Sopyonje* (1993) to an increasingly internationally oriented operation producing mainstream popular genre films with historically engaged narratives. The only national cinema to recover its domestic audience from Hollywood since the Vietnam War,[26] South Korean cinema rose to an international prominence unprecedented for its size.[27] However, it was all the more surprising considering the country's recent experience of 'compressed modernity'[28] (rapid industrialization under military rule, accompanied by massive social unrest and police and military repression during the second half of the twentieth century), and indeed, the country's economic crash during the Asian economic crisis.

During and after South Korea's experience of what became known as the IMF crisis of 1997–2001, several South Korean films explored the impact of compressed modernity on the nation by examining the relationship between recent national history and the present. They include: the high school drama *Yeogo goedam II/Memento Mori* (1999); the art film *Bakha sating/Peppermint Candy* (2000);[29] the goofy science-fiction flick *Jigureul jikyeora!/Save the Green Planet!* (2003); the monster movie *Gwoemul/The Host* (2006); the road movie *Gaeulro/Traces of Love* (2006);[30] and countless others. However, although not alone in their exploration of recent national history, *Calla, Donggam* and *2009* are exemplary in this respect because of their foregrounded examination of national history through time travel narratives. Due to their generic status, these particular films unfold (or, "decompress") the nation's recent history of compressed modernity, to consider social changes brought about by the crisis, enfolding or refolding it in a manner that effects the way in which a number of other considerations (such as changing gender roles) are conceived as part of the national whole.

Calla, Donggam and *2009* belong to an emergent hybrid genre that Anthony Leong identifies in *Korean Cinema* (2002) as 'True Love and Time Travel-Romance Films'.[31] Romance across different dimensions or historical time periods became a popular theme in South Korean cinema after the success of *Eunhaeng-namu chimdae/The Gingko Bed* (1996) that, at that time, was South Korea's highest-grossing film.[32] All three films contain narratives similar to those of recent international hits. *Calla* for instance, repeats one day in the life of its protagonist, as do films as diverse as *Przypadek/Blind Chance* (1981), *Groundhog Day* (1993) and *Lola rennt/Run Lola Run* (1998). *Donggam* is effectively a remake of *Frequency* (2000), makes numerous allusions to *Back to the Future* (1985), and uses the parallel editing typical of films like *Sleepless in Seattle* (1993) to separate historical periods. *2009* for its part was influenced by the international success of blockbusters like *The Matrix* (1999). It is therefore tempting to view this trend of films as the South Korean film industry cashing in on proven international formulas. However, these films are not simply South Korean "rip-offs" of European or North American originals. Although these South Korean films use internationally tested narratives, they do so to negotiate concerns specific to South Korea, in particular by deploying their genre hybridity to unfold and enfold recent national history.

Calla and *Donggam* fold history slightly differently to *2009*. Both emerged during the caesura in economic development created by the IMF crisis, and both use their time travel narratives to unfold and explore the process through which national identity was rapidly formed under compressed modernity. This is a process of unfolding that in both instances hints at the possibility of different pasts found in the time-image's powers of the false. However, while unfolding recent history in this way, *Calla* and *Donggam* ultimately re-enfold it in such a way as to deny their protagonists the ability to change the past. Their melodramatic aspects unfold history, recognizing the sacrifices of the past, while stressing the need to lay the past to rest. Simultaneously their romantic storylines, which enfold or refold in the present, suggest that immanent national rejuvenation is possible. They do so, however, by reaffirming a particular, conservative gender politics that developed under compressed modernity, in which the social and the domestic spheres are normalized as male and female domains. Thus the generic hybridity of these films is crucial to their process of unfolding (melodrama) and enfolding (romance) national history. At once "melodramas of mourning" and "romances of rejuvenation", *Calla* and *Donggam* attempt to neatly enfold complex issues that arose during the crisis, ascribing their gender politics with a supposed legitimacy through time travel narratives that reference recognizable moments in recent national history. By contrast, *2009*, as I will examine at the conclusion of the chapter, folds history differently, to appeal to international audiences.

Melodrama/Unfolding: Mourning the National Past

To inform the exploration of genre hybridity that follows it is worth sketching in the history of South Korea's experience of modernity. Like many Asian countries, South Korea's experience of modernity can be seen to have initially been a colonial invasion. This was consolidated during the Japanese colonial period of 1910–1945. Several historians and anthropologists note how the rapid expansion of capitalism within Korea, particularly in South Korea after the end of the Second World War, took place at an unprecedented rate. Perhaps the most cited of these is Kyung-Sup Chang, who notes that the 'South Koreans have experienced Westerners' historical development of two or three centuries over merely three or four decades'[33]. This rapid economic development was implemented by a strong military state. After the post-war rebuilding period overseen by the US military, and the Korean Civil War of 1950–53, the 1960s saw the gradual implementation of military rule by the right wing dictatorship of President Park Chung-hee. However 1979–1997 was perhaps the most informing period for the present state of South Korea. In 1979 Park was assassinated in a political coup, and General Chun Doo-hwan took advantage of the situation, declaring martial law and dissolving the National Assembly. In 1980 clashes between the military and civilian protestors in Kwangju left several hundred protestors dead.[34] Chun retained control until 1987, when the presidency passed to his successor, General Roh Tae-woo. After over 30 years of military rule, popular protest and violent repression, civilian president Kim Young-sam was elected in December 1992. Although the economy boomed in the 1990s, it was severely hit by the Asian economic crisis of 1997 and was bailed out by the International Monetary Fund. The IMF crisis officially lasted until 2001,[35] and it was during this period that *Calla* and *Donggam* both emerged.

Historically melodrama is the most dominant genre in South Korean cinema, and in the past it has been adept at negotiating the changing historical conditions of compressed modernity. In *South Korean Golden Age Melodrama* (2005), Kathleen McHugh and Nancy Abelmann discuss the golden age of the South Korean melodrama in the wake of the Korean civil war. Noting how effectively 'melodramatic narration conveys the force of a specific historical trauma',[36] they discuss the extent to which the dramatic transformation of post-civil war South Korean society, during a period of rapid economic modernization, finds echoes in the melodrama's exploration of the emotional impact of sudden social mobility.

Neither *Calla* nor *Donggam* is a melodrama in the sense of a narrative focused on the family, although *Donggam* does conform to this generic standard in one half of its temporally split narrative. However, both films contain the narrative conventions – including plot coincidence, suspense, and strange twists of fate – of the golden age melodramas. Moreover, in both there are moments in which the formal elements come to the fore, demonstrating the often mute, visual excesses of the melodramatic mode. In short, *Calla* and *Donggam* are imbued with what various film studies scholars have described as a melodramatic sensibility that, John Mercer and Martin Schingler note, 'struggles to convey charged emotional and psychic states through visual and dramatic means'.[37] This is perhaps unsurprising considering Nancy Abelmann's observation in *The Melodrama of Mobility* (2003) that a melodramatic sensibility is as 'pervasive in contemporary South Korea as it has been in many times and places of rapid social transformation'.[38]

What is remarkable about *Calla* and *Donggam* is that unlike the 'seismic narrative compressions'[39] that characterized melodramas of the golden age as they negotiated the immediate impact of compressed modernity, these recent time travel melodramas are characterized by decompressed or unfolded narratives that experiment with recent national history to contemplate the effect of the past on the present. Consequently, McHugh and Abelmann's formulation is an extremely useful starting point when it comes to examining films emerging in this new historical context. In *Calla* and *Donggam*, again 'melodramatic narration conveys the force of a specific historical trauma'. However, this time the specific moment of the crisis is negotiated through a hybrid of melodrama and time travel narrative that unfolds the 'seismic narrative compressions' of these earlier films.

This difference can be seen to be a direct consequence of the emergence of these films during the IMF crisis. Writing in 2000, anthropologist Hae-joang Cho argued that under compressed modernity: 'People have been pushed and shoved in the rush toward colonial modernization to the extent that it has been difficult to create any space for critical reflection'[40]. Yet, Cho also notes, the economic crisis had the potential to create a degree of pause in South Korea's compressed development for exactly this type of reflection. *Calla* and *Donggam* thus take advantage of a brief pause in economic development, and use time travel narratives to create a reflective space in which to unfold and relive recent history.

Considering these recent films in the light of Cho's argument enables a new dimension to be added to the findings of McHugh and Abelmann. While melodrama was the perfect vehicle for examining the golden age's experience of compressed modernity, the time travel-melodrama hybrid is ideally suited for unfolding and thereby reviewing the IMF crisis period. The additional science fictional element enables the past to be fantastically replayed, facilitating a cinematic working through of a recent trauma in the national past. Indeed, it is in this process that, through the use of conventional techniques that suggest time travel, *Calla* and *Donggam* evoke the thought from the outside to assist their unfolding of history. A subtle, inexpensive evocation of time travel (black screen, white screen, irrational cut) unfolds or decompresses South Korea's recent experience of compressed modernity. This combination is so effective because, as Nancy Abelmann notes:

> The rapidity of post-Korean War development has made for many stories . . . in which small turns of fate – like the "pointer of a railroad switch" or the "casual encounter" in Primo Levi's analogy – spiral into great tragedies or enormous social divides.[41]

In the films in question the "melodramatic" context of compressed modernity is explored through time travel narratives uniquely suited to explore 'small turns of fate'; either by replaying the consequences of a 'chance encounter' differently (*Calla*), or by demonstrating the link between a 'chance encounter' in the past and the present (*Donggam*). For this reason I will now explore the manner in which they both unfold history and, in doing so, evoke the thought from the outside.

Calla (1999)

Calla is the story of a young professional Seon-woo (Song Seung-heon) who, in 1995, regularly sees an attractive young woman on the bus to work. She is Ji-hee (Kim Hee-sun), who works in the 'News Flower' flower shop. Seon-woo begins to find calla lilies left on his desk at work by an anonymous admirer. On 23 December, Seon-woo is to fly to Singapore on business at 7.30pm, but visits News Flower in the meantime. Through a series of misunderstandings he mistakenly confirms his hope that Ji-hee is his admirer, whereas in actual fact it is her co-worker, Su-jin (Kim Hyeon-ju). At the airport he telephones News Flower, and, believing himself to be talking to Ji-hee (it is actually Su-jin), he arranges a meeting in the Plaza Hotel for the following evening. On his arrival he finds the police are there in response to a hostage scenario involving Ji-hee and drug dealer, Min-ook (Choi Cheol-ho). Min-ook throws himself and Ji-hee to their death from a window. Seon-woo is unaware that Su-jin has also gone to the hotel to meet him, or that Ji-hee's presence there is coincidental.

The film actually begins in 1998, when Seon-woo revisits the hotel in a mood of dark nostalgia and reflects upon these past events, which we see in flashback. As he leaves in the elevator he wishes he could live the fateful day over again. His wish is magically granted, and he is transported back to 23 December 1995. He tries in vain to track down Ji-hee, but meets Su-jin instead. They search without success for Ji-hee. Seon-woo attempts to delay Min-ook, only to be hospitalized for his troubles. The story is then replayed again, this time from the perspective of Su-jin, and we learn that she was the one placing the lilies on Seon-woo's desk. Seon-woo discharges himself from hospital, and rushes to the Plaza Hotel. Confronting Min-ook he realizes that the drug dealer is actually Ji-hee's lover. The hostage situation recurs as a result of Seon-woo's actions, only this time as the lovers leap Seon-woo realizes that Ji-hee was a willing hostage. The anguished Seon-woo wonders why he is there if he is unable to change the past, until, in the elevator he sees Su-jin holding a bunch of calla lilies and realizes his mistake. The elevator lights flicker, Su-jin disappears, and Seon-woo is returned to 1998 where fate guides him to the flower shop in which Su-jin now works.

On first appearance there does not seem to be any pretence at historical engagement in *Calla*. However, on closer inspection *Calla* has deliberately situated its narrative in a specific historical moment. On Seon-woo's return to 1995 two historical facts are mentioned to clarify the year to which he has returned. Leaving the hotel, Seon-woo catches a glimpse of a story on television about the arrest of ex-Presidents Chun and Roh – the two military dictators who held power from 1980 to 1988 and 1988 to 1993 respectively – on charges of corruption. In the next scene he hears a news round-up of the year on the radio, which mentions the national disaster of the collapse of the Sampoong department store, which killed over five hundred people and wounded over nine hundred in June 1995. Immediately after hearing this Seon-woo expresses his desire to save Ji-hee. Although these historical pointers primarily function as markers that clarify the historical location of the time traveller, they also place Seon-woo's failed attempt to alter the past in a national context. It is necessary, then, to unpack what mention of these historical events would have meant for South Korean audiences watching *Calla* in 1999.

The Sampoong department store collapse rendered literal the dangers that compressed modernity had created for the South Korean population. The department store was a catalogue of design, construction and development abuses, performed in the service of profit and with disregard for safety. It was built using substandard materials, unplanned changes increased the risk of collapse, and bribery and corruption among city officials ensured its continued existence. Indeed, the dramatic loss of life could have been avoided had warning signs been heeded and the store closed early on the day of collapse. As Chang points out, the Sampoong collapse was one of many that occurred in South Korea in the 1990s, and, along with the collapse of the Seongsu Bridge, prefigured the immanent economic collapse of 1997.[42] The mention of the Sampoong department store collapse in *Calla* is therefore greatly significant. From the vantage point of 1999 the collapse would have appeared symbolic of the "precarious" wealth which rapid development had brought to South Korea. After all, the department store mainly catered to the upper-middle classes, and many of the victims were those who had benefited most from compressed modernity. Therefore, Seon-woo's decision to try and save Ji-hee, which he makes immediately on hearing the radio report, marks a desire (an impossible desire as it turns out) to rewrite the past, and to save the nation from the negative impact of compressed modernity.

The arrest of ex-Presidents Chun and Roh which Seon-woo briefly glimpses on the television was also a major moment in the mid-1990s when the recent national past came under scrutiny. Under Kim Young-sam, the first civilian president since the end of military rule, the trials of Chun and Roh went ahead in 1996, initially on charges of corruption and later for mutiny and treason during the coup of 1979 and the Kwangju massacre of 1980. Chun was sentenced to death and Roh to life imprisonment, although both sentences were later reduced, and both were pardoned and released in 1997 by incoming president, Kim Dae-jung. Thus, by the time of *Calla*'s production (and indeed, of December 1998 when its narrative is set), it was clear that attempts to address political crimes committed in South Korea's recent history were unlikely to lead to satisfactory results. The human cost of compressed modernity was apparently not something that could be readdressed by the courts. This state of affairs is recreated in *Calla*, most clearly in the despondent Seon-woo's failure to influence the past for the better, even though his attempts to do so are prompted by "reminders" of these nationally traumatic events. Unable to save Ji-hee, Seon-woo drifts back to the elevator in a daze, and his voiceover questions why he was granted a chance to revisit the past if he is unable to change it? Here the time travelling Seon-woo appears rather like a South Korean citizen who, in the pause created by the IMF crisis, is suddenly granted a moment of reflection in which to ponder his nation's recent history, only to find himself wondering what can be learned from it if it is unchangeable? Thus even though the economic collapse of 1997 is the major unmentioned event that occurs between *Calla*'s two time periods, its unspoken presence casts a shadow over the entire film.

The scene in the elevator in which Seon-woo slips back in time is the standout moment in which *Calla* simultaneously evokes the outside in the form of a black screen (rendering literal the interstice between images into which a new thought may appear) and yet conforms to established generic conventions to ensure that this process is contained within the film's coherent sense of a national whole, as is typical of the movement-image. On the surface, the scene appears extremely "normal". The event that occurs is nothing more than an elevator stopping and restarting, with the flickering lighting and brief blackout of elevator and screen being con-current with any filmic representation of such a mechanical failure. That this instance also enables a "magical" movement through time for the film's protagonist is also signalled in conventional ways. Seon-woo is clearly in a heightened emotional state as he remembers past events, and he wishes three times that he could relive that day and save Ji-hee. A single tear falls from his face onto the ornate locket he had specially made for Ji-hee (con-taining an engraved likeness of her face), causing it, presumably affected by Seon-woo's love, to transport him back in time. This magical moment is depicted in a momentary rippling effect on the surface of the locket, and a magical flourish on the soundtrack. Finally, between the flickers of light and darkness within the elevator prior to complete blackout we see a close-up of the elevator's floor counter counting downwards, emphasizing the movement backwards through time that is about to occur. This is all typical of mainstream evocations of temporal anomalies, for instance as found in films like *Sliding Doors* (1997).[43] Yet, if we background the mundane/magical events in the diegetic world of a lift breaking down and a broken hearted lover being given a second chance, then we are actually watching the black screen which Deleuze noted as a 'cerebral component' of the time-image when it manifested the appearance of the thought from the outside. The effect on screen is a little reminiscent of a film projector breaking down mid-screening, or alternatively, of an experimental montage in which black frames have been interspersed into the action. Yet, although the interstice is rendered apparent in the film's formal use of the black screen, the splice or fold in time that it enables is contained by representation (Seon-woo is depicted as travelling back in time, rather than a literal evocation of film folding time) within the film's conception of a unified national history. Most evidently, this return to the past, while it provides a new perspective on the past, does not falsify the past in the manner that Deleuze envisioned in the powers of the false. A new perspective on history is provided by this splice in the film, this (un)fold in time, but not a new labyrinthine past.

Ultimately *Calla* provides an upbeat answer to the question of "what can be learned from the past?" In attempting to revise the past for a second time, Seon-woo discovers that he was not as fully aware of different perspectives on previous events as he thought he was, a lesson that again evokes contemporary events. In the period under President Kim Young-sam (1993–1998) in which *Calla* is set, it became evident that the corruption of the military regimes had not disappeared overnight. The Kim regime was also found to be pursuing undemocratic measures at the expense of the population, and was implicated in financial scandal.[44] Seon-woo's confusion over the identity of his admirer, then, and his shock on discovering that he had been labouring under a false impression for several years, replays contemporary feelings of surprise and disappointment that the identities of those in power are not what they may have appeared. In this respect Seon-woo's meeting with Su-jin is key. When the narrative is replayed from her perspective, the audience sees a familiar record of history suddenly turned on its head by a new revelation. This experience matches that of many who discovered that Kim Young-sam, after years of oppositional struggle, was himself not immune to scandal once president. Thus Seon-woo's trajectory as a character – from gloomy nostalgic living in the past to a smiling, carefree young man free of the past – suggests that attempts to revise the past, while essential for the understanding of identity, are not as important as living for the future.

Rather than using its time travel narrative to critique the way in which history is revised by events like the pardoning of Chun and Roh, *Calla* unfolds the past and replays it from a different perspective in order to argue that the past cannot be changed as such, but rather that South Korea must find a way to enfold this period in history and look to the future. Seon-woo comes to this conclusion after realizing that there was something in his past that he did not see (namely, Su-jin), due to his rush to embrace Ji-hee in between business trips to Singapore. Noticeably this enfolding re-emphasizes the power of the whole over the outside. The scene in which Seon-woo returns to the present, after realizing that it was Su-jin who was his secret admirer all along, takes place in the same elevator. Again the lights flicker on and off to illustrate his movement in time, but this time the black screen is "contained" by a close-up on Seon-woo's face. As he shifts in time from 1995 to 1998, and suddenly finds himself alone in the elevator again, this close-up (an affection-image) imposes itself onto the potential interstice into which the outside might otherwise insert itself. The affection-image here contains the black screen, stopping it from totally imposing itself upon the diegetic world, and thereby renders the narrative one of sensory-motor continuity in which the movement of time is expressed in an indirect manner, enclosed within the interval between perception and action in the body of Seon-woo.

Thus *Calla* uses the post-IMF moment as a brief historical pause in which the past can be unfolded and replayed, not in the hope that it can be changed in any significant way, but so that things once forgotten in the rush of modernization may have a chance to resurface. In this way can history be enfolded for the future. In so doing, the film ensures that, while the power of the outside to induce thought is evoked (especially in the notion of time travel), it is ultimately contained within the whole of national history. It is Seon-woo's choice of Su-jin that is essential here, their blossoming romance signalling national rejuvenation in the wake of the crisis. As I will show, this conclusion, which is reiterated in *Donggam*, resonates with media discourses of the time and was itself an expression of the continuing effect of compressed modernity on South Korea.

Donggam (2000)

Somewhat different to *Calla* in its exploration of time, *Donggam* is the story of two young people in their late teens/early twenties who communicate between 1979 and 2000 through a magical HAM radio. In 1979, female college student So-eun (Kim Ha-Neul) attends Shilla University. She is attracted to fellow student Dong-hee (Park Yong-woo), as is her best friend, Sun-mi (Kim Min-ju). So-eun communicates via HAM radio with young male student In (Yoo Ji-tae), attending Shilla University in 2000. So-eun discovers that Dong-hee and Sun-mi are In's parents. When she realizes this, So-eun steps aside to allow their relationship to blossom. This melodrama of personal history is set against the backdrop of the assassination of President Park Chung-hee, which In – after brushing up on South Korean history using his laptop in 2000 – foretells to So-eun in 1979. The inevitability of the marriage of Dong-hee and Sun-mi is thus confirmed by the inevitability of historical events in the national past. In 2000, In, after assisting his wayward admirer Hyeon-ji (Ha Ji-won) back into more respectable ways, makes a brief journey to Chonan University where So-eun works as an English Professor. They pass in a corridor, but do not speak.

Donggam unfolds the recent past by contrasting the different levels of political engagement that exist between the most recent generation and that of the *minjung* movement. The *minjung* movement was 'a collection of radicalised opposition movements of the 1970s and 1980s',[45] whose organized protests for democracy facilitated the emergence of the present state of South Korean government in the face of brutal repression. As Seungsook

Moon has it, 'what distinguished the minjung movement from the social movements of previous decades was its self-conscious concern with radical social change and the utility of theory in guiding collective action.'[46] In contrast to this politically informed opposition, In and Hyeon-ji are products of the 'depoliticization of Korean youth culture in the 1990s'[47]. They represent a generation whose formative years were lived under democracy, and who are considered 'individualistic'[48] and self-centred in contrast to the significant sacrifices made by their parents' generation. Hae-joang Cho's work suggests that this generational difference is largely a result of the greater competition created by compressed modernity, under which children who were exclusively tutored towards financial success by their families gained in exchange, 'the right to become a consumer'.[49] As a consequence, 'children came to judge their parents according to their ability to provide materials, and parents even judged themselves according to their ability to provide tutoring fees and to satisfy the material wants of their children'.[50] *Donggam* uses In and Hyeon-ji to re-introduce this financially oriented generation to its more politically involved predecessor. However, it does so in a way that also reaffirms the gender roles that developed under compressed modernity.

Initially the differences between the generations appear distinct. In's wealthy parents have set him up in a minimalist, luxury apartment in the city, left him the key to their expensive country house, and departed for the USA on business. In is fashionably dressed, has a mobile phone, a laptop, an expensive haircut and very few cares. Through In this generation is represented as "orphaned" from its roots by economic development, leaving it with solely financial concerns. By contrast, in 1979, So-eun lives a quiet, respectable life with her parents. Her father in particular is portrayed as an extremely benevolent patriarch. So-eun's personal decisions are shown to be inextricably linked to those of national history, not only as student demonstrations frequently creep into the background of her story, but also as her decision to sacrifice her own happiness is conflated with her generation's struggle for political freedom. Standing aside for Dong-hee and Sun-mi (Dong-hee is actively involved in the student protest movement) she stands aside for the continuation of national identity in In.

Despite these differences, *Donggam* also goes out of its way to illustrate the continuities between the two time periods, stressing that they belong to the same nation, the same history, the same unified whole. On several occasions *Donggam* deploys formal conventions normally used to create a sense of unified space to suggest a unified, linear national history. Here again the 'cerebral components' of the thinking (time-)image appear, indirectly, contained within the movement-image's unified conception of the (national, historical) whole.

The most obvious of these is the sequence that takes place under the clock tower at Shilla University. On one level it is entirely conventional. When So-eun and In first make contact via HAM radio, they decide to meet at the clock tower the next day. In 1979, So-eun stands beneath the clock tower, which is covered in scaffolding. The camera tracks and pans to create a sense that it is circling So-eun and the clock tower. Simultaneously, a series of dissolves illustrate the prolonged duration of her wait. When In fails to arrive, the camera continues its circling track and pan movement, and a final dissolve reveals In, in 2000, waiting in the rain in front of the now fully operational clock tower. The camera's circling motion and the reappearance of the clock confirm spatial continuity across the two epochs, while the conventional use of the dissolve to denote time passing for So-eun is simply extended (along with a musical flourish) to suggest that a period of twenty years has suddenly elapsed. By using a circling motion around a contemplative character typical of a recollection-image flashback[51] the space around the clock tower is unified by conventions of continuity, as are, by extension, the two time periods. Here *Donggam* creates the sense that these different generations are unified both by place (one continuous nation) and by history (one unbroken, linear time line). South Korea is still considered a unified whole, with a history that links characters in the past and the present. Yet, aside from this conventional rendering of time, this scene also demonstrates the irrational cut and relinkage that occurs in the time-image, in which different layers of time are directly connected to each other in order to suggest a new way of conceiving of history and the people. Although the film works hard to "naturalize" this transformation of character (So-eun into In) using techniques usually deployed to produce the illusion of spatial continuity, what is on display here is the potential cinema has to rethink the people through the metamorphosis produced by the irrational cut. In effect, the film folds together past and present, momentarily enfolding the interim history in the process.

This effect is compounded in various ways throughout the film, most noticeably in the recurring split screen showing So-eun and In talking via HAM radio – a device typically used to illustrate temporal simultaneity between characters talking on the telephone in different physical spaces. Here the very process of relinkage across layers of time is made visible in a single shot, as though the movement-image were flaunting its ability to at once display the same 'cerebral components' as the time-image, and yet to

"get away" with thinking history in this disguised manner by using it to reaffirm its conception of the (national, historical) whole. The split screen
again depicts a literal fold in time, as past and present are brought into
contact by film (different layers of time being connected via the irrational
interstice of the outside), a medium with the ability to reconnect history in
new ways. In *Donggam*, then, the recurrent split screen effect demonstrates
that time is folded by montage, and that when different layers of time are
brought together by this folding of the whole (albeit an organically conceived, unified whole as in the movement-image), history (like the characters on the HAM radio) can communicate across these temporal spaces.

Donggam evokes the irrational cut and relinkage to think history as a
whole, suggesting in the process that underlying continuities exist between
these very different generations. The political protests of the past have
diminished under democracy, but they still inform the present. Thus
Donggam unfolds the recent period of rapid social and economic change
that has seen the end of dictatorship, to reflect upon it and teach a younger
generation of its influence on their very different lifestyle. The fact that
the clock is inaugurated in 1979 (the final montage includes the opening
ceremony) consolidates this effect, suggesting that the history of contemporary South Korea "began" in this defining year, with the assassination of
President Park.

Like *Calla*, *Donggam* also uses this unfolding of history to meditate on the
process of historical revisionism that took place in the late 1990s. Here
again there is a suggestion of the labyrinthine powers of the false, but used
to think a new perspective on the history of the national whole, as opposed
to creating a new past altogether. As the narrative progresses, So-eun's view
of recent events is questioned as she realizes that situations she has lived
through may not have happened quite as she thought. Visiting Sun-mi in
hospital one final time, So-eun reviews the recent past in flashbacks that
acknowledge the growing bond between Dong-hee and Sun-mi, thereby
questioning the validity of the narrative up to that point, and suggesting a
possible alternative history of Dong-hee and Sun-mi's relationship. So-eun
realizes that if she continues to date Dong-hee she will change the course
of history and effectively kill In. She therefore sacrifices her happiness,
allowing history to enfold in its predestined manner, and ensuring that
Dong-hee and Sun-mi become In's parents. So-eun's sacrifice in the face of
this threatened primal scene trades off her personal happiness for the
nation's future. For this reason, although her character is the least politically aware of her contemporaries, she represents a generation's sacrifice
that created the new, democratic world in which In lives. As in *Calla*, then,

in *Donggam* the past cannot be changed (the IMF crisis of the time making such a conclusion seem impossible), but by revising the past it can be enfolded in a "new" way.

The role of melodrama in this particular style of unfolding history is as evident in *Donggam* as it is in *Calla*, as they each render events in a melodramatic mode to evoke a sense of mourning for the personal sacrifices demanded by South Korea's experience of compressed modernity. Both *Calla* and *Donggam* repeatedly deploy lingering facial close-ups and extreme close-ups to illustrate intense emotions, long slow motion sequences accompanied by introspective voiceovers, unspoken sacrifices for others, and emphatic musical accompaniment, all of which contribute to a sense of melodramatic mourning which reaffirms that the past is exactly that, past. These moments elongate cinematic time, as though foregrounding the manner in which time and history are being deliberately unfolded, or decompressed, to enable a greater contemplation of the past. One such moment in *Donggam* is particularly instructive in this respect.

Towards the end of the film, In visits the now adult So-eun at her new position at Chonan University and is overcome with emotion. The scene is filmed for melodramatic effect, as a long, drawn-out sequence of facial close-ups and extreme close-ups with an emotive Bach string accompaniment. Although the scene lasts over two minutes, neither character speaks. Instead, in slow motion, So-eun finally walks past In, and leaves the university building, departing through glass doors into bright sunlight. As she does so she is absorbed into the white light that gradually suffuses the image, eventually disappearing entirely into the bright, all-white background.

Returning to Shilla University, the distraught In is about to smash the HAM radio, believing it to be the cause of his emotional turmoil. He is stopped by the university security guard who crops up at several points in the film, and functions rather like Clarence the angel in *It's a Wonderful Life* (1946), benevolently keeping watch over the young characters. The security guard admonishes him gently, stressing that it will not be so easy to destroy the radio (nor, it is inferred, the past, and the emotions it evokes), and that instead In and Hyeon-ji should 'Go home', because, 'That's how time passes.' In this way *Donggam* both illuminates the "forgotten" past of compressed modernity, emphasizing the links between the past and present through the sacrifice of So-eun, while simultaneously whiting out the past, as though laying it to rest forever. Here once again the Deleuzian 'cerebral component' of the white screen appears, at the moment in which So-eun returns to history, vanishing from the screen back into the outside.

The long drawn out emotional sequence in which So-eun and In meet thus functions as a moment of melodramatic mourning for the past that can only be achieved through its temporal unfolding. In this way the "weepy" aspect of these melodramas provides a cathartic moment in which the past – which, we are repeatedly shown, cannot be changed – is mourned.

In summary, *Donggam*, like *Calla*, unfolds the past in order to create a breathing space for audiences in which to review what may have been lost during compressed modernity. Again the message is that the past can be revisited, and it is an archive (literally represented as such in *Donggam* by In's scholarly research of the past) from which lessons can be learned. However, once again the past cannot be changed. This time the revelation experienced by Seon-woo in *Calla* is granted to So-eun, marking the major difference between the two films. While in *Calla* Seon-woo is able to consider change occurring in the future, in *Donggam* this privilege is not afforded to So-eun, but to In. In both films, instead of investigating the past in order to change it, the past is revisited in order that a certain gender balance can be reaffirmed before the past is then enfolded once again. In *Donggam* in particular a return to a specific type of domestic values is advocated by the security guard, reinforcing the stress already placed by the film on the legitimacy of Dong-hee and Sun-mi's relationship as future parents, and indeed, the sacrifice made by the single professional woman, So-eun. This conclusion, and the importance of the enfolding of the white screen at the film's conclusion, can be better understood when the gender politics of the post-IMF crisis period are considered in greater depth. In fact, these films attempt to enfold history using conservative gender roles, which are reaffirmed by their romantic storylines, to attempt to neatly smooth over the potential uncertainty over gender roles created by the crisis.

Romance/Enfolding: Rejuvenation and Reinforcing Gender Roles

In *Militarized Modernity and Gendered Citizenship in South Korea* (2005) Seungsook Moon summarizes how, during the period of rapid industrialization, women were 'marginalized in production and mobilized to be domestic'[52]. The woman's role was considered as a primarily domestic one, in which she supported her husband, while the male role was that of 'family provider'[53]. Moreover, Cho notes, 'South Korea's modernization created distinct gendered spaces: "a public sphere where men dominate and a family sphere where women dominate" '.[54] As Moon points out elsewhere, these roles were typically normalized through association with traditional 'Confucian gender ideology that functionally assigned women and men to the "inside" and "outside" of the household'.⁵⁵ Thus, when the IMF crisis hit in 1997 and many unemployed or bankrupt fathers found their usual role in society undermined, South Korea's mass media led the cry to 'save the family'⁵⁶ by re-emphasizing these normative gender roles.

In this context, Soyoung Kim notes how contemporary South Korean blockbusters like *Swiri* and *Gongdong-gyungbi-guyeok/Joint Security Area* (2000) represented the nation as a homosocial collective to the point where South Korean women were practically excluded from the screen.⁵⁷ For Kim, this 'disappearance'⁵⁸ of women was a product of the increasing transparency required of South Korea's public space after the economic practices of the *chaebols* (South Korea's business conglomerates) were blamed for the crisis, placing South Korea's predominantly male corporate world under international scrutiny. *Donggam* negotiates this particular context by reaffirming the centrality of the family. Not only does So-eun's personal sacrifice literally save In's family, but In's relationship with Hyeon-ji is also deployed to emphasize the need to "remember" (as in respect) the normative gender roles (and spaces) created by compressed modernity.

A scene occurs early on in the film that perfectly illustrates the normative spheres in which male and female roles are supposed to exist. In, reading a newspaper from 1979 complains: 'It's so complicated. Why did so many complicated and confusing things happen in October 1979?' To this Hyeon-ji, reading In's letter from his mother, replies: 'It's so complicated, the house, the weather, your father.' The different roles to which male and female genders are supposedly suited are here established, suggesting that the two friends are destined to be a couple. However, as we might expect of a romance, they are kept apart for most of the film, and are only able to fulfil these roles after they have experienced first-hand the need for these separate spaces of compressed modernity to be respected.

Throughout the course of the film, Hyeon-ji gradually goes off the rails. Initially she is a nurturing presence, bringing In an umbrella when he is standing in the rain, waiting for him after college, and tracking him down to deliver his parents' letter, all in spite of his constant rebuttals. However, when he becomes more concerned with So-eun in 1979, Hyeon-ji takes a job in a bar, begins to drink, arrives at college in the morning smelling of alcohol, and finally turns up drunk on In's doorstep late at night. This is the turning point for In, who begins to support her. After his emotional visit to Chonan University, and the wise words of the security guard, In finally offers Hyeon-ji his arm in the closing moments of the film. This is the repeat of a scene we first see enacted between So-eun and Dong-heè in a dream So-eun has in 1979. In the dream, the action of taking Dong-hee's arm is the prelude to their first kiss. After the dream, however, So-eun realizes that she must break up with Dong-hee, so that he can instead kiss In's mother-to-be, Sun-mi. When the action is repeated in 2000, it shows that In has learned, through communication with So-eun in 1979, the need to build a monogamous relationship, the basis for a family. He will now, as the security guard suggests, 'go home' with Hyeon-ji to belatedly fulfil So-eun's dream. The ideal of the family thus saves Hyeon-ji from the apparently disgraceful fate of a woman daring enough, or due to the crisis financially needy enough, to enter the public sphere and fashion a living for herself.

In both films the aspect of the past that apparently cannot be changed is the need for stable gender roles. In spite of the crisis, in both films the present sees the continuation of gender roles established under compressed modernity. In *Donggam* in particular the continuity that is created between past and present, as exemplified by the split screen image, suggests that the continuation of these normative roles is inevitable. The only apparent difference is that in the past under dictatorship female sacrifice is necessitated by circumstances, whereas in the present under democracy there is no barrier to the fulfilment of the romantic union, providing normative roles are respected. In this way, In and Hyeon-ji will have the opportunities that So-eun only dreamed of.

Compounding the relationship between In and Hyeon-ji is the fate of So-eun, the representative of a generation whose "passing" is mourned by the film as she is finally whited out of history. As I noted above, So-eun is effectively erased from history by the film, which "thinks" her back into the outside through the white screen. It is her sacrifice at this point in the film that enables the enfolding of the present in a manner that saves In's past, and guarantees his future with Hyeon-ji. Thus although So-eun represents the founding sacrifice of the generation who lived through the 1970s and 1980s (a sacrifice on which In and Hyeon-ji can build their future together), when viewed in the context of the film's unsympathetic stance on Hyeon-ji's economic independence, So-eun's final disappearance from the screen into the outside seems a rather negative reflection of the recent economic 'disappearance' of women from the public sphere. This enfolding of history obscures, or returns to the fold, the productive role of women in the workforce, obliterating such concrete realities as the decline of the women's labour movements in the 1990s,[59] the impact of globalization on South Korea's remaining manufacturing industries,[60] and the targeting of female employees during the massive layoffs that immediately followed the crisis.[61]

The sense of mourning that accompanies So-eun's disappearance, then, suggests that the period she represents is well and truly over. Her erasure from the screen into the outside is a literal 'disappearance', akin to that noted by Soyoung Kim of South Korean women in recent blockbusters, and is a particularly conservative disavowal of the recent importance of South Korean women in the public sphere.

During the 1970s and 1980s, women's movements were an integral part of the struggles for political reform, including coalitions of women's organizations who opposed the family law throughout the period.[62] In the 1990s various women's movements continued to struggle for equal opportunities in the workplace, a decade which saw a series of reforms to the previously inadequate Equal Employment Law.[63] Amongst these groups were educated middle-class women, rather like university professor So-eun, who were instrumental in the legal battle to secure the repeal of the 'extra-points system', a discriminatory employment leg-up that inevitably favoured men who had completed compulsory military service.[64] Yet in the immediate wake of 1997 this process faltered, due in large part to the sudden reduction of women in the workplace. Addressing this changing situation, *Donggam* refigures these years of pressure and reform through its female characters, representing economic independence as either the spinsterly consequence of personal sacrifice (So-eun), or as disgraceful, although recuperable through a return to pre-crisis gender roles (Hyeon-ji). In both instances, female economic independence is rendered as an unrewarding substitute for the company of the ideal man, with only So-eun's sacrifice in the past (the "sacrifice" of not becoming a wife and mother) making it possible for Hyeon-ji to avoid the same fate. Indeed, in both *Calla* and *Donggam* female independence is conflated with a potentially "dangerous" sexuality, both in the death of Ji-hee (the drug dealer's girlfriend in *Calla*) and the risqué behaviour of Hyeon-ji (the alcohol-loving hostess of *Donggam*). This enfolding of history produces a particularly conservative reversal of contemporary representations of South Korean women in various forms of popular culture where, as So-hee Lee has shown, 'a woman's sexuality has become the barometer of her own subjectivity'.[65]

As Kyung Hyun Kim's comparison of the golden age melodrama *The Housemaid* (*Hanyo*, 1960) with *Happy End* (*Haepi-endeu*, 1999) illustrates, what is most remarkable about contemporary representations of gender roles in South Korean cinema is how little they have changed from those of the 1950s and 1960s.[66] While Kim's analysis demonstrates various ways in which *Happy End* offers a more multifaceted negotiation of the gender reversals and public/private sphere ambiguities thrown up by the crisis, in this it is noticeably different from *Calla* and *Donggam*, which firmly uphold established gender divisions in the face of economic crisis. The IMF crisis facilitated a cinematic re-imagining of the national past in line with the 'new conservatism'[67] of the time. Thus, both *Calla* and *Donggam* construct a false continuity between gender roles "then" and "now" that enfolds and eclipses the influence of women in the public sphere during the intervening period. In both *Calla* and *Donggam* a return to established gender roles and the replacement of women in lower income or domestic roles is evoked in response to an economic crisis that potentially threatened the predominantly masculine public sphere. Simultaneously, their romantic element provided their respective protagonists with the capacity to rebuild the future by drawing on pre-crisis family values.

Transforming Time Travel: Folding for National and International Arenas

The chapter concludes with a discussion of how *2009* enfolds national history slightly differently to appeal to international markets, and how the whole that it creates is therefore transnational, rather than national. This difference reflects the shifting position of the South Korean film industry over the last decade, from national growth to international prominence, a shift that is reflected in the move from a nationally to a transnationally enfolded time travel narrative.

For *Calla* and *Donggam*, courting an international audience was something of an afterthought, and as a consequence they had relatively limited success in this respect. Certainly *Donggam*'s moderate overseas success (it gained a theatrical release in Japan and was remade in both Japan and China) was almost entirely unexpected. Both films were products of a film industry in the process of restructuring in the immediate wake of 1997, as several of the major investors pulled out, leaving room for venture capital to invest in production. After the phenomenal international success of *Swiri* – which from an initial outlay of 2.4 billion won garnered $1.3m from sales to Japan and topped the Hong Kong box office for three consecutive weeks[68] – the lucrative nature of the East Asian marketplace was evident. Consequently, South Korean production companies increasingly targeted foreign markets,[69] and total exports of South Korean films grew by over 50 per cent between 1999 and 2000, and again between 2000 and 2001, with Hong Kong, Japan and France being the major importers at that time.[70] *2009*, by contrast to its two predecessors, was the product of the post-2000–2002 boom in the South Korean film industry, and the differences between the two types of film are apparent, as are their respective foldings of national history to target national and international markets respectively.

2009's narrative examines the possibility that twentieth century history has been altered by a Japanese time-traveller, ensuring that South Korea remains a Japanese colony in 2009. *2009* retains the melodrama for mourning (unfold), romance for rejuvenation (enfold) formula of *Calla* and *Donggam*, although the romance plot is relegated to the background to enable spectacular action sequences to dominate. Yet, despite these similarities, in *2009* a science-fiction film with a nationally grounded narrative is deliberately packaged to appeal to international markets, in particular in East Asia. *2009* was clearly engineered with the Japanese market in its sights. Japan is considered the biggest single external market for South Korean cinema, accounting for 70 per cent of exports.[71] Thus, much of the dialogue in *2009* was in Japanese, its narrative engaged with Japanese history (if rather negatively), it co-starred Japanese actor and ex-model Nakamura Toru, and featured a cameo from the famous Japanese director Imamura Shohei. Moreover, the protagonist, Sakamoto, is played by Korean actor Jang Dong-gun, an internationally famous television actor in South East Asia[72], as well as being recognizable abroad for his previous roles in the internationally successful South Korean films *Injeongsajeong bol geot opta/ Nowhere to Hide* (1999) and *Chingu/Friend* (2001). It is perhaps no surprise, then, that *2009*, a film so clearly manufactured to appeal to external audiences was not only seventh in the top ten domestic films at the box office in 2002, but was also distributed directly within Hong Kong by CJ Entertainment and the USA by ADV Films, with its distribution rights being sold to China, Indonesia, Thailand, Malaysia, France, Germany and various of the ex-Soviet Republics.[73]

2009 stretches its nationally specific storyline to appeal to other Asian countries where a reconsideration of modernity often requires a reconsideration of colonial authority. Here the transnational conception of the whole becomes apparent. As in *Donggam*, in *2009* it is the white screen that is the indicator of film thinking the thought from the outside. This time it is a blinding white light that suffuses the image when a portal into the past is opened, its potential for temporal dislocation being emphasized by the appearance of flashbacks experienced by Sakamoto, affirming the virtual slippages in time that the outside makes possible. Noticeably these are not flashbacks to his past, because they show events that will only take place once he has jumped through the portal, in the film narrative's future but the nation's past. These flashbacks, then, are a "national" memory that Sakamoto taps into, memories of the past passed down through the generations. As we might expect by now, the white screen only appears for a few seconds, and is justified diegetically by the build up (the portal takes some time to get ready, with white light getting brighter gradually) and the narrative's focus on the importance of the moment during which the portal is open for the history of South Korea. Fighting to enter the temporal doorway are two cops, previously partners, one South Korean (Jang Dong-gun as Sakamoto) and one Japanese (Nakamura Toru as Saigo). Their personal investments in the past are conflated with their national histories. Whoever is able to re-align time in the past will restore their respective national history, the other standing to lose everything as a result. If Sakamoto gets there first, South Korea will be free of Japanese rule, but Saigo must stop him or else his family will be (or rather, will have been) annihilated during the nuclear strikes on Japan at the end of World War Two. The duel at the heart of this particular action-image, then, is a duel between national histories, ensuring that the whole which is at stake in the opening of the temporal doorway is a transnational, colonial history shared by South Korea and Japan. This is emphasized when the two characters discover the truth, that they are living in a "falsely" realigned time due to Japanese intervention in the past, as the film cuts back and forth between them, using parallel montage in the manner in which, as discussed in Chapter 1, Griffith previously constructed a unified national whole in films like *Birth of a Nation* (1915). When the duel is finally won by Sakamoto in the past, history enfolds once more in the separation of the two nations after World War Two, reaffirming an independent, post-colonial (South) Korean history.

Thus this transnational whole that makes an action spectacle of the thought from the outside is at once a post-war whole that relates to East Asia generally, and also a product of this specific moment in history when South Korean cinema became a strong international force. As East Asia's previous existence as a buffer between communism and capitalism was redefined with the end of the Cold War, the cinemas of countries like South Korea, Hong Kong and Japan all variously reconsidered the rapid changes that had effected national identity. For this reason the market for films like *2009* is larger than just South Korea, a factor that clearly influenced its packaging of the previously popular time travel narrative formula as a blockbuster with transnational appeal, the manner in which it deploys its time travel narrative to examine colonialism, and its conclusion, which sees South Korean national history triumphally restored by Korean cop, Sakamoto. This is an optimistic ending to a film that could otherwise be read as a criticism of the neo-colonial perpetuation, in the form of South Korea's post-war dictatorships, of the military rule imposed on Korea by Japan during the occupation. Instead, in the victory of South Korean history over a falsifying labyrinthine past forced on the nation by Japan, *2009* renders the whole transnational and postcolonial. The white screen thus evokes the outside, providing a glimpse of the falsifying powers of the labyrinth that are available when time is folded, only to enfold time once more to think a new, triumphalist post IMF crisis history for South Korea.

Conclusion: Folding History

All three films demonstrate the same process of unfolding and enfolding time in order to think history cinematically. They all deploy the 'cerebral components' of the thinking image which Deleuze isolated in the time-image, but use mainstream conventions to contain these aspects (black screen, white screen, irrational cut and relinkage) within a unified conception of the whole typical of the movement-image. In this way the whole enfolds the outside, providing a way of thinking history that does not correspond to either of the positions that Deleuze outlined – on universal history in *Cinema 1*, or on minor cinema in *Cinema 2* – drawing on Nietzsche and Kafka respectively. As was the case in Chapter 2, then, a different cinema illustrates the difficulty of upholding Deleuze's movement-/time-image distinction beyond the boundaries of certain, often rather specific cinemas.

Space:

Geopolitics and the Action-Image

Chapter 4

Not Just Any-space-whatever: Hong Kong and the Global/Local Action-Image

The next two chapters examine action-images from Hong Kong and the USA respectively, exploring the deployment of Deleuzian any-space-whatevers in the cinematic construction of urban milieus. Following on from the concluding analysis of *2009* in Chapter 3, I argue that while the any-space-whatever plays a particular role in the negotiation of a crisis in the national whole, it can also function transnationally. In this case it can be seen to demonstrate the impact of more widespread forces, such as imperialism or globalization, on various parts of the world. Thus, while the subject matter is specific (Hong Kong), the ramifications are far broader (global/local).

In this chapter I examine the any-space-whatever in Jackie Chan's stunt-filled *Ging chat goo si/Police Story* (1985). While many Hong Kong films of the 1980s and 1990s have been analysed in terms of their negotiation of a very specific period in Hong Kong's history – the years leading up to the handover to the People's Republic of China (PRC) in 1997 – their any-space-whatevers can be interpreted as having a slightly different emphasis. It is entirely possible, in line with the conclusions of various scholars discussing films like John Woo's *Ying hung boon sik/A Better Tomorrow* (1986), to read the exploration of affect in these films, and the difficulty of constructing a continuous sensory-motor continuum across distinctive urban any-space-whatevers, as a product of their engagement with a time of "national" identity crisis (Hong Kong's problematic "national" status notwithstanding).[1] Here, however, I argue that it is also fruitful to examine how any-space-whatevers in films like *Ging chat goo si* address the global economic concerns that impact on Hong Kongers at a local level. Thus I view *Ging chat goo si* as an exploration of the global/local wealth disparities created by the economic and geographical transformation of Hong Kong wrought by the onset of globalization, as they were manifest in the 1980s.

This distinction has major ramifications both for our understanding of how the any-space-whatever functions in action-images, which would otherwise seem to exclude the affective nature of the any-space-whatever *by definition*, and also for Deleuze's *Cinema* books when they are conceived of as a historical project. This latter is especially the case when Deleuze's remarks about the emergence of the time-image in the various new waves, as expressions of national mutations, are weighed against the broad thrust of *Cinema 2* and its exploration of a post-war time-image cinema in (predominantly) European art cinema. This chapter, then, focuses on the contested status of the any-space-whatever in the action-image, arguing that in many cases the cinematic any-space-whatever should be understood as being of concrete geopolitical significance. In spite of its inevitable actualization in the movement-image, I demonstrate that the any-space-whatever still has the potential to open up a space in which to negotiate, expressively, a global/local meaning from the apparently "anonymous" spaces of globalization. In this way the development of the action-image under globalization demonstrates the continued need to reconsider the conclusions drawn in the *Cinema* books, which primarily focus on the action-image as it appears in classical Hollywood cinema.

First I discuss the Deleuzian concept of the any-space-whatever. I then situate this concept within a global context, engaging with Ackbar Abbas's *Hong Kong* (1997), in which Abbas uses Deleuze's work to explore the 'disappearance' of Hong Kong in films made in the run-up to the handover, and to develop the concept of *déjà disparu*. Next I draw together a range of critiques and developments of Deleuze's notion of the any-space-whatever to demonstrate how it is increasingly understood to be linked to globalization. Finally I argue that *Ging chat goo si* can be interpreted as an action-image attempting to find local ways of mapping Hong Kong in its transition from Crown Colony to global city, whose ASA' narrative is bracketed by spectacles in which the any-space-whatever becomes prominent. Through the expressive physical movements that play across the "face" of these any-space-whatevers they are rendered simultaneously both anonymous spaces typical of globalization, and yet very much localized spaces. They are at once specific to Hong Kong, but also able to resonate with the physical experiences of a number of other cities (especially in East Asia) experiencing the impact of globalization at a local level.

Any-space-whatevers

The any-space-whatever, a term Deleuze credits to Pascal Augé,[2] appears in both *Cinema 1* and *Cinema 2*, and exists in a slightly different form in the movement- and time-image. In *Cinema 1*, Deleuze discusses the any-space-whatever in relation to the affection-image. The affection-image is an integral part of the movement-image's sensory-motor regime. As Deleuze argues in chapter six, it often takes the form of a close-up of a face. This might be, for instance, the reverse shot in a sequence of shots that introduce a person or object from a particular character's point of view. The initial point of view shot, a perception-image, is followed by a reverse shot of the face of the character viewing the person or object, often in close-up. This is the affection-image. In the affection-image we might expect to see the person reacting physically to what they see. As an expression plays across their face, the micro-movements of their facial muscles are magnified, as though the face were a landscape reacting to events it perceives. Conventionally, the sequence is then concluded by an image of the action the character decides to take as a consequence of their encounter with the person or thing, an action-image. However, Deleuze notes that affect, while normally "overcome" by action in this way, also has the potential to pause the sensory-motor continuum. In so doing, space becomes divorced from the defining coordinates of action. Deleuze argues that:

> [T]he close up retains the . . . power to tear the image away from spatio-temporal coordinates in order to call forth the pure affect as the expressed. Even the place, which is still present in the background, loses its coordinates and becomes 'any space whatever . . .'[3]

This is the very specific sense in which the any-space-whatever is defined by Deleuze in *Cinema 1*, not solely, as the term might suggest, as random, anonymous spaces (although by *Cinema 2* Deleuze is discussing them in this way, as 'disused warehouses, waste ground, cities in the course of demolition or reconstruction'[4]), but as spaces whose spatio-temporal coordinates have become suspended or detached from an action-oriented sensory-motor continuum. Relating such affection-images to the semiotic categories of Charles Sanders Peirce, Deleuze argues that they express powers or qualities, existing as pure potentiality, rather than end results of actions.[5] Claire Colebrook's work is helpful here, as she notes of the any-space-whatever that:

> One no longer sees this city or building, in this historical, narrative moment, nor this event as part of a series for a collection of bodies, but perceives a power as such, a power to be seen, an extended quality that is not located in *this* space, but is 'a' space.[6]

Thus, an affection-image has the ability to both divorce character from situation, and to abstract a space from its usual milieu, rendering it in terms of its powers or qualities. However, in action-image cinemas, or with the completion of a movement from perception- through affection- to action-image, this affective function of the any-space-whatever is "completed" (its virtual potentiality having been actualized) by the dominance of the sensory-motor continuum. From 'a' space it returns, through action, to *this* space.

In chapter seven of *Cinema 1*, Deleuze continues this line of argument, moving away from the face and focusing on any-space-whatevers that are, he argues, 'capable of inducing non-human affects'.[7] Of most relevance for this chapter, Deleuze draws upon Béla Balázs's analysis of Joris Ivens's films, including *De Brug/The Bridge* (1928) and *Regen/Rain* (1929), to demonstrate how a specific structure like a bridge in Rotterdam, or the rain-soaked city of Amsterdam, can be rendered affectively in cinema. Here, for Deleuze, the space is depicted in terms of its potential for 'virtual conjunction'[8] rather than its actual use or function.[9] As D. N. Rodowick clarifies in *Gilles Deleuze's Time Machine* (1997), the affective nature of these images depends on the absence of any reterritorializing specificity, such as the cinematic construction of 'a definite place, historical origin . . . or narrative exposition'.[10] Any such contextualizing device would actualize the any-space-whatever, transforming it from 'a' space into *this* space: into a specific bridge in Rotterdam, or a city (Amsterdam) defined in terms of their particular use-function within a national, historical or narrative context. Instead, these any-space-whatevers provide an affective impression of a bridge in terms of its power (for Rodowick, 'the potential of rail transportation itself'), and a city seen through the qualities of 'wetness, rippling, reflection, a hundred associations without specific reference to the concept of rain or rain specific to a time and place'.[11] Thus, as Ronald Bogue summarizes in *Deleuze on Cinema* (2003), the any-space-whatever 'is a virtual space, whose fragmented components may be assembled in multiple combinations, a space of yet-to-be-actualised possibilities'.[12]

After discussing the construction of any-space-whatevers through various cinematic techniques (through the use of shadow, 'lyrical abstraction', and colour to extract the any-space-whatever from its 'determinate space'[13]), Deleuze concludes chapter seven by gesturing towards *Cinema 2* and the increased importance the any-space-whatever will take on in post-war cinemas like Italian neorealism and the French New Wave.[14] In this context, Deleuze argues, the any-space-whatever moves beyond being a 'disconnected' space to become an empty, or more accurately, 'emptied' space.[15] He states:

It is no longer, as before, a space which is defined by parts whose linking up and orientation are not determined in advance, and can be done in an infinite number of ways. It is now an amorphous set which has eliminated that which happened and acted in it. It is an extinction or a disappearing . . .[16]

For Deleuze, in post-war cinemas these emptied any-space-whatevers would give rise to the pure optical and sound images that marked the crisis of the movement-image, and ultimately the arrival of the time-image, expressing the 'modern affects' of 'fear, detachment . . . freshness, extreme speed, and interminable waiting'.[17] Indeed, Deleuze returns to the any-space-whatever in the final chapter of *Cinema 1* (after first discussing the action-image), to reiterate his point.[18]

By the start of *Cinema 2*, then, the any-space-whatever has become of key importance to the shift Deleuze charts from movement- to time-image cinemas in the post-war era. Accordingly, Rodowick situates any-space-whatevers as one of several indicators of the inherently unstable nature of the movement-image, and in particular of the action-image, in relation to the virtual potential cinema contains for the emergence of the time-image.

For Deleuze, the cinema is marked from the beginning by a tension wherein the open surges to undermine the whole and the Whole is defined by the open. The simple durations of early cinema, the dynamic and mathematical sublime of German Expressionism and French Impressionism, *the emergence of any-space-whatevers in the affection-image*, and the episodic nature of the small form of the action-image: all are harbingers of time, as it were, signs of openness within an emerging desire for totality.[19] [my italics]

Alongside these other factors, then, any-space-whatevers, while ultimately actualized in the action-image, are a symptom of the instability of the sensory-motor whole. They are 'harbingers of time', in the sense that they indicate the potentially destabilizing effect of the virtual whole of time on the movement-image's ability to construct a unified, very often national, whole. As such, they retain their virtual potential in the time-image. The any-space-whatevers of post-war European cinema are emptied of significance for the sensory-motor incapacitated seers who populate them, the irrational linkages that join them together suggesting more the emergence of a thought from the outside than the existence of a unified whole. The any-space-whatever thereby illustrates our existence in time, as opposed to the actualized spaces of the action-image which are given purpose and meaning by the sensory-motor actions of protagonists. The any-space-whatever is thus not evidence of the spatialized time found in the movement-image, but of the virtual 'movement of world'[20] (of Bergson's duration) in which we are all caught up once our sensory-motor continuity becomes destabilized and actions are no longer capable of altering situations. In the first chapter of *Cinema 2*, Deleuze argues:

> The optical and sound situations of neo-realism contrast with the strong sensory-motor situations of traditional realism. The space of a sensory-motor situation is a setting which is already specified and presupposes an action which discloses it, or prompts a reaction which adapts or modifies it. But a purely optical or sound situation becomes established in what we might call 'any-space-whatever', whether disconnected or emptied.[21]

Any-space-whatevers are therefore of great importance for time-image cinemas because when they are encountered by the seer they are, as I noted in Chapter 2 when discussing the child, 'invested by the senses'[22] as characters struggle to make sense of situations which are beyond their physical power to control. They are integral to the ability of the pure optical and sound situation to confront situations 'intolerable and unbearable', whether 'something too powerful or too unjust' or 'sometimes also too beautiful'.[23] These situations beyond individual human control are what give rise to the mutations that Deleuze observes in the cinemas of the post-war world as though in waves, 'in Europe after the war, mutation of an Americanised Japan, mutation of France in '68',[24] illustrating, again as I argued in Chapter 2, that the whole that Deleuze considers to be mutating is apparently a national whole. In such films the any-space-whatever retains the potential to be as expressive as a face in close-up, as the urban milieu forms itself into an expression that fills the void between perception and action for the (national) whole.

Hong Kong

Abbas's *Hong Kong*, which explores the city's mutation in the years leading up to the handover in 1997, directly draws upon and furthers the Deleuzian line of thinking regarding the proliferation of national 'mutations' in the post-war world. Abbas situates Hong Kong cinema of the 1980s and 1990s as the next in line of Deleuze's mutations, after post-war Europe, Japan, post-'68 France, post-Vietnam USA, etc. *Hong Kong* was published in the year of the handover, and meditated on the changing shape of Hong Kong culture in the immediately preceding years, in cinema, architecture, photography and certain forms of writing. For Abbas, in the years following the Sino-British Joint Declaration of 1984, which included the Tiananmen Square Massacre of 1989, Hong Kong became 'a space of disappearance'[25] producing a 'culture of disappearance'[26] in anticipation of its imminent change of identity. This was an exploration of the uniqueness, or specificity of Hong Kong culture, prompted, ironically, by its anticipated end. Abbas situated this moment in the city's history as a juncture between 'imperialism and globalism', where 'the previous colonial cities, have been primed to perform well as global cities'. [27]

In fact, numerous scholars have interpreted works of Hong Kong cinema after 1984 as attempts to negotiate the city's identity crisis provoked by the immanence of 1997.[28] What is interesting for this discussion is the manner in which Abbas situates the city's disappearance, as it is negotiated in Hong Kong cinema, as the latest example of Deleuze's trajectory of cinematic explorations of such transformations or mutations that marked the spread of the time-image.[29] Abbas seems to be noting the correlation between the broad shift that Deleuze identifies with the Second World War, as marking the caesura between a movement- and a time-image cinema, with an increasingly widespread economic transformation in the post-war world, one that has, since the 1970s, and increasingly since the end of the Cold War, become synonymous with neoliberal globalization. The mutation of 'space and affectivity'[30] that Abbas observes in certain works of pre-handover Hong Kong cinema appears to give credence to the idea that the time-image marks the emergence of a new episteme, a new post-war image of thought. Yet, whereas Deleuze was somewhat vague about precisely what context this new image of thought might potentially be thinking about, the disappearance of Hong Kong suggests that this context could be conceived of as the post-war reconstruction of spaces previously conceived of as national (or in Hong Kong's case at least imperial) towards an increasingly globalized economic situation, whose transformative powers are seen in Hong Kong cinema in the run-up to 1997 through its any-space-whatevers.

In line with Deleuze's thinking on modern political or minor cinema in *Cinema 2*, Abbas considers the role of pre-handover Hong Kong cinema to be the avoidance of clichés (recognizable representations of "old" Hong Kong that leave the viewer with the sense that what they are seeing has already disappeared – Abbas's '*déjà disparu*') in favour of a self-conscious cinematic exploration of Hong Kong's shifting cultural space.[31] Accordingly, he favours the more contemplative art films of directors like Wong Kar-wai in which, he argues, 'affectivity . . . is the index of a space that cannot be grasped directly'[32] over the popular genre films that many associate with this period in Hong Kong cinema, such as the gangster movies of Woo. Even so, I would argue, there is a great deal to be gained by analysing how the any-space-whatever is explored in these genre films. For instance, Julian Stringer's analysis of the way action and melodrama are intertwined in Woo's *Ying hung boon sik* and *Dip huet seung hung/The Killer* (1989), and how they function to negotiate pre-handover anxieties, suggests that the interplay between affect and action in genre films provides more than just a 'simplification' of the situation, as Abbas somewhat dismissively states of such approaches.[33] Moreover, consider Jenny Kwok Wau Lau's critique of the widespread critical conflation of 1997 with a supposed "awakening" of Hong Kong popular cinema to issues of cultural identity, whereas, as she demonstrates through her analysis of Cantonese comedies, these popular genres have a much longer history of negotiating Hong Kong identity on screen. As she concludes, '1997 became one (but not the only) issue in some (but not all) of the best films coming out of Hong Kong'.[34] For this reason, although as Ka-Fai Yau has shown, there is much to be gained from studying the thoughtful films of Hong Kong director Fruit Chan as works of minor cinema,[35] there is just as much intellectual ground to be uncovered by exploring the any-space-whatever in popular films like *Ging chat goo si.*

In these popular genre films the any-space-whatever is not self-consciously investigated in terms of its virtual potentiality, in the manner of Wong's films. Yet it is still negotiated, even if it ultimately disappears through its overcoming by action. Put another way, in Jackie Chan's *Ging chat goo si* the any-space-whatever of pre-handover Hong Kong is explored as a spectacle that provides an affective hiatus in the sensory-motor regime. In the any-space-whatever, the virtual "potential" (a word which now begins to seem potentially politically problematic) of unseen or absent global forces – like waning imperialism, or increasingly widespread globalization – emerges, only to be renegotiated into an actualized form by representatives of Hong Kong, the "national", although in this case, regional, but in any case, local, whole. Thus these movement-images examine the mutation of the local in its engagement with the global through the contested nature of the any-space-whatever. This is most evidently apparent if we focus on the expressive nature of emptied urban any-space-whatevers as they encounter the forces of globalization, their resulting "facial" reactions demonstrating their emotive attempts to actualize these spaces in a way that will be meaningful for a developing global/local whole, Hong Kong.

Global/Local versus National

As several scholars have observed, historically Hong Kong cinema has been a site for negotiating conflicts between the local, national, transnational and global.[36] Abbas, after all, notes that during the period in question (approximately 1984 to 1997), Hong Kong held a unique position as a city at the juncture between 'imperialism and globalism'. It was at this time that Hong Kong began to negotiate its shift from being one of the last outposts of British colonial wealth to a global city and Special Administrative Region (SAR) of an economically resurgent PRC. Indeed, the PRC was at that time prospering under, as David Harvey defines it, 'neoliberalism with Chinese characteristics'[37] (Harvey is here deliberately reworking the oft-quoted description of the economic development of the PRC under Deng Xiaoping as "Socialism with Chinese characteristics"), a particular blend of authoritarian politics and neoliberal market economics.[38] However, this process of global/local reterritorialization in cinema is also an increasingly widespread phenomenon.[39] Thus, the emptied any-space-whatever that appears in *Cinema 2*, marking the shift to a new cinema, is usefully seen in many instances as an indicator of global forces temporarily rendering characters within a nation (or in the case of Hong Kong, a city or region) incapacitated seers, who must then consider how they will respond to these debilitating any-space-whatevers.

Various critics have drawn similar conclusions concerning the geopolitical nature of the any-space-whatever. In *The Skin of the Film* (2000), Laura U. Marks considers the political relevance of post-war films set in any-space-whatevers for 'inter-cultural' characters: diasporic or otherwise displaced characters that exist in a space that is not necessarily informing of their present-day identity. Observing the Eurocentrism of Deleuze's position on the emergence of the any-space-whatever in post-war Europe, Marks points out that 'any-space-whatevers are not simply the disjunctive spaces of postmodernism, but also the disruptive spaces of postcolonialism, where non-Western cultures erupt into Western metropolises, and repressed cultural memories return to destabilise national histories'.[40] Unable to turn perception into action in these potentially alienating any-space-whatevers, these characters exist in a more affective relationship with them. In addition, in *Cinema and the City* (2001), Mark Shiel explicitly positions the any-space-whatever as an indicator of globalization.

> This space, whether taking the form of a shopping mall, a corporate headquarters, a hotel lobby, a downtown street, or indeed, a multiplex

cinema, is not notable simply because of its ubiquity or familiarity but more particularly because if, as Foucault suggests, all space is controlled, the any-space-whatever is a space in which the source of control, the center of power, is curiously difficult to apprehend. It is a space in which the intangibility of global capitalism is particularly apparent.[41]

As in Abbas's work, in Shiel's argument there is a direct acknowledgement that the any-space-whatever, while by definition a space detached from specific historical coordinates, is also a politically 'controlled' space that directly expresses the absent presence of global forces. Finally, Martine Beugnet, exploring contemporary French cinema through a Deleuzian filter, also considers the any-space-whatever to express a new 'global age'[42] of late capitalism, structured by the forces of neoliberal globalization.[43] This is seen in particular, for Beugnet, through the depiction of the 'post-industrial', 'transnational corporate world of customised global architecture'.[44]

As the works of Abbas, Marks, Shiel and Beugnet variously demonstrate, Deleuze's overwhelming any-space-whatevers of modernity experienced by the seer in the post-war time-image, often seemingly the product of an absent guiding hand, are now increasingly acknowledged as products of an equally 'intangible' global capitalism that has become increasingly widespread in the postcolonial and now also post-Cold War era. To understand the, as it were, "post-national" nature of the global any-space-whatever it is perhaps helpful to consider that the types of spaces least likely to be considered any-space-whatever are those recognizable (usually urban) landmarks which are typically identifiable precisely because of their association with a certain national location and identity (the Eiffel Tower in Paris, the Empire State Building in New York, the statue of Christ the Redeemer over Rio, Tiananmen Square Beijing, The Sydney Opera House, and so on). Any-space-whatevers are, by contrast, spaces that recur across nations, but are not nationally specific, including airports and shopping malls on the one hand, and shanty towns and refugee camps on the other.

These spaces are, precisely, the proliferating 'non-places' that anthropologist Marc Augé has noted as characteristic of globalization, especially in his influential book *Non-Places* (1992), the correlations of which with Deleuze's idea of the any-space-whatever are often discussed.[45] Augé develops his idea of the non-place by discussing how the world has been spatially condensed by the rapidity of mass transport and technological developments, like satellites, cable networks and computer chips, which enable a global flow of people, information and image.[46] For Augé, non-places are not located in a cultural context, but exist outside or beyond a defining sense of location or history. Non-places include spaces associated with either end of the wealth spectrum. On the one hand mass transit hubs like international airports, commercial centres, hotel chains, supermarkets, shopping malls, and so on, and on the other, refugee camps, shanty towns, slums, etc.[47] As Augé further argues in *A Sense for the Other* (1994), in these non-places the individual existing in or encountering these often transitory spaces becomes a 'witness' as opposed to an 'actor',[48] a stance that also seems very similar to Deleuze's interpretation of the protagonist in the time-image as a seer, rather than an agent. As Ian Buchanan summarizes in his contribution to *Deleuze and Space* (2005):

> Augé's point, I think, is that jet travel has lightened our step on earth; we no longer dwell as heavily as we once did. We swim through places more than we dwell there and consequently a new type of social space has emerged whose precise function is to facilitate a frictionless passage – airports, train stations, bus terminals, fast food outlets, supermarkets and hotels. Because they do not confer a sense of place, Augé calls these places non-places.[49]

Although there are important differences between Deleuze and Augé's ideas (the most significant being Deleuze's focus on cinematic constructions of space), and indeed, a great deal more to Augé's work than solely his conception of the non-place, it should be clear that, although Deleuze does not discuss its global geopolitical ramifications for his conception of cinema in any depth, the any-space-whatever is extremely similar to Augé's non-places. Accordingly, the any-space-whatever can also usefully be considered as expressive of the anonymous spaces of globalization which, although possible to reterritorialize through local actions, are no longer the historically defined and definitive milieu of the nation, even while they exist within nations.

Contextually this provides a slightly different understanding of the any-space-whatever than is evident at the start of *Cinema 2* where Deleuze discusses Luchino Visconti's *Rocco e i suoi fratelli/Rocco and his Brothers* (1960), and the attempts made by a family of Italian rural immigrants to invest their new urban settings with meaning through their senses.[50] By the time of the handover of Hong Kong to the PRC, the geopolitical significance of the any-space-whatever has shifted. It is no longer exemplified by an exploration of the rapidly mutating post-war industrial city (Milan) through the eyes of the incapacitated seer (a poor family arriving from the rural South) overwhelmed in the face of the impact of modernity on the nation. Now it

is more accurately an attempt to make sense of the equally rapidly transforming post-imperial/global city (Hong Kong), in a way that re-forms a
local whole in relation to the proliferation of global any-space-whatevers.

This understanding of the any-space-whatever as it appears in action-
images from parts of the globe experiencing the impact of globalization,
as an emptied space of late capitalism in need of negotiation by the local
population, falls in line with definitions of globalization that emerged in
the early 1990s which stress the interactive relationship between the local
and these globally determined spaces. These include Mike Featherstone's
observations on how 'the processes of globalization and localization are
inextricably bound together'; Roland Robertson's work on 'glocalization',
which acknowledges that 'globalization – in the broadest sense, the compression of the world – has involved and increasingly involves the creation
and the incorporation of locality, processes which themselves largely shape,
in turn, the compression of the world as a whole';[51] and David Morley and
Kevin Robins' argument concerning how 'globalisation . . . is about the
achievement of a new global-local nexus, about new and intricate relations
between global space and local space'.[52] After all, it is increasingly in
the any-space-whatevers of globalization, be they anonymous, hi-tech air-
conditioned malls and airports or, as I will discuss further, what may appear
to be equally interchangeable shanty towns and slums that people make
sense of their local identity (even if this line of reasoning illustrates the
Western, metropolitan bias of Deleuze and Augé, as these areas undoubtedly appear distinct to their inhabitants). Thus the negotiation of a shifting
national identity in the face of rapid modernization seen in the any-space-
whatever that is at the forefront of *Rocco e i suoi fratelli*, and which informs
Deleuze's allusion to the post-war world as somehow different from the pre-
war one, is nowadays most usefully seen as an indicator of a broader shift
towards the local negotiation of identity under globalization that has
become most apparent several decades later.

To conclude this section, it is helpful to consider popular films from
Hong Kong, like *Ging chat goo si*, in terms of spatial politics because they
illustrate the link between the any-space-whatever and global forces (imperialism, globalization) in the action-image. This is especially clear if we
consider how Deleuze formulates the any-space-whatever as at once, and by
definition, divorced from specific historical coordinates (a space expressing a quality or power, a space with as yet unrealized virtual potential), in
Cinema 1, and yet and at the same time, a defining aspect of mutating or
transforming cinema in a range of *national* post-war contexts in *Cinema 2*.
Understood in terms of spatial politics it is precisely when the any-space-
whatever becomes 'a' space that it also allows for the potential to become

very definitely *this* space once again, especially in the action-image. While this may initially seem paradoxical, because the any-space-whatever is, I would argue, by definition an "any" space typical of those which proliferate under globalization, it is in the interaction between the potential 'a' space of globalization and the negotiation through action of a recognizable local *this* space (be it national, or in this instance, within a global city) that a geopolitical notion of place returns to the any-space-whatever. Accordingly, in *Ging chat goo si* the any-space-whatever appears as a landscape or location which functions like that of a close-up of a face – following Deleuze, a ' "faceified" [*visagéifée*]'[53] image – across which the struggle for global/local identity plays out in an expressive mode, through actions of characters which are rendered micro-movements across its surface.

Ging chat goo si (1985)

Ging chat goo si is an action-image in the small form, with an ASA' structure. We are dropped into the action at the start, and from the fragmented, elliptical events that take place a situation is gradually revealed. As in the large form action-image (SAS') the narrative is ultimately sensory-motor, but here the trajectory is reversed, with motor actions seemingly driving perception or cognition of the situation.[54] Deleuze considers the burlesque, along with the costume drama, detective movie and certain types of westerns (which I discussed in Chapter 1), to epitomize the action-image in its ASA' small form.[55] In many respects *Ging chat goo si* is akin to a detective film in that its investigation narrative reveals the extent of the situation, although the burlesque is also a very good way of describing Chan's acrobatic/comedic movement, that which carries the various episodes that constitute the film. In any case, in *Ging chat goo si* the situation that is revealed to us through Chan's actions is one of self-serving greed on the part of the already wealthy Hong Kong business elite, pursued through international trade, at the expense of the less well off in the local population. This is a situation that the Crown Colony's legal system is shown to be unable or unwilling to deal with, leaving outstanding individuals to take action in their own defence. *Ging chat goo si* is, thus, a film that explores local resistance to the wealth discrepancies of globalization. The film's most apparent 'indices', Deleuze's term to refer to the indicator or sign of the broader situation,[56] are the opening car chase through the shanty town and the concluding punch-up in the shopping mall. These spectacular sequences are key to the film's revelation of this situation. They are the film's A and A' moments in which the actualizing of the any-space-whatever is most apparent. They also clearly demonstrate the process through which the 'a' space of globalization is reterritorialized locally into *this* space, Hong Kong.

A plot synopsis provides the first step towards understanding this process. The film opens with a police operation to arrest a local drug baron with connections in Thailand, Chu (Chor Yuen). Chu is engaged in a heroin deal in a hillside shanty town, and when confronted by the police he and his henchmen make their getaway by driving down the hillside, straight through the shanty town. Chu is pursued and finally apprehended on a local bus by the incredibly agile Chan (Jackie Chan). Chu's secretary Selina (Brigitte Lin) is held in police custody as a witness for the prosecution, protected by Chan, although this causes mayhem in Chan's private life. The criminal courts are unable to convict Chu, and Selina's life is once again endangered when she is recaptured by Chu. Chan is framed for the murder of a corrupt fellow officer, and arrested, but escapes, determined to clear his name. Selina prints out information from Chu's computer relating to his criminal undertakings, and escapes with it into a local shopping mall. There, Chan single-handedly fights Chu's numerous henchmen, apprehending Chu, and physically beating both Chu and his lawyer.

However, this plot synopsis does not do justice to the mixture of spectacles that constitute *Ging chat goo si*. As was the case with the spaghetti western, the episodic nature of the Hong Kong action movie is the product of very specific industrial conditions and aesthetic traditions. In *Planet Hong Kong* (2000), David Bordwell notes how, historically, the nine reel structure of the typical Hong Kong feature film became the basis for an industrial norm of an episodic narrative of spectacles that is still evident in Chan action movies, like '*A' gai wak/Project A* (1982). Moreover, the popularity of this format can be explained by its similarity to other popular forms well known to Hong Kong audiences, from oral epics to pulp adventure stories[57] and the spectacle-driven aesthetic of the Peking Opera tradition[58] in which Chan received his hard physical apprenticeship and training. Accordingly, although the opening action sequence is extremely tense, with a bloody shootout and one of the most famous action stunts in cinema history (the drive through the shanty town), the film rapidly becomes a series of comic situations, sight gags, slapstick, stunts, brawls and kung fu fights. This parade of burlesque spectacles includes: Chan in a variety of police uniforms taking part in a PR photo shoot; Chan and a colleague faking an attempt on Selina's life in which their fighting forms appear akin to two entwined dancers; Chan receiving a birthday cake in the face from his girlfriend May (Maggie Cheung); Chan stepping in cow dung, and moonwalking in the style of Michael Jackson to wipe it off; Chan driving different cars in various states of disrepair (effectively collapsing clown cars); Selina jumping from a high rooftop into a swimming pool; and Chan's incredible leap and seventy foot slide down a steel pole (through electric lights and into a glass house) to apprehend Chu in the shopping mall.

Despite Chan's amazing physical prowess these comedic and spectacular situations ultimately demonstrate his sensory-motor weakness in the face of global any-space-whatevers, as well as the risks involved in policing, or reterritorializing them on behalf of the local populace. Through the often amazing actions of protagonists in these scenes the situation revealed is one of Hong Kong residents struggling to survive in the face of the global wealth represented by Chu, with his international contacts and expensive lawyer. This is epitomized in the court room sequence, where the traditional wigs and gowns synonymous with the British legal system adorn Hong Kong lawyers disputing the guilt of Chu, demonstrating the peculiar role of the Crown Colony as a structuring absence in the city. This system is seen to function to keep Chu at large, despite his evident guilt and in the face of the everyday heroism of the ordinary citizen, Chan, when confronting the international power of Chu. The role of the any-space-whatever in revealing this situation is most clearly seen in the two giant urban facial expressions that begin and end the narrative, indices that express globalization's impact on the local population. The first of these is the shanty town, a setting which has a very specific relevance to Hong Kong.

A – Shanty Town

At the start of the film we are dropped into the action, as Chan is deployed as part of a team of police, attempting to arrest Chu in the shanty town. Discussion of shanty towns appears in the *Cinema* books on several occasions, particularly in relation to the any-space-whatever. In *Cinema 1*, Deleuze discusses the emergence of the emptied any-space-whatever in post-war cinema with specific reference to the destruction wreaked on Europe's major cities by the war. He notes:

> . . . the post-war situation with its towns demolished or being reconstructed, its waste grounds, *its shanty towns*, and even in places where the war had not penetrated, its undifferentiated urban tissue, its vast unused places, docks, warehouses, heaps of girders and scrap iron. [my italics][59]

Yet, as Marks' work suggests, this description could equally be applied to the growth of urban poverty throughout the world in the second half of the twentieth century, and the displaced wandering postcolonial seers who increasingly inhabit the shanty towns of its expanding metropolises. It is also possible to consider this description as relevant to Hong Kong.

Shanty towns are not uncommon to Hong Kong action-images, having featured prominently in numerous and varied Hong Kong films, from *Saang Gong Kei Bing/Long Arm of the Law* (1984) to *Heung gong yau gok hor lei wood/Hollywood Hong Kong* (2001). In Hong Kong cinema shanty towns have generally functioned to demonstrate the wealth and social inequalities that exist in different parts of the city. Therefore, due to the release of *Ging chat goo si* in 1985, the shanty town is perhaps intended to represent the result of the Crown Colony's economic policies, and as an any-space-whatever it initially seems to relate more to imperialism than globalization. After all, in spite of Hong Kong's prosperity in the latter half of the twentieth century, and its degree of government-supported social planning, in particular in the realms of education and housing,[60] there was social unrest among the population directly relating to wealth and social inequalities. The most well-known example of this is the Star Ferry Riots of 1966, which were prompted by a rise in the first-class fare rate for the cross-harbour Star Ferry. According to Steve Tsang, in *A Modern History of Hong Kong* (2007):

[T]he protest was started and supported mainly by young people of the lower social and economic strata who would usually not have travelled first class on the Star Ferry. Most took part in the riots not because the fare increase directly affected their own livelihood but because they were frustrated and bored, and they resented the idea of businesses appearing to make excessive profits while their own lots were neglected.[61]

However, despite this history of social inequality in the Crown Colony, of excessive profits for some and a sense of social neglect for others, the shanty town that appears in *Ging chat goo si* can also be considered indicative of a larger urban transformation. It is, after all, a product of economic decisions made in the 1970s that would lead to Hong Kong's development into a global city. Therefore, much as the shanty town can be considered an any-space-whatever of imperialism, it is also equally possible to interpret it as an any-space-whatever of globalization. Some further historical context is necessary if we are to understand this distinction.

By the end of the 1960s Hong Kong enjoyed prosperity based primarily on its successful manufacturing industry. In the 1970s, however, it began to transform its economy in order to, as Tsang summarizes, 'upgrade and develop its already impressive network of banks, shipping and insurance agencies into a modern financial centre and regional hub for business services'.[62] An integral part of this process was the opening up of the banking sector, to allow foreign and international banks to establish offices in Hong Kong; although several other factors played a part, including the supportive but generally non-intrusive government and the Crown Colony's emphasis on entrepreneurial economic activity.[63] For Tsang the transformation of Hong Kong is in actual fact a tribute to the efforts of the local Hong Kong community as opposed to the colonial authorities, the latter's major contribution being, he argues, the provision of a political framework and social stability, conditions in which entrepreneurial activity could flourish: 'The management of Hong Kong's economy in the 1980s might have made it look like the only place where Thatcherism was applied in its purest form, but it was in place well before Margaret Thatcher came to power in Britain in 1979.'[64] Thus, whether we consider the entrepreneurialism of Hong Kongers to be due to a government of 'positive non-intervention', or simply of 'benign neglect'[65] Hong Kong began to develop into a 'modern international financial centre'[66] well before the immanent handover became a reality in the early 1980s. Accordingly, Hong Kong's cinematic any-space-whatevers, including its shanty towns, can be seen to function as much to negotiate the city's transformation into an integrated part of the global economy, a global city, as they do to explore the imperial legacy of British rule in the Crown Colony.

In *Global Hong Kong* (2005), Gary McDonogh and Cindy Wong observe that the city's economic transformation, in the wake of the riots of 1966–7, directly contributed to income and class inequality in Hong Kong.[67] In this Hong Kong was not unusual. As Saskia Sassen has demonstrated, the shift away from manufacturing to producer service based economies in cities like Hong Kong in the latter decades of the twentieth century, a shift that is typical of globalization, has led to marked wealth inequalities among the population of such globally interconnected cities.[68] This conclusion falls in line with David Harvey's contention, mentioned in Chapter 2, that wealth inequality is the aim, rather than a by-product, of neoliberalism; an economic policy effectively designed to ensure that a numerically small elite class accumulates the majority of the world's wealth.[69] Again, as Robert H. Wade finds in his contribution to *Global Inequality* (2007), in the period 1980–2000 globalization and market liberalization failed to increase economic growth rates worldwide compared to the period 1960–1978.[70] Indeed, with the exception of the PRC these measures did not facilitate a reduction in income inequality either. Rather, income inequality grew throughout the world during this period,[71] including in Hong Kong. Typically for a global city in Hong Kong this economic expansion deepened existing social and economic inequalities, the boom of the 1970s producing not only a new generation of entrepreneurial billionaires, but also expanding the middle classes more generally.[72] The division of the city into shanty town and shopping mall that we see in *Ging chat goo si*, then, was an emerging by-product of Hong Kong's transformation into a global city.

Events in the PRC also played their part in this transformation of Hong Kong, especially after the instigation of the 'open door' strategy of 1979.[73] In the years leading up to the handover, particularly after the period of economic slowdown and inflation that led to the Tiananmen Square protests in 1989, wealth inequality in Hong Kong increased as a direct result of changes in the PRC.[74] As James K. Galbraith notes, after 1989 the impact of Deng Xiaoping's open door policy on Hong Kong included increased migration to the city, an increase in Chinese export business (in particular from the Southern province of Guangdong), that was handled through Hong Kong, and the property bubble; all of which furthered wealth inequality in the city.[75] Hong Kong businesses also took advantage of the PRC's new Special Economic Zones, with manufacturing firms relocating most of their production bases to Southern China in the years 1980–1987 at a cost of around 60,000 jobs per year in Hong Kong.[76] Financing production in these areas of the PRC enabled increased profit margins due to the cheaper costs of production they offered, while firms retained their offices in Hong Kong, the region's financial, information and export hub.[77] Hence the city's transformation from a manufacturing to a financial services industry employing 60 per cent of the population by the 1990s,[78] focusing on 'financing, insurance, real estate and business services',[79] which was fostered by events in the PRC, directly contributed to the increased wealth inequalities of Hong Kong.

This change became clearly evident in the city's physical landscape. In *Planet of Slums* (2006), Mike Davis comments on the urban overcrowding that beset Hong Kong during this period, while noting more generally that the increased prevalence of shanty towns and slums that typically evidence the wealth inequalities of globalization result especially from neoliberal economic policies:[80]

> The challenge was to reconcile a continuing supply of cheap labour with soaring land values, and the preferred solution was not high rents – which would have forced up wages – but peripheralization and overcrowding.

By 1971, writes [Alan] Smart, one million squatters had been resettled 'on land equivalent to only 34 percent of the land previously occupied, and on peripheral land of much lower value.' . . . Although conditions improved in projects built later, Hong Kong maintained the highest formal residential densities in the world: *the price for freeing up the maximum surface area for highrise offices and expensive market-price apartments.*[81] [my italics]

Despite the reputation of Hong Kong's social housing programme, with the government rehousing over 1.5 million inhabitants by 1969[82] and the initiation of the Ten Year Housing Program in 1972,[83] a report published in *Third World Planning Review* in 1985 noted that the number of squatters continued to rise (up to 700,000 by 1981 from 450,000 in 1978[84]); that the government's rehousing programme prior to 1972 was, in effect, a 'smoke-screen' designed to clear land for development;[85] and that after 1972, 'urban renewal was selectively carried out for the same reason'.[86] McDonogh and Wong seem to concur with this view in *Global Hong Kong,* observing that developers made major profits after the signing of the Joint Declaration in 1984 created 'an artificially limited supply of land' that pushed property prices well above income levels.[87] Indeed, the squatter clearances that accompanied rehousing disrupted communities, families and businesses, leaving many feeling worse off than before as income inequality continued to rise.[88]

As this evidence demonstrates, the poor quality of life experienced by those in Hong Kong's projects, slums and shanty towns in the latter decades of the twentieth century can be seen to be a result of the planning preference given to offices and apartments for the wealthier employees of the services industry as Hong Kong transformed itself into a global city. Indeed, this was a life lived in immanent danger of land clearance, as is seen in the opening of *Ging chat goo si.*

Not only is the shanty town as much a product of globalization as it is imperialism, but so too does the violent destruction of this particular any-space-whatever demonstrate the impact of broader, global forces on the local area. As the effects of this transformation were particularly felt by the people excluded from the wealth on offer, the film fantastically restages, in the destruction of a shanty town that enables the entrepreneurial Chu to escape the law, the clearing of the land in order to enable the interests of a select few to prosper.

Chu is identified by the police voiceover as a nightclub owner, trader and property developer. Hence, even before he is discovered to be an

international drug dealer, his legitimate business "front" is associated with
activities that prompted the rapid wealth increases of 1970s and 1980s Hong
Kong, thereby conflating his criminal activities with this particular form
of entrepreneurial wealth accumulation. As Gina Marchetti argues, it is
extremely common in popular cinemas, including those made in Hong
Kong, to see business interests represented allegorically through the machi-
nations of gangsters.[89] The opening of *Ging chat goo si*, then, should be
understood as a fantastic rendering of the manner in which Hong Kong's
economic transformation led to the subjugation of one sector of the population to the interests of another, as Chu literally destroys the shanty town
in order to escape the law with his ill-gotten gains.

Thus the overrunning of the shanty town by the gangsters demonstrates
not anxieties over the handover, but concerns for the people of Hong Kong
when the interests of the wealthy minority (whether understood as formed
under conditions pertaining to imperialism, or as I am arguing a product
of globalization) ride roughshod over their lives. After all, as Tsang argues,
while the Crown Colony's British administration created the conditions
that fostered this economic transformation, it was the energy of the local
inhabitants who propelled it with their business acumen and entrepreneurial endeavours. Therefore, although Chu is able to manipulate the Crown
Colony's legal system to enable him to remain at large, he is ultimately a
Hong Konger himself. His destructive getaway through the shanty town,
then, is not an image of imperial abuse, but rather of the division of Hong
Kong as a potentially unified whole due to the wealth inequalities that
accompany the rapid development of a global city, and the abuses perpe-
trated on the majority by the local elite in search of a share of global wealth.
With this historical context in mind, then, I will now turn to analyse the
expressive nature of the shanty town chase.

Facial Expression – Agony

The opening shot of the film is of the hillside shanty town. For a moment
this image, although a conventional establishing shot, exists as an any-space-
whatever *par excellence*. Not only is it a location entirely devoid of action, or
any sort of narrative frame placing it in a specific geopolitical context, it is
also, quite literally, an entirely constructed location-space, designed and
built for the filming of the destructive opening car chase. A small tilt of the
camera reveals Chu arriving in his chauffeur-driven car, and the any-space-
whatever is overcome by the action of the film, morphing imperceptibly

into a perception-image (eventually we discover, when the reverse shot arrives, that we are seeing the shanty town from the point of view of the police staking out the terrain from a dilapidated high rise), and thereby reterritorialized within the film's constructed whole, Hong Kong. In short, it is imperceptibly actualized, transformed from 'a' space to *this* space, within the narrative of the police operation to trap Chu in the midst of a drug deal.

The opening sequence draws out this process, making a spectacle of the reterritorialization of the any-space-whatever through action. The shot of Chu freezes, a voiceover switching us in an instant to a police briefing room prior to the stakeout in the shanty town, where Chu's image is presented on a big screen to the assembled officers as that of a seemingly successful businessman whose assets are based on criminal activities. This process repeats several times, the montage cutting back and forth between events slowly advancing towards the drug deal in the shanty town in the present, and the police briefing room in the recent past showing enlarged photographs of Chu conducting business. In the process the back story of Chu's ill-gotten wealth (and indeed, of the police operation) are filled in by the voiceover in a conventional manner that effectively "polices" the space of this encounter. Yet, while this constructs the national whole in the manner typical of the action-image, our visual experience of the shanty town remains that of a fragmented any-space-whatever. Although this is nothing like the pure optical or sound situation of the emptied any-space-whatever as it appears in the time-image, neither is it precisely the fluid movement from perception to action that typically contains, or reterritorializes the virtual potential of the affection-image within the action-image's constructed whole. Rather, somewhat akin to the construction of space in the affection-image (here think of the discontinuous spaces of Ivens' *De Brug* and *Regen* that provide an affective impression of a bridge in terms of its power and a city seen through the quality of wetness), the shanty town is presented at ground level as a disconcerting series of disconnected spaces suggestive of its potential for amorphous spread.

This affective cinematic construction of the shanty town is compounded during the shootout that follows in the shanty town's seemingly anonymous, interchangeable labyrinthine alleyways. It is as though we experience the any-space-whatever as at once 'a' space, fragmented and retaining its virtual potential, awaiting its forthcoming engagement with the forces of global capital, and simultaneously becoming *this* space, a shanty town somewhere in Hong Kong as defined by the narrative and the imminent destruction that Chu's thirst for financial gain brings with it. Thus, although *Ging chat goo si*'s depiction of the shanty town is diegetically motivated, the as-yet unactualized potential of this any-space-whatever (expressed in its virtual conjunctions), is the shanty town's power for perpetual movement, be it through spreading growth or, in this instance, destruction and displacement.

When Chu and his men find themselves trapped by the police, who have blocked off all roads leading to the shanty town, they take their only available option and drive down the hillside, destroying the temporary dwellings as they do so. Fearlessly, Chan jumps into the nearest available car and gives chase. On the one hand this sequence again demonstrates how the action-image typically reterritorializes the any-space-whatever through action, in this case literally destroying its virtual potential in the process. On the other hand, this very process is rendered as a spectacle by the editing, in a somewhat unusual manner, thereby retaining something of the any-space-whatever's fragmented, expressive nature.

As is typical of many Chan films, but unusual for continuity editing more generally, the spectacular nature of the stunt is emphasized by the use of the double take. This technique involves the filming of a stunt from various angles using different cameras, and the footage then being assembled in sequence (or, at times, repeatedly) through montage. In fact, in the most discussed example, of Chan's fall from the clock tower in *'A' gai wak*, the same stunt was performed several times and the different versions then edited together in sequence, entirely destroying any sense of narrative realism. This technique, akin temporally to the non-continuous attraction-image, enables the viewer to marvel at the stunt several times in succession, or indeed, at several versions of the same stunt. As we might expect of the any-space-whatever, for Rodowick a 'harbinger of time', time is manipulated in this process in a very conscious manner. It stutters momentarily our sense of the action-image's existence as an unproblematically continuous, sensory-motor whole, and draws attention to the process through which the potential of the any-space-whatever is reterritorialized (in a self-conscious manner that is closer to the cinema of attractions than Brechtian distanciation). Thus, while undoubtedly intended as a means of maximizing the screen time dedicated to the financial investment and human risk involved in Chan's amazing stunts, this technique also places the any-space-whatever on display due to its ability to offer different possibilities. It is a space with potential powers of physical expression or movement under the geographically reshaping forces of globalization. For this reason, the various different trajectories that the cars take across this space become the micro-movements that make up the agonized expression on the "face" of the shanty town's any-space-whatever.

The shanty town's latent power, its potential for constant de- and reterritorializing movement in response to the pressures of global capital, is most evident in the destruction of the squatter factory that is a prominent feature of the chase. The factory, producing lengths of dyed cloth, is typical of those forced into constant migration by land clearances, for development purposes, at the time of the film's shooting.[90] Its vivid red and yellow drying cloths appear numerous times during the sequence, most noticeably in the foreground to tracking shots following moving bodies, and their hanging forms are shown repeatedly being knocked to the ground by the various speeding cars. The reterritorialization of the any-space-whatever is thus rendered as a spectacle that also expresses the economic development of Hong Kong. The destruction of the shanty town is the micro-movement across the "face" of the any-space-whatever that expresses the destructive, or deterritorializing, power of globalization to shift or clear the physical landscape of the global city at the expense of its local population. In this way, the interval in narrative continuity opened up by this repeatedly edited spectacle of destruction provides the shifting expression, writ large on the urban landscape through the any-space-whatever, of Hong Kong's encounter with the overwhelmingly transforming force of globalization.

The opening sequence, then, provides the clearest image of the impact of global capital on the local inhabitants of Hong Kong in this period, as the shanty town is literally raised to the ground to make way for Chu and his criminal greed for wealth. Indeed it is filmed in such a way as to encourage us to view it as a spatial expression of this transformation, rather than a psychological narrative. During the chase sequence, with the exception of one or two close-ups of Chan driving his car (intended primarily to demonstrate the authenticity of his presence in the scene), characters are almost entirely absent from the frame. Instead, we see the destruction in an alternating montage of long shots capturing the big picture, interspersed with close-ups of individual cars crashing through different buildings at various points on the hillside. The significance of this process for this reading of the film as an expression of the shaping of Hong Kong's physical landscape can be better understood with reference to the work of Michael J. Shapiro.

In *Cinematic Geopolitics* (2009), Shapiro draws on Deleuze to make a case for analysing the geopolitical significance of films by focusing on the aesthetic as opposed to the psychological story. The actions of characters on

screen, then, assist in revealing this story as it plays out in various historically and politically determined spaces, the characters themselves becoming somewhat 'transparent' figures in the process.[91] Shapiro states:

> [A] focus on the aesthetic rather than the psychological places an empha-
> sis on images rather than film narrative, and turns the analysis of a film
> away from personal drama and toward the changing historico-political
> frame within which the drama takes place.[92]

Thus cinema, for Shapiro, maps 'the contemporary violent global carto-
graphy'[93] as though creating a story through the combination of any-space-
whatevers, or at the very least, by offering the viewer the opportunity to
read these images in this way. In the shanty town sequence, in which characters practically disappear in order to foreground the spatial narrative,
there is an exploration of the virtual potential of the any-space-whatever in
this ASA' structured film. In this large-scale "facial reaction" of the physical
space to the forces of globalization we become aware that we are watching
the transformation of 'a' space into *this* space, a process in which the reterritorializing power of action becomes divorced from human co-ordinates,
becomes simply spatialized images, or any-space-whatevers. Although in
Ging chat goo si this viewing experience suggests once again the crisis of the
movement-image, this is not specifically for the reasons Abbas and others
state (the immanent handover of Hong Kong to the PRC), but because of
the transformation of Hong Kong into a global city which began prior to
this historical moment.

Global/Local Action Hero

In *Ging chat goo si* the shanty town does not function as a location within
which to produce a people yet to come, as in the modern political or minor
cinema which Deleuze discusses in *Cinema 2*. Instead, it demonstrates the
overpowering of the local population in the global any-space-whatever.
Even so, the manner in which Chan works to reterritorialize the any-space-
whatever, in particular by using his acrobatic skills, emphasizes the power of
the local population to negotiate and even triumph over globalization. The
destruction of the shanty town with which the film commences, after all,
finds its correlative in the devastation of the shopping mall with which it
concludes. In this way the film reveals the situation, of a Hong Kong increasingly engaging with globalization, through action – ASA'. The correlative to

the agonized facial expression of the shanty town's destruction is provided by Chan's movements in the shopping mall as he defeats the odds to finally "catch up" with Chu (a process which began with the initial shanty town chase), to reterritorialize the any-space-whatever of globalization through almost impossible, potentially life-threatening localized physical action. If the shanty town is Hong Kong's expression of agony on encountering globalization, the shopping mall is its look of steely determination as it summons up its courage to act in protection of the local. Before analysing the film's shopping mall finale, however, it is necessary to consider exactly how Chan's star persona enables us to understand the appeal of his actions, local reterritorializations of global any-space-whatevers, transnationally.

As numerous critics have noted, Chan's star persona has been built on his ability to physically negotiate his position as a Hong Konger, existing at once between forces of the local and the global, be they Britain and the PRC, or perhaps more importantly, Confucian traditions and capitalist enterprise. In *Action Figures* (2006), discussing the famous bus chasing sequence that immediately follows the shanty town escape in *Ging chat goo si*, Mark Gallagher draws on Esther Yau's work to observe parallels between the acrobatic skills of Chan's malleable, mobile body and the survival skills needed by the average, upwardly mobile Hong Kong citizen in a situation where 'Hong Kong has long combined the cultural heritage of mainland, Communist China – emphasising family ties and other Chinese historical traditions – with capitalism's emphasis on economic wealth and consumption'.[94] David Bordwell, designates Chan a 'Hong Kong everyman', whose 'urge to overcome all obstacles' combines with his 'calculated cosmopolitanism' to construct a 'modern image of Hong Kong'.[95] Steve Fore, perhaps the foremost critic to assess Chan's status in both Hong Kong and Hollywood, seems to agree, arguing that 'his character from film to film is usually a "typical" Hong Kong resident who finds himself between cultures . . . in his own backyard (e.g., *Project A* and its sequel [and] the first two *Police Story* films . . .)',[96] a reading that also resonates with Yingchi Chu's interpretation of *'A' gai wak* and its sequel – which Chan directed and starred in either side of *Ging chat goo si* – as revealing 'Hong Kong's perception of self in the triangular relationship' between the city, the PRC and Britain.[97]

This critical weight suggests that Chan's persona facilitates a local engagement with the global any-space-whatever of a kind that is very specific to Hong Kong. His physical actions within and across the any-space-whatever are therefore the local micro-movements that constitute the urban facial expression as Hong Kong encounters globalization. However, Chan's crossover appeal also implies a more transnational element to his 'dynamic movement and reconfiguring of space'.[98] This further suggests that *Ging chat goo si* be read as a story of global/local engagement that is understandable elsewhere, as much as a film specifically about Hong Kong's handover anxieties. As Fore notes, Chan's films are specifically designed to reach out beyond Hong Kong, a home market of only seven million people in which it is extremely difficult to recuperate costs or achieve profitability. Accordingly, although his films are well known globally, they are most popular in East Asia, the shanty town presumably being enough of an any-space-whatever to be understandable to audiences in various East Asian countries, and further afield, where the impact of globalization was effecting the urban environment in similar ways.[99] Fore states:

> In East Asia, where Chan is already a major star, the "Chineseness" of his persona is, of course, more closely aligned with the cultural heritage and life experiences of the average moviegoer, whether at a primary level of cultural proximity (for audiences in Hong Kong, Taiwan, and the PRC), or at a secondary level (for non-Chinese audiences in Asian countries where Hong Kong movies are widely distributed).[100]

For broader audiences, then, Chan's films 'had a regionally based attraction based on historical connections between Chinese culture and other East Asian cultures',[101] including a negotiation between (Chinese) tradition and (Hong Kong) modernity that would seem pertinent in neighbouring countries experiencing the impact of globalization. Chan's ability to, as Kenneth Chan observes, 'insert himself into the contemporary discourses of globalization and diaspora',[102] while particularly true of his later works, as he spread beyond Hong Kong to make films in various parts of the world (including Australia and the USA), is also extremely pertinent to *Ging chat goo si*. The film's engagement of the global/local in Hong Kong, after all, is transferable to many East Asian cities experiencing their own encounter with globalization, and indeed, beyond the region in various parts of the world.

A' – Shopping Mall: Facial Expression – Determination

In its closing sequence, *Ging chat goo si* contrasts the degraded any-space-whatevers of globalization, specifically the shanty town, with the shiny, metal and glass shopping mall. It does so specifically to explore how Chan, the representative Hong Konger, negotiating between the global and the local, is able to react to globalization at a local level. Here again a spectacle is created out of the global any-space-whatever, the mall's seemingly interchangeable floors and connecting escalators creating a confusing, fragmented sense of the building, as though the action occupying each store or hallway could be taking place either right next to the previous scene, or equally on another floor entirely. This disorientation is compounded in the moments when either Chan or one of Chu's henchmen is suddenly thrown from a landing, the viewer being forced to immediately renegotiate their sense of space in light of the extent of the drop the falling body experiences, only to once again lose their grasp of the space as a coherent whole when the film cuts to fighting resuming elsewhere. The sequence also concludes with an amazing stunt, as Chan's leap from a high balcony above the atrium and his slide down a giant steel pole is replayed three times in quick succession in a way that further fragments our sense of the mall as a continuous unified space-time.[103] As in the opening sequence, then, there is again an any-space-whatever in evidence, in some ways akin to the spatial fragmentation of films like *De Brug* and *Regen*, only this time expressing the potentially disorienting powers of ubiquity and interchangeability that characterize consumerism, amidst and against which the movements of Chan's body (rendered micro by comparison) battle to express the city's determination to fight illegal and unequal commercial gain at a local level.

Aside from the spectacle of the mall's destruction in which we see various metal and glass display cases and their brand name consumer goods being smashed to pieces (everything from jewellery to sports equipment to a Yamaha motorbike), the action sequence in the mall has one objective, the struggle over the briefcase containing the financial data that Selina has downloaded from Chu's computer. By finally recovering this evidence, albeit through death-defying courage and by taking the law into his own hands, Chan demonstrates the ability of the local Hong Konger to conquer the any-space-whatever of globalization. In the process of obtaining evidence of the guilt of the greedy transnational capitalist Chu, evidence in the form of financial information typical of the services industries of the global city, Chan destroys the shiny palace of consumerism. Therefore, although Chan was ultimately outpaced by Chu in the chase through the shanty town, in the mall, with the situation now revealed to be that of the abuse of certain sections of the local populace by representatives of global capitalism, Chan is able to fight back on behalf of Hong Kong. His actions have exposed the situation (A-S), and indeed, enabled a further shift to a new type of action, A'.

In fact, throughout the film Chan is forever trying to uncover and master the situation through actions that ultimately reveal that the situation (globalization's impact on Hong Kong in its division of the city into shanty and mall) is almost too big for him to conquer. Previously, Chan's frenzied attempts to investigate or uncover the situation behind his rapidly changing circumstances were most apparent in his attempt to catch and board the speeding double-decker bus, on which Chu makes his getaway from the shanty town, using nothing more than an umbrella and his muscular finesse. These acrobatics further the film's exploration of the economic impact of global forces on the nation/region. It is noticeable that Chan is first knocked off the bus by Chu's briefcase full of ill-gotten US dollars, and then, having finally arrested Chu, is offered the money again as a bribe. Indeed, even though he refuses he is still betrayed by the apparently inadequate justice system of the Crown Colony. Thus, in *Ging chat goo si* the forces of globalization, typically absent by definition from the any-space-whatever, have transformed Hong Kong into what the film renders as a choice between localized actions within a global anywhere shanty town, or localized actions within an equally global anywhere shopping mall. In either case it is a continued confrontation with the almost overwhelming forces of globalization that is affectively expressed.

In the final instance, Chan, no longer reliant on the absent guiding hands of the Crown Colony's ineffective justice system (Chan has quit the police force, and taken the law into his own hands in spite of the instructions of his former superiors), physically beats both Chu and his lawyer for their financial offences against the local Hong Kongers. Here Chan's star persona as a global/local everyman enables him to demonstrate the ability of the local to reterritorialize the global, as this representative of the "typical" Hong Konger uses his malleable, acrobatic body to overcome the any-space-whatevers of international capitalism that he encounters in the emergent global city. Noticeably, Chan's particular brand of individualism, while retaining Hong Kong's emphasis on entrepreneurial activity, contrasts sharply with the selfish greed of Chu. Unsurprisingly, then, Chan's final kick knocks Chu into a shopping trolley that tips him unceremoniously into a display case. Indeed, it is noticeable that the film's famous closing image is a freeze frame on Chan's contorted face, as his ex-colleagues restrain him from further beating Chu. The freeze frame provides a final affective index that encapsulates the greater "facial expression" of the global/local conflict being played out in Hong Kong's cinematic any-space-whatevers.

Conclusion: Global/Local Any-space-whatevers

Although *Ging chat goo si* does to a certain degree negotiate Hong Kong's position in relation to British imperialism, it is distinct from its immediate predecessor, *'A' gai wak*, because it focuses far less on a "national" identity that exists in contrast to (but is mutually interconnected with) those of the PRC and Britain, and far more on the wealth inequalities experienced by different sections of the Hong Kong population as the city transforms into a global hub for producer services, banking, export and trade. Viewing the any-space-whatevers of *Ging chat goo si* enables us to see the film less as a reaction to the immanent handover, than as a comment on Hong Kong's emerging global/local identity. The film's opening and closing any-space-whatevers are therefore readable as at once affective, anonymous and global ('a' space), and yet simultaneously local, as in concretely, geopolitically and historically determined (*this* space), the latter status becoming apparent in their actualization through the actions of Chan. Chan's localized micro-movements play across these expressive spaces of global power, through the agony of pursuit (A – shanty town), to the determination for retributive justice (A' – shopping mall). In the next chapter I will continue this line of argument, exploring the changing face of the ASA' action-image in the global gateway city of Los Angeles (as seen in the Hollywood blockbusters of Michael Mann) in order to reconsider the transformation of the action-image under globalization.

Chapter 5

Globalization's Action Crystals: Los Angeles in Michael Mann Blockbusters

This chapter continues the exploration of the any-space-whatever under globalization by examining two big budget Hollywood blockbusters, Michael Mann's *Heat* (1995) and *Collateral* (2004). Both films are set in Los Angeles, a global gateway city through which international trade flows from and to the Pacific Rim. In both films the any-space-whatevers of globalization are integral to the narrative and aesthetic. This time, however, rather than a global/local renegotiation of the any-space-whatever, as in the Hong Kong action movie *Ging chat goo si/Police Story* (1985), in *Heat* and *Collateral* there is a central crystalline component to the action. In both cases this is a crystal formed by male characters oscillating around the dividing line of the law, whose struggle explores exactly which form of professionalism will most effectively serve the environment of any-space-whatevers (Los Angeles as gateway city) in which the crystal exists. Around this oscillation of the crystal the any-space-whatevers coalesce to form a complementary 'movement of world',[1] albeit one that is reterritorialized by each film's sensory-motor narrative.

These contemporary ASA' form action-images transform the duel at the heart of the SAS' form action-image into an "action crystal", and surround it with a world of globalized any-space-whatevers. Vying for control of the any-space-whatevers of globalization, oscillating (as opposed to duelling) characters determine how the environment of the gateway city will be sowed with a new seed, born out of their reaction to the uneven economic flows that play across the city. In this process the any-space-whatever performs a prominent role in the construction of a narrative that at times verges on a semi-autonomous movement of world, only to be reterritorialized as environment (although significantly, not encompasser) by the sensory-motor actions of the male professionals at the centre of the action.

Complementing this process within the diegetic world, an affective aesthetic of coloured lights simultaneously renders the city an expressionist shimmering any-space-whatever, an amorphous sea of lights at the heart of which is situated the action crystal. It is the molecular potential of this shimmering any-space-whatever that will be sown with the (molar) seed of the action crystal.

Accordingly, continuing the book s theme of critiquing Deleuze's image categories, neither film falls neatly into one specific category. Rather, they exist somewhere between action-image (ASA' structure) and time-image (crystals of time, any-space-whatevers) due to the environment of globalization that they negotiate.

Initially I discuss my decision to examine Mann's Los Angeles films. I then proceed to explore the way in which any-space-whatevers function in these films, which have more similarities with the (ASA' form) film noir than, as is often claimed, the (SAS') western. In this section I examine how the process of crystallization works in these films, suggesting not that they are time-images (they are not), but rather that they are contemporary, transformed US action-images, their transformation being a result of globalization and its impact on the notion of an encompassing milieu or (national) whole that was previously evident in large form (SAS') US action-images. It is here that I explain what I mean by the potentially paradoxical expression, "action crystal". The two films are then examined in turn to draw out their depiction of Los Angeles through the crystalline internal limit of oscillating masculine characters and surrounding any-space-whatevers (the play of seed and environment), their engagement with the recent, historically determined transformation of the city under globalization, and their use of an affective aesthetic of coloured lights to construct the city as a molecular any-space-whatever.

Deleuzian *Auteur*

In the past I have been critical of Deleuze's *Cinema* books for the problematic elitism of their structuring emphasis on an assumed canon of directors as a way of organizing discussion of cinematic images.[2] In spite of extremely convincing arguments that Deleuze treats directors like philosophers,[3] his approach has the disadvantage of detrimentally decontextualizing many of the films he discusses. Why, then, this chapter's focus on a director whose work is increasingly given *auteur* status? The answer lies in the pertinence of these Mann films for this book, due to their engagement with the spaces of globalization.

Mann is a mainstream director increasingly "elevated" to *auteur* status, an inheritor of the Alfred Hitchcock, Howard Hawks or John Ford mantle of industrially situated, genre director-cum-*auteur*. Both the films under discussion were bankrolled by major Hollywood studios, *Heat* on a budget of US$60m[4] for Warner Bros (although produced by Mann's production company, Forward Pass), while *Collateral* was a Dream Works/Paramount movie made for US$65m.[5] Mann worked as producer and director on both films, as well as a writer on *Heat* (which was developed out of his original script for the television movie *L.A. Takedown* (1989)). His keen involvement in the editing of his later films,[6] not to mention their consistency of themes and aesthetic treatment, further suggests the appropriateness of considering them works of a mature *auteur*. Nick James, for instance, in his 2002 monograph on *Heat* compares Mann to such esteemed predecessors as Jean-Pierre Melville, John Woo, Ingmar Bergman and Robert Bresson,[7] while others have cited Michelangelo Antonioni,[8] Stanley Kubrick,[9] Hawks and Brian De Palma,[10] Hitchcock, Ford, Clint Eastwood,[11] etc.

Yet this canonization of Mann as *auteur* can potentially distract attention from the specific engagement of these two films with Los Angeles. Although certain critics view *Heat* as part of a larger series of Mann films dealing with US history (*The Last of the Mohicans* (1992), *Heat*, *The Insider* (1999), *Ali* (2001)),[12] I personally consider *Heat* and *Collateral* to constitute two parts of a story about Los Angeles under globalization designed to appeal to international markets, a story about international trade flows which Mann later transfers to Miami and South America in *Miami Vice* (2006). They are thus the perfect examples for this book, bringing us back to the opening work on the spaghetti western, its orientation towards a global market and its engagement with issues of pertinence to audiences around the world. Accordingly, as big budget genre vehicles with world-renowned stars, whose director works within the Hollywood film industry, *Heat* and *Collateral* also further discussion of the applicability and adaptability of Deleuze's work to all kinds of cinema from around the world, providing requisite attention is paid to the broader context in which they emerge. The question addressed by examining this brace of Mann films in this way is, what happens when the encompassing milieu previously found in large form (SAS') action-images like the classical Hollywood western, with its nationally constitutive whole (something that Mann critiqued earlier in his career with his remake of *The Last of the Mohicans*), are replaced by the any-space-whatevers of globalization?

Contemporary Western or Contemporary Noir? The Duel Becomes a Crystal

A number of critics have noted the similarities between Mann's urban films and the western. For example, James draws on Mann's description of the sound created by the machine guns in the shootout in Downtown Los Angeles, as noise rebounding off 'concrete canyons', to make this point about *Heat*.[13] For their part, in *Michael Mann* (2006), F.X. Feeney and Paul Duncan note how the emergence of *Heat* after *The Last of the Mohicans* invites comparisons between the two, with contemporary Los Angeles functioning as a new 'lawless frontier' in which 'cop tribe' are pitted against 'criminal tribe'.[14] Interestingly, however, these two films are not SAS' westerns like those of Ford. Rather, they can be productively seen to correspond to Deleuze's description of the small form (ASA') action-image in the films of Hawks (perhaps not surprisingly Mann is often compared to Hawks due to his emphasis on masculine professionalism), which Deleuze describes thus:

> In Hawks, pure functionalism tends to replace the structure of the encompasser. . . . in the obliteration of the encompasser this is no longer (as in Ford) communication between an organically situated interior and an outside which surrounds it, giving it a living milieu which is a source of assistance as much as aggression.[15]

With respect to their rather sudden dropping of the spectator into the midst of the action, both *Heat* and *Collateral* are closer to the ASA' structure of the action-image in its small form, as found in Hawks' later westerns like *Rio Bravo* (1959), which Deleuze discusses in the above quote. Alternatively, the 'successive situations' which Deleuze describes in Sam Peckinpah's ASA' westerns, which replace an encompassing milieu with disparate but abutting locations to construct the 'skeleton-space' of the small form action-image[16] (albeit without quite becoming the parade of spectacles found in the attraction-image), could equally be applied to the construction of Los Angeles from any-space-whatevers in both *Heat* and *Collateral*.

Furthermore, *Heat* and *Collateral* can also be considered to correspond to the ASA' format typified by certain types of film noir, again including those of Hawks. Towards the end of *Cinema 1*, Deleuze confidently places film noir among the SAS' action-images.[17] However, he then discusses certain film noirs – specifically those that follow detectives investigating and uncovering criminally defined situations – as ASA' small form action-images. In fact, the noir aspects of the two Mann films resonate with previous noir classics that Deleuze identifies precisely as ASA' action-images, including Hawks' *The Big Sleep* (1946).[18] In *Heat* these include the film's twin focus on criminal underworld characters and the police who pursue them, the intertwining of struggles in familial life with the professional lives of policemen and professional thieves, and the standout emotional moment in the film (even more so than the attempted suicide of a teenage girl) during which Lt. Vincent Hanna (Al Pacino) comforts the mother of a murdered prostitute in close-up, to a crescendo of melodramatic music, their distraught faces shot against a background of darkness and coloured neon lights. Such features of the film can be considered similar to the characteristics of noir that were directly inherited from its German Expressionist roots, as Mark Bould notes, for example, in the films of Fritz Lang,[19] whose *The Big Heat* (1953) is presumably alluded to in the title of Mann's film.

This small form action-image format is somewhat similar to Jackie Chan's ASA' form *Ging chat goo si*, discussed in the previous chapter. For example, in both cases it is a police investigation that uncovers the larger situation and in Mann's Los Angeles-set films again the situation that is revealed is not one of the graspable national whole, as it is in the SAS' western, but of a city entangled in international trade flows which traverse the proliferating any-space-whatevers of globalization. For this reason once again the crisis of the action-image that Deleuze identifies after World War Two can be considered – at least in certain films that explore the new geopolitical landscape of global (Hong Kong) or gateway cities (Los Angeles)[20] – to have shifted under globalization (approximately since the 1970s and increasingly post-Cold War) towards an aesthetic expression of the post-national in the transformed, contemporary action-image.

Without the encompassing (national) milieu of the SAS' form, in these contemporary ASA' form action-images set in Los Angeles the duel at the heart of the action-image becomes akin to a crystal of time. However, rather than connecting up with other images characteristic of time-image cinemas, such as recollection-images, dream-images or world-images,[21] it is a crystal that is reterritorialized by the sensory-motor regime of the action-image. Nevertheless, it retains its crystalline form and potential (it does not become a duel, as in SAS' action-images) because it is surrounded not by an informing milieu, or encompasser, but by an environment constituted by the any-space-whatevers of globalization.

In *Cinema 2*, when discussing the crystals of time, Deleuze begins by noting that: 'The cinema does not just present images, it surrounds them with a world.'[22] At the internal limit of this world is the crystal of time, which expresses the division of time into an actual present that passes and a virtual past that is preserved.[23] Deleuze explores the 'elements' or 'figures'[24] of the crystal image, which are made manifest in images that show their mutually interchangeable or exchangeable nature in terms of the following indiscernible, reversible oscillations: virtual/actual, limpid/opaque or seed/

environment.[25] These crystals are best understood as relating to individual shots within a given film, but are also applicable to an entire film.[26]

Deleuze, then, appears to be searching for a way to describe an entire film in a manner that is different from his SAS' and ASA' formulations at the end of *Cinema 1*. He goes on to outline certain of the states of the crystal found in the works of various *auteurs*, including Max Ophüls, Jean Renoir, Federico Fellini and Luchino Visconti. It is here that things become slightly unclear, however, as the crystals of time are seemingly divorced from the sensory-motor schema of the movement-image, but in many cases the films in question might well be described as movement-images. Ronald Bogue attempts to clarify this matter:

What Deleuze identifies in Ophüls, Renoir, Fellini, and Visconti is a particular vision of the world-as-reflection, as infinite mirrorings, stagings, performances, spectacles, rites and ceremonies. More than a mere theme, the world-as-reflection is a way of seeing and one that issues from a particular conception of time.[27]

The crystal, it seems, is an expression of time as a force that is perpetually dividing, although this may or may not be presented as such in the image, but rather rendered through an acknowledgement of, say, the performance of life. This is what might cause the confusion over whether many of the films Deleuze discusses are actually movement- or time-images. While I am not claiming that Mann's films be considered quite like this, they do occupy a position between ASA' action-image and crystal of time. They retain the sensory-motor thrust of the small form action-image, but reterritorialize within it the crystal of time, "characterising" it, as it were (in the sense of, presenting the crystal in the oscillation between characters) as a seed with the potential to sow the any-space-whatever environment of the gateway city. They are thus identifiable as crystalline elements, but not properly speaking, crystalline states.

Put another way, the 'particular conception of time' that Bogue notes to have been identified by Deleuze in the *auteurs* in question is also evident in Mann's films, but is reterritorialized as a spatio-temporal, as opposed to purely temporal, division. Thus Mann constructs action crystals. Within the action crystal the division enabled by time is used to represent a narrative of professionalism that functions not through a duel within an informing encompasser, as in the large form action-image, but through a crystalline seed that populates its globalized urban environment. In this way the crystal is brought into the ASA' action-image as it transforms under the conditions created by globalization.

The emergence of the crystal image can thus be seen to be as relevant to a discussion of the transformation of the contemporary action-image as it is to the formation of time-images. The shift from an action-oriented duel within a surrounding milieu or national whole (SAS' action-image) to a crystal and its any-space-whatevers (contemporary ASA' action-image) could be said to demonstrate less the birth of the time-image than the transformation of the movement-image under the conditions of globalization. To return to D. N. Rodowick's words, along with the any-space-whatever the small form of the action-image is also one of the 'harbingers of time . . . signs of openness within an emerging desire for totality'[28] that indicate the tension inherent in cinema for the movement-image to be disrupted by the emergence of time. Contrary to what Deleuze thought, however, perhaps this potential for transformation or de/reterritorialization of the movement-image was the 'phantom' that haunted cinema from its inception, rather than the time-image as such.

As I discuss further in relation to popular Indian cinema in Chapter 6, Deleuze's division between movement- and time-image is not flexible enough to hold for all films or all cinemas. It is noticeable, then, that contemporary action-image cinema that engages with globalization develops in a way that brings it closer to popular Indian cinema (discussed in Chapter 6), in that the sensory-motor drive of the narrative begins to take place against or across a world constructed of any-space-whatevers that is itself also in movement, rather than within an encompassing (national) whole.

In the Mann films in question, the movement of world that Deleuze finds in the works of directors like Fellini to express the many facets or entrances of the crystal, is now made manifest in the any-space-whatevers of globalization. These spaces provide the environment, too large to be a graspable encompassing national whole, for which Mann's masculine action crystals will provide the seed. Both *Heat* and *Collateral* construct limpid and opaque crystals (the two tightly knit teams of cops and robbers and the hit-man/cabbie duo respectively) that function as internal limits, as seeds that oscillate to determine precisely whose form of professionalism will populate their environment. In both instances they inhabit a city seen through the 'movement of world' of its globalized any-space-whatevers, rather than of any graspable national whole. Accordingly the sensory-motor actions of these men are not so much duels as they are oscillating crystalline facets mirroring and reflecting each other as they struggle for control of the wealth that flows across the any-space-whatevers of Los Angeles.

Mann's films, then, contain recognizable elements of the crystal, such as its limpid/opaque and seed/environment oscillating couplings, and its replacement of the encompassing milieu with an almost independently moving parade of any-space-whatevers. This is the case even while they retain sufficient emphasis on sensory-motor action to stave off the full-blown time-image. Hence they never fully realize the (temporal) state of the crystal, even while being structured by many of its elements, and expressing its power to divide.

The Structure of Los Angeles

If the crystal of time can be considered another way of describing an entire film apart from the SAS' or ASA' action-image structures, it is perhaps not such a surprise to find a crystalline structure to a transformed ASA' action-image. Such a view of the contemporary small form action-image may also go some way towards clarifying why, when writing *Cinema 2*, Deleuze did not feel the need to emphasize that movement-images continued to exist in parallel with the birth of the time-image, i.e. that mainstream Hollywood continued in spite of the growth of the European art cinema circuit in the post-war years. As his passing suggestion of a 'beyond the movement-image' in the chapter on the crystal image[29] indicates, he may have felt that in writing about the emergence of the time-image he was also implicitly discussing the transformation of the movement-image.

To further understand how a temporal division can be reterritorialized to such an extent that it comes to represent a spatio-temporal choice over the most appropriate form of professionalism that will succeed in the gateway city, it is worth considering one or two of the instances in Deleuze's discussion of the various elements and states of the crystal where such a reading is possible. For example, Deleuze discusses the ship in Federico Fellini's *E la nave va/And the Ship Sails On* (1983) as a crystal. For Deleuze, the ship expresses precisely the crystal's power of 'splitting in two',[30] a power that is inherent to the crystal, which by definition captures the dividing in two of time. However, beyond the purely temporal, Deleuze's choice of Fellini's film also suggests that the crystal in question expresses another kind of power within the figure of the ship, that is, a power to divide along lines marked out by wealth. In *E la nave va*, the ocean liner divides into an opera of rich passengers and lowly workers who keep the ship running, the two sides of the income divide mutually intertwining and oscillating because, 'This is the circuit of two mutual images which continually become actual

in relation to each other, and are continually revived'.[31] Deleuze notes of
E la nave va that:

> It initially splits in two according to the division of bottom and top: the
> entire visible order of the ship and its sailors is at the service of the grand
> dramaturgical project of the singer-passengers; but, when these passen-
> gers from the top come to see the proletariat at the bottom, it is the latter
> who become in turn spectators, and listeners to the singing competition
> which they impose on those at the top, or to the musical composition in
> the kitchens.[32]

In the crystal there is thus always the possibility of an imperceptible slippage from seer to seen, from spectator to spectacle, which may in turn
reverse class or wealth polarities, even if it is only a temporary oscillation.

Deleuze's examples also include the theatrical nature of the actual/
virtual division that engages with class divisions in Jean Renoir's country
house in *La règle du jeu/The Rules of the Game* (1939). Here Deleuze describes
'the actual image of the masters and their virtual image in the servants, the
actual image of the servants and their virtual image in the masters'.[33] Indeed,
this is a film which Deleuze had previously described in *Cinema 1* as a pre-
war movement-image.[34] As I will demonstrate, this type of analysis of the
intertwining or precarious oscillating of wealth and social status found in
the crystal by Deleuze, irrespective of whether a temporal divide is immediately apparent, could equally be applied to the division of Los Angeles
around the crystal formed by the masculine protagonists in the Mann films
under discussion. This suggests that, along with the ship (operatic) and the
country house (theatrical), the global or gateway city becomes another
figure with the power to express the division inherent within the crystal,
only this time through the performance of professionalism. In the Mann
films in question this occurs through the crystallization of oscillating characters (actual/virtual, cops/robbers, working man/hitman) who exist on
either side of a legal, and in *Collateral*, wealth, divide. It is these couplings
that form the seed from which the environment (the gateway city's any-
space-whatevers) will be populated.

For this reason, of most relevance for this chapter is the crystal discussed
by Deleuze that is formed by the relationship between two men at the heart
of Krzyztof Zanussi's *Struktura krysztalu/The Structure of Crystals* (1969).[35]
These two men, visibly depicted as different through the simplest of formal
devices (a light sweater and a dark sweater), are not seen by Deleuze to be
engaged in a duel. This in spite of their costumes' variation on the "white
hat versus black hat" theme of the SAS' western. Instead, for Deleuze these

two men create a limpid/opaque crystal that forms the seed which will populate the environment, the anonymous snowy expanses of rural Poland as an any-space-whatever, which they inhabit. Their mutual oscillation concerns the right way to live as a man of science, whether through personal advancement (albeit at the expense of others) in the capital, or perpetually "pausing for breath" in the sticks. This question is explored in an any-space-whatever, which is, for the purposes of the film's exploration of national identity at least, depicted as existing at a distant remove from the "progressive" narrative of the nation.

Within this crystal the two men spend the majority of the film in verbal discussion (on topics ranging from science to philosophy), mostly within the confines of a single isolated house and surrounding countryside. Yet, although time passes in the film in a manner that suggests a loosened sensory-motor regime, actions are an important part of the inner workings of the crystal. At one point the two men compete physically in a boyish manner, first in a running race, then through the muscular test of pull-ups, followed by the shot put, sliding on ice, and finally arm wrestling. Although in a sense these are micro actions within the crystal that demonstrate the competing oscillation (as opposed to duel) of the two men, nevertheless, the crystal consists of the relationship between the two men in the same physical space, rather than the direct engagement with the division of time that we see, for example, in the indiscernible slippages between fantasies, flashbacks and dreams of Fellini's time-images. There is a degree, then, to which the crystal contains an element of action, even before we come to consider Mann's more explosive action crystals.

Admittedly, Mann's action crystals are somewhat akin to the duel at the heart of the action-image, in that situation and characters are 'simultaneously correlative and antagonistic'.[36] Yet they are distinct from this in that the way they manifest the relationship between 'milieux that actualise and modes of behaviour which embody'[37] (in this instance, characters and the globally interconnected gateway city) is closer to that found in the seed/environment relationship of the crystal of time. The transformations of the ASA' action-image, due to the disruptive force of time or the time-image, that we see in Mann's films thus illustrate its engagement with the impact of globalization on Los Angeles, the global gateway city.

Los Angeles as Gateway City

Before turning to look at the two films it is necessary to consider the recent history of Los Angeles' transformation into a global gateway city. This will

help clarify why the any-space-whatever of globalization plays such an important role in these films. Although at time of writing the state of California
is suffering from the impact of the recession of the late 2000s, the recent
history of Los Angeles is one of remarkable growth and transformation in
the latter decades of the twentieth century. Los Angeles became a gateway
city, a node through which international trade flows are processed, many of
them physical, as distinct from the global city status of Hong Kong, which
was based primarily on the services industry, global banking and finance, or
information flows. In the preface to the 2006 edition of Mike Davis's *City of
Quartz* (1990), a seminal critique of the impact on Los Angeles of Reagan-
Bush era USA originally written pre-Rodney King, Davis traces the origins
of the transformation of Los Angeles into a gateway city to the early 1970s,
under Mayor Tom Bradley. For Davis, Bradley governed by 'elite consensus'
in order to transform Los Angeles.

> [T]he greatest single achievement of the Bradley era was the immense
> program of new investment in ports and airports that allowed L.A. to
> become a dominating hub of Pacific Rim commerce, and, thus, to survive
> the eventual post-Cold War downsizing of its aerospace economy.[38]

Like Hong Kong, then, Los Angeles transformed from the 1970s onwards[39]
to take advantage of the conditions created by globalization, but this time
as a global gateway city. The impact of global finance on the city was felt
spatially, as alongside the 'high levels of public investment in container
docks, terminal buildings, and downtown skyscrapers'[40] came an influx of
foreign investment, in particular in the 1980s from Japan, whose skyscrapers helped transform the landscape of Downtown Los Angeles.[41] As Steven
P. Erie notes in *Globalizing L.A.* (2004), in the decades immediately before
the shift towards increased security brought about by the 9/11 attacks[42]
Los Angeles became the primary gateway city for US trade with East Asia
and beyond.[43] Its container ports, airports and rail networks consolidated it
as a city of flows into and out of the country that reaped the benefits of
global trade. By the early 2000s, Los Angeles had 'the world's third busiest
port and airport facilities',[44] and ranked either in the top 10 or top 20 economies in the world, depending on how you calculate the area of Los Angeles.[45] Unsurprisingly perhaps, the transformation of Los Angeles into a
gateway city ensured the proliferation of the any-space-whatever. As I will
demonstrate momentarily it is no coincidence that Los Angeles's container
ports and LAX airport, which were vital to the transformation of the city,[46]
figure prominently as locations in *Heat*, as the two teams of men attempt to
negotiate these new any-space-whatevers of globalization.

The major social consequence of the economic transformation of Los Angeles was a rise in economic inequality among the different sectors of society, akin to that experienced in most major global cities. In a much-discussed quote from 1989, Edward W. Soja notes that:

One can find in Los Angeles not only the high technology industrial complexes of the Silicon Valley, and the erratic sunbelt economy of Houston, but also the far-reaching industrial decline and bankrupt urban neighbourhoods of rust-belted Detroit or Cleveland. There is a Boston in Los Angeles, a Lower Manhattan and a South Bronx, a São Paulo and a Singapore.[47]

Similarly, for Davis there emerged in Los Angeles a 'Dickensian social polarization between rich and poor'[48] that reached 'almost Latin American extremes'.[49] During the Reagan-Bush era, along with the disinvestment in public spaces that accompanied the liberalization of the economy there was a corresponding segregation of space in the city along lines demarcated by wealth. This created a 'spatial apartheid'[50] whose borders were policed by the LAPD,[51] a 'technopolice' that has enjoyed a 'long and successful liaison with the military aerospace industry'.[52] This is a theme I will return to in my analysis of *Heat*. Even so, despite the rising unemployment of the early 1990s (a consequence of the military cutbacks that followed the end of the Cold War), and indeed, the Los Angeles riots of 1992, by 1994 Los Angeles had 'surpassed New York as the nation's busiest trade hub'. This was increasingly due to import trade from the growing economies of the Asian Pacific as opposed to US exports.[53] In effect, then, Los Angeles has been transformed under globalization in a manner that equates its spaces precisely with Marc Augé's non-place's. More pertinently, they equally correspond with the descriptions of the any-space-whatever offered by Laura U. Marks, Mark Shiel and Martine Beugnet in Chapter 4, especially with what Beugnet describes as the 'post-industrial', 'transnational corporate world of customised global architecture'[54] and its 'corporate any-space-whatevers'.[55]

For the purposes of this discussion of the way in which any-space-whatevers function in the two Los Angeles-set small form action-images, it is important to understand that Los Angeles is a city of such diverse spaces that it is extremely difficult to summarize as a totality. It is best understood instead as a patchwork of spaces that lack any sense of coherent whole. To quote Soja once more, as a city, Los Angeles

spatiality challenges orthodox analysis and interpretation, for it . . . seems limitless and constantly in motion, never still enough to encompass, too filled with 'other spaces' to be informatively described. Looking at Los Angeles from the inside, introspectively, one tends to see only fragments and immediacies, fixed sites of myopic understanding impulsively generalized to represent the whole. To the more far-sighted outsider, the visible aggregate of the whole of Los Angeles churns so confusingly that it induces little more than illusionary stereotypes or self-serving caricatures – if its reality is ever seen at all.[56]

Accordingly, in Mann's films Los Angeles is similarly unable to function as an encompassing milieu in the manner of the large form action-image. Our understanding of the movement of this world around the characters in the action-image therefore requires further development. The organic whole is now no longer determining of the action within it, or vice versa, at least not in the same manner as it was in the large form action-image. Instead, in the contemporary small form action-image the duel at the heart of the action-image, that which constitutes its very action, transforms into an action crystal as the deterritorialized flows of people and trade that characterize globalization play across its increasingly frictionless any-space-whatevers. To uncover how these spaces are negotiated in the films I begin with *Heat*, and its two elite teams of cops and robbers.

Heat (1995)

Mann's atmospheric thriller is set in contemporary Los Angeles and pits two teams of men against each other. On the one hand there is Neil McCauley (Robert De Niro) and his crew of highly skilled robbers. This includes Chris Shiherlis (Val Kilmer) whose private life is in turmoil due to his gambling debts, and McCauley's right-hand man, Michael Cheritto (Tom Sizemore). Their main source of information and intelligence is Nate (Jon Voight). On the other side is Lt Vincent Hanna (Al Pacino), of the LAPD, and his team. McCauley's hi-tech crew attempt to divert the wealth flows of the city into their pockets, while Hanna and his team strive to keep these flows moving smoothly using the intelligence, technology and military arsenal at their command.

The film opens with McCauley's team robbing an armoured car of US$1.6m in bearer bonds, a job on which they are joined by a man who has not worked with them before, Waingro (Kevin Gage). When Waingro kills one of the security guards McCauley's crew execute the remaining guards before escaping. Furious, McCauley decides to kill Waingro, but Waingro flees when McCauley is distracted by a cruising police car. The remainder of the film interweaves the plotlines of McCauley's crew's attempts to rob a precious metals depository and a major bank; Hanna's attempts to track them (including occasional visits to police informants); Shiherlis's marital problems; Hanna's marital problems (including the attempted suicide of his step-daughter); and McCauley's relationship with Eady (Amy Brenneman), a young woman he meets in a diner. Although a minor character, Waingro is pivotal, reappearing intermittently as a serial killer of prostitutes wanted by Hanna, and finally betraying McCauley's crew when in the employ of a crooked businessman, Roger Van Zant (William Fichtner). Van Zant's bearer bonds were in the armoured car that McCauley's crew robbed at the start of the film. Ultimately Waingro is used as bait when Hanna makes one final attempt to catch McCauley, who is fleeing to New Zealand with Eady in the wake of a bloody bank robbery, giving Hanna the opportunity to kill McCauley in LAX in the film's final scene.

Environment – any-space-whatevers

Heat renders Los Angeles as a city of any-space-whatevers that move around the protagonists, thereby illustrating the existence of these spaces as an environment to be populated by the cops/robbers crystal, rather than as an encompassing milieu. In *Film Noir and the Spaces of Modernity* (2004), Edward Dimendberg notes the centrality of city spaces to classic Los Angeles-based film noir, including the prevalence of those designed for their functionality in a post-war urban environment increasingly defined by its ability to facilitate the growing circulation and movement of people and trade.[57] In *Heat* this focus on the movement of flows is key to understanding the prevalence of any-space-whatevers, which now express the greater global movements into and out of Los Angeles towards the end of the twentieth century, as it vigorously inserted itself into Pacific trade.

The opening shot is of a train arriving in a station. The train initially appears as an undifferentiated triangle constructed of three lights. The shape of the train then emerges into the shot through a haze of darkness and smoke, fluorescent lights cutting into the night as it crosses a bridge bordered by undifferentiated structures (steel towers and masts strung with electric cable), all of which provides no determining sense of spatial location but the impression of a mass transit flow intersecting with the city. As an opening establishing shot, the train suggests something of the movements and flows that now characterize space in Los Angeles. Rather than a fixed or definitive space, the city has become a process of flows. This is most clearly seen when the train finally comes into focus in the foreground, and we see the words "Los Angeles" in neon light written across its front. The city is thus characterized as much by its flows as its spaces.

This introduction to Los Angeles as a city of transient movement is compounded by the opening armoured car robbery. We later learn from Hanna's conversation with his wife that this takes place off Venice Boulevard,[58] but initially this space is rendered anonymous by the film, as an any-space-whatever underneath three massive, parallel freeway overpasses. It consists of a road, used car lot and patches of deserted wasteground inhabited by the homeless. Hence it appears as another non-place or any-space-whatever of intersecting flows. This is evident both in the movements made possible by the freeway overpasses, but also more literally, as Cheritto and Waingro use their truck to ram the armoured car side-on, before the crew make their getaway in a stolen ambulance after first blocking off the pursuing police using a spike strip strung across the road. The crew, then, literally taps into a flow of wealth before using the city's urban geography to make their escape in its myriad traffic flows.

The proliferation of any-space-whatevers accelerates as the film introduces numerous of Los Angeles's varied and disparate spaces. Many of these are the staple of action-image cinemas in general, such as suburban homes, apartments, restaurants, nightclubs, etc. What is significant, however, is that a number of these spaces are related to Los Angeles's position as a gateway city. They include the diners, motels and hotels that facilitate the movement of people; but also power stations, container ports, oil refineries and the airfields of LAX into which Hanna chases McCauley in the final shootout. These are all spaces associated with Los Angeles's position as a facilitator of international trade. In fact, they are joined by spaces associated with flows of wealth, such as McCauley's extremely expensive beach house, Van Zant's high-rise office in which he organizes the offshore investment portfolios in the Cayman Islands of his clients in the drug trade, and the bank which McCauley's crew rob. Moreover, we should include Kelso's (Tom Noonan) hi-tech house in this category. When Nate and McCauley visit Kelso, who has obtained information to enable them to set up the bank robbery worth over US$12m, he tells McCauley how he is able to insert himself into the information flows that surround Los Angeles.

It just comes to you. This stuff just flies through the air. They send this information out, its just beamed out all over the fucking place, you just gotta know how to grab it. You see, I know how to grab it.

Noticeably, Kelso's house overlooks a major freeway, an automobile flow, and is covered in antennae and a variety of different sizes of satellite dish to enable him to capture these financial information flows. Thus, these any-space-whatevers, including both Hanna's and Waingro's hotel rooms are spaces marked by movement and transience, non-places designed to facilitate the frictionless flow of people and trade under globalization.

In particular McCauley's beach house demonstrates his purposeful adoption of a life lived in a non-place. The house looks directly onto the sea, as though this amorphous environment into which McCauley stares reflects back his uncentred identity. The main room is kept practically devoid of furniture or belongings due to McCauley's strict professional robber's credo: 'Have no attachments, allow nothing to be in your life that you cannot walk out on in thirty seconds flat if you spot the heat around the corner.' The fact that he learned this from a fellow convict while in prison suggests the cell-like nature of his living space (Hanna even teases McCauley by asking him if he is a monk), but also that McCauley has turned his life into an anonymous any-space-whatever. His beach house, then, is a non-place without memories or attachments, just a transitory, empty, frictionless space through which his life can momentarily flow.

These any-space-whatevers are also used to express the markedly different social conditions and wealth inequalities of Los Angeles. In this, *Heat* again demonstrates similarities with film noir. In *More Than Night* (1998), James Naremore observes that a typical characteristic of film noir is the movement back and forth of the action between 'rich and poor areas of town', offering predominantly white audiences (at least during the classic noir cycles of the 1940s and 1950s) a chance to thrill at the experience of slumming among the city's "Others".[59] In the era of globalization, these spaces are also juxtaposed to note the end of the city's previous, internationally defined position within US history (the logical conclusion of westward expansion) now that it has transformed into an entrepôt for global trade. Thus, if we again follow Michael J. Shapiro's work, as outlined in Chapter 4, and take note of the spatial narrative of the film as much as we do the psychological story of the characters, we see how the any-space-whatevers move quasi-independently. It is as though they complement the movements of the characters, to create an environment for their crystalline oscillations. Like Soja's physical description of Los Angeles, this environment of any-space-whatevers is ungraspable as a coherent totality or whole. Although corresponding to the larger movement of world typically constrained by the continuity of sensory-motor movement in the large form action-image, in these small form contemporary US action-images, actions reveal the dispersive, frictionless nature of the globalized situation. For this reason they give the spatial narrative of the city a quasi-independent nature in relation to the narrative of the people who crystallize within it.

For example, consider some of the dramatic shifts of locations that occur early on in the film. In one of the most obvious we are initially situated on the terrace of Eady's apartment above Sunset Boulevard, with its amazing view of the city lying beneath it, rendered as a sea of twinkling lights. There McCauley tells her of sea-dwelling iridescent algae in Fiji, a suggestive comparison for the sea-like city below them, in an exotic location he states his intention to visit in the future. This space of wealth overlooking the city is then provided with an immediate contrast when we are transported to a dusty location beside a railroad track, next to which are cacti and palm tress and a man in a cowboy hat riding a horse. Hanna and Sergeant Drucker (Mykelti Williamson) arrive at this location, an illegal automobile chop shop constructed from corrugated iron, to brace their informant, Albert (Ricky Harris). As they do so they are framed against a montage of contrasting surroundings, as this "Other" side of Los Angeles reveals itself.

As Drucker leaves the car he is pictured in front of a pile of bright yellow sulphur next to an industrial conveyer belt, dominating half of the screen, while the other half is taken up, in the middle distance, by an industrial plant. Hanna and Drucker take separate routes into the building's courtyard, walking past several resting manual labourers and pick-up trucks. Hanna strides through a kennels, in the background of which is an old bus, seemingly from the 1950s or 1960s, now converted into a dwelling or storage unit, but still bearing the words Central Baptist. In this sequence, then, the space not only represents the underside of luxurious Los Angeles, with its surviving industrial sector, manual labourers and illicit industries, but both the cowboy figure and the incongruous presence of the bus suggest that Los Angeles is a place where US history has been overwritten by the divisive economic forces of globalization and left semi-derelict in an abandoned part of town. The USA, it seems, is now only a poverty-stricken national relic, subsisting in the shadow of the global lights of Los Angeles.

These wealth contrasts proliferate throughout the film. We move from McCauley's expensive, minimalist beach house to the diner where fellow ex-convict, African-American Donald Breedon (Dennis Haysbert) reports to work only to find that his status as a parolee means that he will be denied the rights of any normal worker, and have to work harder for less pay. Another such contrast occurs when Hanna is called away from a meal in an expensive restaurant to a crime scene across town where the body of a teenage prostitute has been dumped by the murderer, Waingro. Again juxtaposing spaces are used to great effect when, after Van Zant's double cross in a deserted drive-in fails, McCauley, situated in a busy restaurant kitchen, calls Van Zant in his luxury office to tell him that he is a dead man.

In the process of juxtaposing these various spaces of contrasting wealth, *Heat* demonstrates the end of any singular, national historical identity to the city (witness the seemingly discarded elements of US history in and around the automobile chop shop), and the emergence instead of an environment, as Soja puts it, defined by historical 'fragments and immediacies'. This is a whole that now only 'churns . . . confusingly', as though moving around the characters, awaiting a crystallization of the seed that will populate the environment.

Seed – Action Crystal

Central to the film is the crystal constructed by the two teams of men. Although we find out very little about most of the crew members on either side, the two teams are clearly intended to mirror each other in terms of their ethnically diverse construction. Hanna's five-man team consists of three Caucasians, an African-American and a Native American. McCauley's regular crew consists of three Caucasians and a Mexican-American, and on their final bank robbery they are joined by an African-American, to bring the two teams into their closest oscillation. In the shootout following the robbery in Arco Plaza,[60] although several of the crew die the death of Hanna's right-hand man Bosko (Ted Levine) is mirrored by Hanna's shooting of McCauley's long-time friend, Cheritto (Bosko and Cheritto are of similar age and physique), while the injury to Shiherlis's shoulder is mirrored by the wounded arm of Schwartz (Jerry Trimble), conflating the two youngest, prettiest and blondest members of the respective units.

Aside from the gun battle outside the bank there are three key moments in which the oscillating, crystalline nature of the two units is emphasized. The most obvious is the face-to-face meeting of Hanna and McCauley in a diner. By this point in the film it has already become obvious that these characters are intended to be counterparts. Matching McCauley's minimal beach house and avoidance of attachments, Hanna has demonstrated that his role in his family home is that of a casual visitor. He criticizes his wife's absent ex-husband for not considering their troubled teenage daughter, but he himself is not prepared to perform the role of either father or even husband. His only attachment to their home, which he describes as his wife's 'ex-husband's dead tech postmodernistic bullshit house', is "his" small television set, a virtual window onto the outside world through which he keeps track of news of crime in Los Angeles. Indeed, at the end of the film he will eventually decamp to a hotel room that he has kept even while married, its minimal nature clearly marking his similarity to McCauley and his choice of a lonely life in his minimalist beach house.

During their conversation in the diner this equation or oscillation between the two professional men continues. They demonstrate their mutual respect for one another's professionalism, shared rejection of a 'regular-type life' of family, 'barbeques and ballgames', and their joint decision not to show mercy should they ever meet again. The conversation in the diner is therefore rather like those between the two scientists in Zanussi's *Struktura krysztalu*, men who have a shared interest in science, but who are divided on what is the best way to go about pursuing its advancement in their engagement with the world. For McCauley and Hanna, similarly, their shared workaholism is not enough to unite them over the best way to work, cop or robber. At the centre of *Heat*, then, is not quite a duel, but an action crystal. Indeed, the scene in the diner is well known because it was shot in such a way that at no point do both characters' faces inhabit the shot together, prompting numerous conspiracy theories suggesting that Pacino and De Niro were not together in the same space when the scene was filmed. The effect of this is to create the impression of two interchangeable facets to the crystal, never coexisting, always indiscernible, separated into limpid and opaque only by the dividing line of the law.

The two other defining moments of crystallization also occur in any-space-whatevers that emphasize the interrelationship between the seed crystal and the environment of globalization's any-space-whatevers that it will eventually come to populate. The first of these is the aborted police sting at the precious metals depository. As McCauley, Cheritto and Shiherlis arrive and break into the building, they exist on the actual side of the crystal. In a closed container trailer across the street sits Hanna and his team, inhabiting the virtual side. With no way of seeing out of the enclosed trailers they have constructed a virtual window onto the outside, watching the activities of the robbers on two monitors, one of which is an infrared heat detector. In a very self-consciously stylized moment, McCauley, keeping watch outside the building, steps back into the shadows. As he disappears from view entirely, his face slowly reappears in negative on the infrared monitor inside the trailer. From an actual (McCauley)/virtual (Hanna) circuit we here move imperceptibly to a virtual (McCauley)/actual (Hanna) circuit. The crystal at the heart of the film, then, once again illustrates the interchangeability of Hanna and McCauley, two dedicated professionals

existing on different sides of the law vying for control of the wealth flows
that traverse the city.

Finally, there is the sequence in the container port at Long Beach
harbour.[61] Aware that they are under surveillance by the LAPD, McCauley
and his crew turn the tables on Hanna and his team. They act as though
they are staking out the container port, discussing escape routes as though
preparing a score, and we see members of Hanna's team in an elevated
position in a neighbouring oil refinery recording their conversation. After
they withdraw, Hanna and his team enter the same space in the container
port, and are similarly dwarfed by the massive containers. As it dawns on
Hanna that McCauley has simply drawn his team into a trap in order to
gather counter-intelligence, McCauley is revealed on a high gantry taking
photos of the LAPD. Once again the two sides of the crystal have oscillated,
with those under surveillance only playing along with this role, in a virtual
form, before oscillating into the active/actual role of those able to oversee
the space and those within it.

The scene is evocative of Deleuze's description of crystalline divisions in
Renoir's *La règle du jeu* and Fellini's *E la nave va*, with the interchangeable
actual/virtual oscillation of servants and masters here giving way to that of
cops and robbers. Noticeably, like the interacting opera singers in *E la nave
va*, not only are McCauley's crew performing for Hanna when they dummy
run a dummy heist in the container port, but so too does Hanna, when he
realizes he is being watched, also play up to his viewer, gesticulating wildly
and shouting in appreciation at McCauley's professional ingenuity. Shot in
the container port, an any-space-whatever representing an era, since the
1960s, in which 'containerization' has placed a greater emphasis on 'port
and airport facilities', and seen the rise of the global gateway city,[62] this
sequence demonstrates that what is at stake in the crystal is the ability to
control the trade flows that make Los Angeles prosperous.

The final shootout occurs between Hanna and McCauley in LAX, the
airport matching the container port for significance both as an any-space-
whatever of globalization and as an indicator of Los Angeles's wealth from
trade flows.[63] Accordingly it is not precisely a duel in an action-image, but
an action within a crystal that lies at the internal limit of an environment of
global any-space-whatevers. Although Hanna is the victor, he and McCauley
have by now imperceptibly changed places. Hanna is the one leaving his
family to live alone in his hotel room (taking the place previously occupied
by McCauley in his minimal beach house), and McCauley the one performing the cop's role, attempting to hold together his relationship with Eady
while chasing down the serial killer Waingro. When McCauley dies holding

Hanna's hand, then, this is not a victory for the law, but an interchange between McCauley and Hanna, such that Hanna is the one finally left with nothing in this life he cannot walk out on in thirty seconds flat, ultimately embodying McCauley's uncompromising professional credo.

The crystal that will come to populate this environment, then, is finally found by Hanna in the limpid face that he inhabits once McCauley has crossed into the opaque, and been eliminated by Hanna. It is no accident that this moment in the shootout is one in which light and shadow betray position, light eventually giving Hanna the edge needed to shoot McCauley, who is betrayed by his own shadow. When Hanna shoots McCauley, Hanna's face is shown in close-up, bathed entirely by the runway lights that McCauley had hoped would hide him from Hanna. In Hanna's illuminated face, we see that he has become the limpid side of the crystal. McCauley's extreme, alienated professionalism, which had previously been presented as the opaque facet (as seen in his blue filtered any-space-whatever beach house in the Pacific Palisades), has oscillated into its limpid facet, crossing over the line of the law to the "correct" side, to be embodied in Hanna.

Indeed, it is not only in the shootout at LAX where Hanna finally outdoes McCauley by moving imperceptibly to the side of the professionalism crystal previously inhabited by McCauley. In the container port, McCauley showed Hanna how to police the any-space-whatever most effectively, baiting a trap into which Hanna walks in order to be photographed by McCauley. It is this very tactic that Hanna uses to catch McCauley at the end of the film, when he lets it be known where Waingro is hiding in the hope that it will lure McCauley into the open. In so doing, Hanna finally dedicates himself to McCauley's credo when he leaves the hospital where his step-daughter is recuperating after her suicide attempt to pursue McCauley, and this at the very point at which McCauley is moving back to the other side of the crystal after being affected by Eady into an emotional desire for vengeful justice (to kill Waingro) previously embodied by Hanna.

Policing the Action Crystal

It is the process of oscillation at the heart of the film that integrates crystal as seed with environment. The cops and robbers struggle for control of the most lucrative gateway any-space-whatevers of globalization, those from all the possible spaces of Los Angeles depicted in the film's semi-autonomous movement of world that would construct an appropriate accompanying environment for wealth creation. Admittedly, both McCauley's crew and

Hanna's team would seem to belong to the wealthy side of any such divide, such that their crystal might be considered to skim along the surface of this environment rather than inform or populate it. After all, one might pause to wonder why someone who can advance US$100,000 for information to set up a score would need to steal further. Even so, the crystal at the heart of *Heat* is concerned with the policing or control of the spaces of wealth that are of most importance to the gateway city.

In *Heat* the other side of the wealth divide, spaces like the automobile chop shop, become bit part actors in the parade of any-space-whatevers. Those of real importance are those in which the identity of the cops/robbers crystal solidifies, the container port and LAX, in which it is McCauley's brand of dedicated professionalism that triumphs on both occasions (in the last instance because it has become embodied by policeman Hanna). These are the entrances to the crystal that *Heat* settles upon as the most viable way of replacing the previously encompassing national milieu that has been shattered into crystalline fragments by globalization.

Historically, the revenue from the airports and harbours that transformed Los Angeles into a gateway city were used to 'pay for a massive build-up in the city's police force',[64] including the first police helicopters in the US.[65] In *Heat*, their technological mastery is shown to be such that, at the precious metals depository stakeout their surveillance technology can see into the shadows and make out McCauley's face. Mann's representation of the LAPD in *Heat* is thus far more forgiving than in many movies of the 1990s. Although on the one hand Hanna's team is equated with MacCauley's criminal crew, the aspects with which the two units crystallize are their professionalism and teamwork, rather than any criminal wrongdoings on the part of the cops. This positive depiction stands in sharp contrast to the more sinister representations of the LAPD that emerged in the wake of Rodney King and the Los Angeles riots of 1992, in such films as *Strange Days* (1995).[66] In *Heat*, by contrast, the resurgence of Los Angeles and the growth of the LAPD are shown to be inextricably intertwined, as the police find their identity in the container port and airport, crystallizing therein as defenders of the city whose trade flows, entering through these particular any-space-whatevers, perpetuate their existence. The correlation between the policing of the city and the prominence of Los Angeles's primary gateway spaces in *Heat* is therefore far from accidental.

Indeed, it is noticeable that both McCauley's crew and Hanna's team are the elite of their respective fields, the reason for their interaction being, specifically, that McCauley's team are a threat to the financial stability of Los Angeles, due to their ability to steal sums in the millions. They therefore demand more attention from Robbery-Homicide than the serial killer Waingro who preys on lower class prostitutes. Hence the film begins with McCauley arriving on the train, but ends with him missing his flight out of LAX, as his attempts to steal from the gateway city must be foiled. In the interim, however, we witness the ease with which an entrepreneurial professional can apparently create wealth in the gateway city.

City/Sea of Colours

This analysis of *Heat* as an action-crystal draws to a close with a discussion of the film's cinematography, its extremely expressive rendering of Los Angeles through darkness and coloured lights contributing to its construction of the gateway city as an any-space-whatever. Most apparent in this process is the use of racking (or pulling) focus, which switches our attention intermittently from the narrative of the men in the action crystal to the quasi-autonomous movement of Los Angeles as environment of globalized any-space-whatevers.

Racking focus is an extremely conventional cinematic device, an integral aspect of cinematography in many action-images, and a common feature of Hollywood films. In most shots in Hollywood films the focus will be on a character or characters, and the rest of the scene will be, to a greater or lesser extent, out of focus. The term racking focus refers to a change in focus that alters the appearance of a scene, often from a clearly defined object or face in the foreground against a blurry background, to a blurry foreground and clearly defined objects or faces in the background (or indeed, vice versa). The standout example of racking focus in *Heat* is a scene that occurs in the wake of the armoured car robbery and McCauley's failure to kill Waingro, in which McCauley returns home and places his gun on a small, glass-topped table in his minimalist beach house in the Pacific Palisades. The scene references Canadian artist Alex Colville's painting *Pacific* of 1967, although the introduction of a new space through a close up on a gun is a celebrated recurring device in *The Big Heat* (and the technique itself is typical of classical Hollywood cinema generally, with its noir variant focusing on guns, telephones, smoking cigarettes in ashtrays, and alcoholic drinks).

We are immediately disoriented as to what we are looking at. The shot is filmed with a blue filter, and all that it is really possible to make out are windows and other glass surfaces. When McCauley's hand enters the frame and places his gun and keys on the table immediately in front of us it becomes clear from the size of the objects that we are positioned fairly near to the floor, looking onto a low, glass-topped table, in a room the picture windows of which look out onto the sea. McCauley's seemingly "giant" legs walk forward across the left-hand side of the screen, out of focus. Initially, then, it is the space that is in focus, not the man. As the camera tilts to take in the full height of McCauley in the background, focus racks onto McCauley, and the space loses its definition. A cut follows to a close up of McCauley's face in profile, before another rack causes his face to blur, and the sea to come into focus. A final cut returns us to the original shot, with the gun and keys in the foreground and the room in focus once more as McCauley walks out of the space.

In this sequence the racking focus draws our attention alternately to the room, the man, the sea, and the room once more. Although James reads the use of racking focus in this scene as marking a transition in the film 'from pure thriller procedure to interior drama',[67] I prefer to consider it, following Shapiro, as an exemplary moment in which the film demonstrates the parallel narratives that exist between the people and the city's spaces. In this evocative instance the cinematography enables us to see the quasi-independent existence of the environment (the bare beach house is an any-space-whatever par excellence) from McCauley, the man who, as I noted above, has constructed a life without an informing past or any sense of connection to his surroundings as though he were himself a frictionless non-place. The movement of focus from one to the other notes their simultaneous, but independent existence, as McCauley flows through a space that pre-exists and outlives his presence in it. This particular entrance to the crystal is a blank, then, in that McCauley uses it solely for a temporary base from which to exploit the city for its wealth flows before moving on again. Finding him wanting, the any-space-whatever rotates again in search of another facet of the crystal (ultimately to be found in Hanna once he is becoming-McCauley) that will police and protect the city's flows.

This alternating movement into and out of focus demonstrates the coexistence of city environment and the action crystal that oscillates at its inner limit. It positions the environment as a yet to be actualized molecularity most clearly seen in the sea of coloured lights (or as McCauley notes, iridescent algae) panorama shot of the city at night seen from Eady's rooftop terrace. This image of the city is reiterated on numerous occasions throughout, in aerial helicopter shots of the city at night, and indeed, in beautifully crafted shots of blurry neon lights used to background the characters. Cinematographer Dante Spinotti worked painstakingly on the lighting for *Heat*, in order to capture, or if necessary, artificially reproduce, the various different lightscapes that exist throughout the city of Los Angeles. Across the 95 locations used[68] this includes everything from the reflection of bright sunlight off tall metal and glass skyscrapers to the different night time colours and shades from fluorescent, sodium and mercury-vapor lights,[69] as well as the carefully constructed lighting in the bank, to recreate a sense of realistic "daylight robbery" in a room surrounded by high windows.[70] Most importantly for this discussion, however, the film's two standout lighting scenes were shot using greenscreen to ensure that the correct lighting effect could be created afterwards: both the rooftop terrace sequence at Eady's apartment[71] and the final shootout against the runway lights of LAX.[72]

Viewing the city as a molecular sea of lights in this manner is to follow Beugnet's argument (itself the latest in a growing tradition of Deleuze-inspired cinema critiques that include Steven Shaviro, Barabara Kennedy, Marks, Anna Powell et al.) that there is a molecular and molar distinction within some contemporary films between moments of sensation (molecular) and the drive of the narrative (molar). Beugnet argues that we should consider such films not solely in terms of their narrative content, but also in light of their affective aesthetic qualities, their 'concrete and aesthetic qualities as film matter – the choice of framing and camera movements; the variation in light and sound; the rhythm of the editing'[73] and so on. This distinction is clear in the contemporary French art films she discusses, narrative films which contain moments in which the aesthetic comes 'forth in its material actuality, as an event in itself'.[74] It also emerges in Mann's Los Angeles-set thrillers, where the aesthetic of light at times renders Los Angeles visible in terms of its molecular materiality, as more than solely a conventional location in the manner we would expect of the informing milieu of a movement-image. In its very title, *Heat* is suggestive of an atmosphere, a molecular sensation which is made visible in the aesthetic, and which corresponds throughout to the gateway city as a space in constant movement. This is evident from the very first shot of the train approaching as a blur of lights, ill-defined shapes and colours, and again, in the closing shootout in the all-encompassing airport lights.

Collateral (2004)

Collateral was made nearly 10 years later, but is also an action crystal. The film involves one night in Los Angeles during which a hitman, Vincent (Tom Cruise) arrives by plane to fulfil a contract for an international drug cartel. The cartel's representative in the USA, Felix (Javier Bardem), faces a federal indictment, and is paying Vincent to kill four witnesses and a state prosecutor, so that he will not be prosecuted. Vincent pays an initially unwitting cab driver, Max (Jamie Foxx), to drive him to the five destinations where the hits will take place. Prior to picking up Vincent outside a sky-scraper in Downtown, Max had given a ride to a state prosecutor, Annie (Jada Pinkett Smith), who, coincidentally, is to be Max's final hit. During the course of the night, Max drives Vincent to various different locations across Los Angeles (including a brief stop to visit Max's mother in hospital), and with each hit Max becomes increasingly involved in trying to stop Vincent. The LAPD and the FBI become aware of the activity of Max's cab, but not of the identity of Vincent. Only one local cop, Fanning (Mark Ruffalo), realizes the whole story, but he is killed by Vincent. In the film's finale, after purposefully crashing his taxi, Max chases Vincent back to Downtown to try and avert the murder of Annie. He wounds Vincent, and he and Annie escape on a subway train. Vincent pursues them, and in a final shootout Max mortally wounds Vincent, who dies sitting on the train. Max and Annie walk away together as dawn breaks.

Wealth Divide Crystal/Professionalism Crystal

In *Collateral* the crystal at the inner limit consists of Max and Vincent in the cab. Through their contrasting economic status this crystal expresses precisely the power of the crystal that forms in the gateway city to divide along lines demarcated by wealth. Even so, as in *Heat* the two characters begin to oscillate over the question of professionalism, which is again seen as a matter of performance that has the potential to seemingly eradicate this financial difference. Once this happens they enter into a mutual process of becoming-(each)-other, very much akin to that of McCauley and Hanna in *Heat*, which ends with Max inheriting a new professional aspect from Vincent.

Initially Vincent and Max are respectively established as the limpid and opaque facets of a crystal. Vincent is clearly wealthy. He sits in the back of the cab, on the left of the screen as we look at it. His white hair and expensive silver-grey suit serve as a stark contrast to Max, in the front seat and to the right as we look, with closely cropped hair, dressed down in dark green hooded-top, green t-shirt and loose-fitting sweatpants. They are clearly divided by wealth, and indeed race: Vincent is Caucasian, Max,

African-American. Their common ground, and what impresses Vincent about Max (a clear similarity with Hanna's respect for McCauley in *Heat*), is their professionalism.

Vincent is the consummate cold-blooded killer, and is considered very highly in his profession. Cabbie Max matches Vincent's uptight ruthlessness with his own anal retentiveness. As Vincent observes, Max has the cleanest cab in Los Angeles, and can predict how long a cab journey will take to the nearest minute. The difference between the two is that Vincent has the drive required to become the best in his field (limpid professionalism), whereas Max has been procrastinating over starting up his own limousine company ('Island Limos') for the 12 years he has worked as a cabbie (opaque professionalism).

Once this difference has been established early on, the film charts Max's becoming-Vincent, as he gradually learns to take the risks needed to be a successful entrepreneur in the gateway city. Island Limos, after all, is a venture that proposes to use the city's traffic flows (something Max knows intimately), to make money. All Max has to learn, from Vincent, is how to successfully perform the role of entrepreneur and turn a profit from these flows.

Accordingly, Max's becoming-Vincent begins with the first lesson he learns from Vincent, the need to perform a professional role, believably, to succeed at work. When Max and Vincent are pulled over by the police, Max knows that should they find the body of Vincent's first victim in the trunk, Vincent will undoubtedly kill the two cops. Vincent instructs him to effect his own destiny, stating, 'You're a cabbie, talk yourself out of a ticket.' The faltering Max is unable to do so, however, and is only saved by luck, when the police are called away elsewhere. In the wake of the police calling in his damaged cab to his employer, Max is given his second lesson by Vincent, on the need for a confident professional performance. Vincent speaks to Max's boss over the cab's CB radio, effortlessly performing the role of an assistant US attorney. With clipped, threatening tone and confident rapid delivery he berates the dispatcher for attempting to 'extort a working man', citing that the cab company's 'collision policy and general liability umbrella will cover the damages'. This time, while tied to the wheel of his cab and fed his lines by Vincent, Max is able to begin to stand up for himself.

The crystal finally begins to oscillate, however, when Max takes the initiative, and disrupts Vincent's work. Max and Vincent visit Max's mother in hospital. She reveals Max's false front, exposing the fiction he has maintained for his mother of his successful limo company operating in Los Angeles and Las Vegas. She also notes, humorously, that Max never had many friends, and was always talking to himself in the mirror. Max is exposed as having a fantasy Vincent side (a ruthless, successful entrepreneur), but of only being able to perform this role for his mother. He is revealed to be an otherwise introverted character without an enabling double with whom to crystallize and oscillate (only his own mirror image). Max retaliates to this exposure of his faults by throwing Vincent's laptop under the wheels of a truck. In retaliation, Vincent grabs Max by the lapels, and pins him to the floor. He positions himself on top of him, and the camera cuts to close-up on their two faces, centimetres apart, as Vincent looks down into Max's frightened face. Like the recurring shot of the two men in the cab, this is another literal rendition of the two facets of the crystal in one shot, the blurred lights of the freeway traffic seemingly emanating from it like a river of coloured light. Rather than killing Max, as we might expect of two characters involved in a duel, Vincent instead tells Max that they will 'see what else you can do'. From this point on, on Vincent's insistence, Max will begin to perform the role associated with Vincent, finally taking his place as the victor in their last shootout. The consequence of this is that Vincent will imperceptibly and unwittingly mirror this becoming-other, and will ultimately find himself in Max's position at the film's close.

Max is forced to enter El Rodeo nightclub, posing as Vincent, to retrieve a copy of the intelligence 'work-ups' he has destroyed. Vincent needs these to complete his contract killings for the drug baron Felix. Trying to rapidly establish a back story for his role, Max asks Vincent if he gets benefits, insurance or a pension in his line of work. Clearly this is a ludicrous question to ask of a hitman, and its purpose in the film is to conflate Max (who states earlier that he claims no such assistance for his job) with Vincent as two facets of the same entrepreneurial crystal. After much faltering, Max is able to successfully imitate Vincent's confident, threatening professional demeanour and obtain the necessary computer files from Felix. As a consequence of Max's growing sense of himself as a capable performer, however, Vincent increasingly finds himself losing control of the situation. After Vincent kills Fanning, Max's only hope of salvation from outside the crystal, Max is forced to rotate the crystal in his favour himself. He therefore crashes his cab on purpose to escape Vincent. Here Max shows that he has adopted Vincent's self-serving pseudo-philosophy on life (Vincent rationalizes his career due to the seeming insignificance of his actions in relation to the dropping of nuclear bombs on Hiroshima and Nagasaki, or genocide in Rwanda), but does so, he says, mainly in retaliation to Vincent's cutting assessment of his prevarication over the starting up of Island Limos. Indeed, further illustrating Max's adoption of Vincent's role, when he disarms the cop who attempts to arrest him, Max paraphrases Vincent, holding the cop at gunpoint and asking, rhetorically, 'When did this become a negotiation?'

Finally, like Hanna in *Heat*, Max is the unlikely victor in the shootout with
his double, this time on the subway train rather than LAX. Although the
gunfight suggests a duel, here the crystal is clearly seen in the death of
Vincent, in a stylized reflection in the subway train window. This is a new
crystalline formation, in which Max and Vincent have completed their
movements of mutual becoming-other. After Max has mortally wounded
Vincent, the two sit opposite each other in the train carriage. A reflection
of Vincent appears behind Max, in the train window. The shot of the crystal
which dominated so much of the film, of Max in the front seat of his cab,
on the right of the screen as we watch, and Vincent a passenger on the
left-hand side in the back, has found its inverse, mirror image. Now we see
the reflection of a ghostly Vincent seemingly sitting behind Max and
on the right as we look. The cab dynamic has found its virtual double, its
mirror image, with Vincent's previously limpid form giving way to Max (who
is now framed by the lights of the buildings passing behind him), while
Vincent fades into the opaqueness of the virtual double. The process of
becoming-(each)-other has thus been completed. Max has adopted the
role of killer that Vincent first forced him to perform when he sent him
into El Rodeo. Vincent, as a consequence, has become the man he talked
about at the start of the film, who boards the MTA, dies, and rides the train
for a further 6 hours before anyone notices. This is an image of isolation,
stasis and failure that echoes the dystopian future vision of Max that
Vincent predicted for him due to his procrastination over the starting up
of Island Limos, of sitting in a Barcalounger, 'zoned out', hypnotized by
daytime television until death.

In the becoming-Vincent of Max the two sides of the wealth divide
are shown to exist in a mutually reinforcing relationship, a becoming-
indiscernible in which the two men express two facets of the same potential, two ways (better and worse) of developing professionally, with the
legitimate but plucky risk-taking entrepreneur finally validated in Max and
the limo company venture he will now undoubtedly pursue. As in *E la nave
va*, this crystal is a performative one, shown to rotate imperceptibly when
one side of the wealth divide confronts another, and the seer is suddenly
the one seen, or in this case, the professional killer the one killed.

Environment – Entrances to Los Angeles

The environment which the Vincent/Max crystal encounters is again, as in
Heat, made up of any-space-whatevers that express the globalized nature of

Los Angeles and the flows of people and trade that traverse them. As opposed to the wealthier hillside and beach areas depicted in *Heat*, *Collateral* takes place almost entirely in the basin.[75] The any-space-whatevers on display include Vincent's arrival at a busy LAX, the multiethnic *mise-en-scène* of the cab company garages (different languages and cultures being evident in the newspapers, television coverage of soccer, and conversations on cell phones), various shots of Los Angeles' freeways, the garage attendant whose market is covered with Latin murals and with whom Max speaks Spanish, certain anonymous urban exteriors (such as back alleys where shootings occur), the hospital interior, three nightclubs, several parking lots, skyscrapers and finally the subway. Passing through these frictionless spaces on a one-night-only contract for an international drug cartel, Vincent expresses precisely the international flows of finance that pass through the gateway city. To make this point more firmly the FBI agents rapidly fill Fanning in on the transnational nature of private sector security companies who hire out extremely well-trained assassins like Vincent (possibly ex-special forces or former KGB agents) to international drugs cartels in Colombia, Russia and Mexico, who then appear in US cities to commit murder.

What marks *Collateral* out from *Heat* is that this time there is a greater emphasis on the various ethnic histories of Los Angeles expressed by the different any-space-whatevers that offer possible entrances to the city. *Collateral*'s ethnically and historically coded spaces all provide different entrances to the crystalline environment that is the city of Los Angeles. They function in a similar manner to those which Deleuze analyses in Fellini's *Roma* in which, he argues,

> There are geographical entrances, psychic ones, historical, archaeological, etc.: all the entrances into Rome . . . by entering into coalescence the images constitute one and the same crystal in the course of infinite growth.[76]

Yet, *Collateral* is also slightly different to *Roma* in that the narrative is more singular, consistently linear and does not, as it does in *Roma*, appear to begin again several times over with each new entrance. In this it could be considered to again fall in line with the ASA' vector (previously discussed in Chapter 1) which appears in the '*skeleton space*'[77] of US westerns like those of Hawks. In fact, however, the film's use of these entrances to Los Angeles positions *Collateral* somewhere in between Deleuze's definitions of time-image and ASA' action-image (it is, after all, an action crystal), but verging more towards the time-image in that, as in *Roma*, the parade of entrances to

Los Angeles are varied in their geographical and historical nature. Indeed, as in *Roma*, in *Collateral* each entrance could be considered one more dead end in an attempt to express a city in its totality that is effectively impossible, in this case due to its perpetually morphing nature as a gateway city.

There are three primary instances when different entrances to Los Angeles are explored by Vincent and Max, all of them nightclubs. They are, the African-American jazz club, *Daniel's*, off Crenshaw; *El Rodeo*, on Washington Boulevard in Pico Rivera; and *Fever*, the disco in Koreatown, off Sixth St and Alexandria. The first two spaces are historically positioned through the telling of stories that relate to personal histories. At *Daniel's*, the club owner, trumpet player Daniel (Barry Shabaka Henley), relates the personal highlight of his life, the night in the 1960s when he played alongside legendary jazz trumpeter Miles Davis. Although Vincent kills Daniel, the chance he gives him to save his life is a question about Miles Davis's background, which Daniel answers correctly. Here is the first entrance to Los Angeles offered by the film: an African-American history of an "Other" Los Angeles and indeed, an opposing history of the entire USA, evoked through Daniel's personal memories of meeting Miles Davis.

The second entrance is the *El Rodeo* nightclub, a Latino venue in which bouncers speak Spanish, the music is Latino, and the clientele wear cowboy hats. In this instance the story is an old Mexican tale told by Felix, and relates to one Pedro Negro, an "anti-Santa Claus", whose job was to punish misbehaving children (at the same time as Santa Claus was rewarding good children) and who Felix associates with Vincent (albeit in this instance played by Max). Here the history that is alluded to is one of Los Angeles', and indeed West Coast USA's, identity in relation to other, Spanish-speaking parts of the continent America, for instance, in its previous existence as part of Mexico in the nineteenth century, and its current, at-times fraught, cross-border relationship with people and trade passing into the USA through its neighbour.

The third and final entrance is *Fever*, the Koreatown disco in which the FBI are taken out of the picture by a gunfight, Fanning is killed, and Max is saved from Felix's men by Vincent. This Korean club is not associated with a long history of integration within US culture in the same manner as the other clubs, no matter how fraught these histories may have been. This absence may reflect the more recent, diasporic history of Korean-Americans in Los Angeles, or may simply have been expediency as the film notches up another gear of violence and races towards its conclusion in Downtown.

Each of these entrances provides a dead end, not least because *Daniel's* and *Fever* are the locations for two of Vincent's hits, but also because *El Rodeo* nearly leads to the death of both Vincent and Max when a suspicious Felix sends his men to track, and if necessary kill, Max (who they believe is Vincent). In fact the penultimate location, Downtown, does not provide the successful entrance to the crystal either, even though it is a location that resonates with Los Angeles' most recent makeover, including through foreign investment, into a gateway city since the 1970s.

Thus in *Collateral* there is no single entrance to Los Angeles, but instead, a tour of its many possible portals. This also facilitates an introduction to something of the city's demographic diversity. In classic film noir it is not uncommon for exoticizing treatment of the "Other", especially in Los Angeles-set films, to be considered symptomatic of a more general middle-class white male panic at the erosion of Anglo-American influence in the city.[78] To reiterate Naremore, diegetically motivated visits to poorer neighbourhoods typically offer the noir spectator a kind of thrill-seeker's chance to briefly slum it with the exotic, ethnic, criminal "Other", rather than to consider the economic conditions that create such parts of the city. Anglo-Americans are now a minority in Los Angeles,[79] and in the wake of the Los Angeles riots of 1992, apparently embattled white collar male protagonists remained the subject of anxiety in films like *Falling Down* (1993).[80] Over a decade later, in *Collateral* there is a greater acknowledgement of a multi-cultural, ethnically diverse Los Angeles. Yet, the ethnic mixture that characterizes Los Angeles in *Collateral* is a product of the witness list against Felix's international drug cartel, and while this undoubtedly corresponds to the exploitation of minorities for the kind of thrill-seeking viewing that Naremore identifies, it also reflects the inter-, multi- or transnational nature of the drug cartel that is being federally indicted. Hence these various ethnically coded entrances to Los Angeles represent the importance of trade flows (albeit illicit, criminal activities in this instance) moving within and through Los Angeles, rather than any specific hierarchy of spaces or ethnically defining national histories. Most tellingly, at the centre of this crystal with many entrances is a couple of African-American survivors, Max and Annie, whose identities seem as much defined by their professionalism as by their racial identity, the ideal couple being, apparently, the lawyer and the entrepreneur. It is, after all, ultimately they who will populate the environment of the gateway city.

Tellingly, the entrance to the crystal through which Max and Annie are finally able to pass is the mass transit system of the subway, a frictionless non-place designed for commuter travel. Whereas in *Heat* McCauley arrives by train and attempts (but fails) to leave by aeroplane, Vincent touches down in LAX, and fails to leave on the train (the Metro Rail Blue Line, running from Seventh St in Downtown to Long Beach). This, it seems, is the end of Mann's two-film visit to Los Angeles, as the subway train pulls out across a similar bridge to that on which McCauley's train arrived in *Heat*. The city of Los Angeles, then, is an environment seemingly without history, in that it is not a defining, historically determined national space with single, identifiable entrances that is of most importance, but the ability to move or flow through the gateway city (as seen in Max's cab routes, the train system, and ultimately the business venture, Island Limos).

Moving Lights

As in *Heat*, in *Collateral* the city is also expressed as a molecular sea of lights, although this time with a greater emphasis on the flowing lights of the freeways and roads through which Max drives his cab. This is seen continually throughout, but is most evident early on as Max's car is tracked from high angle and helicopter shots, appearing as one more light among the many that flow through amorphous streets constituted solely of the darkness between the lights of buildings and traffic. It is also emphasized again later when the FBI become involved, the heightened action including extended shots of cars and helicopters racing through the city at night, a city once again expressed through coloured lights.

The vast majority of the film, in particular the night time exterior sequences, was shot on High Definition (HD) video.[81] This was to enable greater visibility at night, to capture the city's different light and colour schemes,[82] and, according to Mann, to depict the kind of brightness that is possible in Los Angeles in the early hours of the morning when cloud cover causes the city's lights to bounce back and illuminate the streets.[83] *Collateral* is often credited with on-set development of digital technology and film-making know-how, especially in the modifications that Mann required of the Thomson Viper FilmStream camera to shoot the night-time scenes.[84] Emphasizing the importance of the film's expressive depiction of space, of the city as a molecularly defined any-space-whatever, Mann directed his cinematographer, Dion Beebe (the second to work on the film after Paul Cameron departed), to use light to fill the space, rather than (as is usually the case) to key the actors.[85] This resulted in some unusual lighting innovations, such as the use of Electroluminescent Display (ELD) panels containing laminated phosphors that cast light much as the displays on mobile phones do, mounted on Velcro, to light the taxi interior.[86] Thus Los Angeles again features as an expressive entity or environment, rather than a location or milieu for the action. What it expresses is the molecular coming-into-being of the environment as it coalesces around the crystal formed by the cab and its two oscillating, limpid and opaque characters Max and Vincent.

It is this coalescence of world around the action-crystal that differentiates *Collateral* from the 'impulse-image' that Deleuze discusses in *Cinema 1* in relation to the films of Erich von Stroheim and Luis Buñuel. This in spite of the similarities in terms of the rendering animal of Vincent and the use of light in a manner that could be seen as constructing an 'originary world'.[87] Rather, *Collateral* shows how the any-space-whatever (which completes the transition of space from defining milieu in the SAS' action-image, through originary world in the impulse-image, to any-space-whatever in the time-image) functions in relation to the action crystal. Here again the phenomenal attention to detail in the shooting was integral to the construction of a crystalline seed that reflected back its environment, with six differently painted cars being used to ensure the shade of the cab's colour looked right in the city's differently lit landscapes (plus another 50 or so painted samples to use to test the cab colour under different city lights), during the 3 months night shooting.[88] The aesthetic effect of this is twofold. First, the cab drives through a sea of coloured lights as seen from above, suggesting it is a seed in an amorphous environment in precisely the same way that Deleuze describes the ship in *E la nave va*.[89] Secondly, the cab is also surrounded by lights seen through its windows, which on numerous occasions reflect off the outside of the cab, as though the city is entirely immersing the characters in light.

However, it is in the finale, from the point at which Vincent tracks Annie through the library of her law offices in a skyscraper in Downtown to the final shootout on the subway train, that the city's lights are most expressive in terms of the film's crystalline formation. The blackout in the office is diegetically motivated, as Vincent cuts the power to ensure that Annie cannot telephone out of the building and stalks her in the dark. Yet specially constructed glass panels were added to the law office library location to make the sea of lights which fills the background – seen through the law library's windows – all the more pervasive in the space. The law library becomes, in effect, as flooded by the lights of the city as the cab was previously. In the confrontation between Max and Vincent within this non-place (Max initially wounds Vincent before he and Annie escape), the city of lights expresses the molecular formation of the any-space-whatever, in particular through a solitary racking focus on Vincent's face as he hunts Annie. This again (as in *Heat*) draws our attention to the parallel narratives of people and space in the gateway city. In fact, in *Collateral* this distinction was flagged in the very opening shot of the film, in which Vincent walks through LAX on arrival, the only person in the shot who is in focus amidst the shifting blurry crowds.

Finally, when Max kills Vincent on the train, strobe lighting is used to create a bewildering flashing image of alternating light and darkness, as Max and Vincent unload their guns simultaneously, just as the lights momentarily go out in the carriage. When Max is ultimately victorious, like Hanna before him he is associated with the light, becoming the limpid facet of the crystal. This time, however, rather than an all-suffusing light illuminating his face, Max is shot against a brightly lit city background, while Vincent, dying, is shot against a dark sky devoid of lights or structures. Here again the lighting is far from accidental, as greenscreen was used to customize the background in these final scenes. During the shootout in particular a parking structure near LAX was deployed to telling effect, its very particular form of strip lighting illuminating Max and Vincent as the crystal revolves imperceptibly to reveal a new limpid side in Max.

Conclusion: Action Crystals and the Gateway City

In both *Heat* and *Collateral*, crystals exist at the internal limit of the films, action crystals that retain the sensory-motor nature of the action-image, even though they are not the duels within an encompassing milieu of previous action-images. Indeed, in this they are not alone, but demonstrate a movement that has been explored by David H. Fleming in relation to contemporary films like *Fight Club* (1999) and *The Machinist* (2004) that also surround a central, all-male crystal with the non-place/any-space-whatevers of globalization. This is the case even though Fleming's choice of film demonstrates the transformation of the time-image as much as Mann's films do the action-image, both *Fight Club* and *The Machinist* being focused on schizoid virtual doubles as opposed to the oscillating professionals of Mann's action crystals.[90]

In Mann's films the crystals are reterritorialized such that they demonstrate the temporal division inherent to the crystal as a spatio-temporal choice between different styles of performed professionalism, and in this they vie for control of the wealth-creating any-space-whatevers of the gateway city. In both instances we witness an ASA' structure in which the outcome is not a new situation (which it is no longer possible to effect once the national encompasser has been demolished by globalization) but a new professional form of action (A' being the professional's isolationist credo of *Heat*, or the entrepreneurial ruthlessness of *Collateral*), that is also a new way of populating the environment from the crystal.

Mann's films thereby throw up a further challenge to Deleuze's definition of the movement-image/time-image split. Somewhat like the attraction-image discussed in Chapter 1, the transformed small form action-image under globalization provides a parade of any-space-whatevers, albeit a far more reterritorialized one. Indeed, like the South Korean time travel movies discussed in Chapter 3 it provides what might be considered an actualized version of the time-image. The very nature of Deleuze's divisions of images is thus called into question once again. Accordingly, in Chapter 6 I focus specifically on popular Indian cinema, an examination of which demonstrates the potential not only for refining or revising Deleuze's conclusions, but for reconsidering them altogether.

Spectacle II:

Masala-Image

Chapter 6

The *Masala*-Image: Popular Indian (Bollywood) Cinema

This concluding chapter is the second to focus on spectacle. In Chapter 1 I identified another type of movement-image, the attraction-image. This particular movement-image is peculiar to cinemas of spectacle (including early silent cinema and spaghetti westerns) that present an indirect image of time and express a non-continuous temporal whole. In this concluding chapter I pursue a related but different direction, using popular Indian cinema to directly question the movement-image/time-image distinction that shapes Deleuze's *Cinema* books.

Popular Indian cinema, often a little problematically referred to as Bollywood cinema,[1] offers the most comprehensive challenge to the boundaries of Deleuze's categories of the movement-image and the time-image. An aesthetically, culturally and industrially specific cinematic tradition, popular Indian cinema appears at once time-image and movement-image. It demonstrates that there is a greater fluidity between these images than is evident in the US and European films on which Deleuze based his categorization, and points the way towards a reconsideration of this very divide.

In fact, I argue, a cinema of spectacle that I am calling the "*masala*-image" emerges in popular Indian cinema. It appears similar in certain respects to the attraction-image. Indeed, as was the case with the attraction-image, to fully understand the genesis, function and impact of the *masala*-image (not to mention its specific conception and expression of time), requires a comprehension of the historical, cultural, industrial and aesthetic context from which it emerged. Yet the *masala*-image, for this very reason, remains distinct from the attraction-image, and is not either movement- or time-image. Thus, although it is possible to identify aspects of both movement- and time-image in popular Indian cinema, because of its culturally specific origins popular Indian cinema actually creates a different type of image to those categorized by Deleuze. This throws open the question of whether movement- and time-image exist alongside a number of other potential images, like the *masala*-image, which can be uncovered when different cinematic traditions are explored.

Popular Indian cinema is marked by the fluid interaction of two movements. First the 'movement of world'[2] (as explored throughout this book in various contexts) that is discussed by Deleuze in *Cinema 2* in relation to the time-image. For Deleuze, this type of movement demonstrates the independent movement of discontinuous spaces that characterizes the time-image. Secondly, a unifying movement across otherwise discontinuous spaces (often seen as a sensory-motor movement, most clearly evident in the movement of characters in the action-image) typical of the movement-image. In popular Indian cinema these movements alternately mesh and separate, taking it in turns to dominate and drive the narrative, which proceeds circuitously, alternating between spectacles or interruptions and linear progression. This is an alternation between on the one hand an often dominant sensory-motor movement that unifies and drives the narrative forward across the otherwise discontinuous spaces of the world, and on the other, an independent movement of world that suddenly "catches up" sensory-motor movement, in the sense that it is almost suspended, or made to tread water in the moment, often in a song and dance sequence. This is not, however, because the spectacles of popular Indian cinema are akin to dreams or other moments of sensory-motor suspension within Western movement-images, but, rather, is due to the different conception of the temporal whole found in popular Indian cinema. This can be understood, I propose, as being in certain respects akin to a *dharmic* whole. It is this very different conceptualization of the whole that creates what might otherwise appear to be an interplay between what Deleuze separated out as movement- and time-images. It also distinguishes the popular Indian narrative structure from Western, Aristotelian forms like classical Hollywood cinema.

The fluid interaction of these two movements enables popular Indian cinema to explore the potential fluxing of identities that emerges during moments of historical complexity. To illustrate my argument I examine song and dance sequences from three popular Indian films spanning the sound era of the twentieth century, *Toofani Tarzan* (1936), *Awaara* (1951) and *Dilwale Dulhania Le Jayenge* (1995). Through analysis of these different moments of spectacle, popular Indian cinema is examined as a limit case that facilitates a constructive, historicized engagement with Deleuze's categories of movement- and time-image. Neither movement- nor time-image, the popular Indian film instead exposes the Eurocentric reterritorializing that Deleuze's image categories prematurely impose on cinema.

Examining this particular popular cinema, then, throws into question Deleuze's understanding of what cinema actually is, demonstrating that it is a far more fluid entity than his two broad image categories suggest. It also sheds further light on the history of cinema that his categories construct; the Eurocentric underpinnings of the conclusions he draws from his analysis of predominantly European and US films; and the at times limiting theoretical basis for the *Cinema* books provided by Henri Bergson's model of time. In short, popular Indian cinema demonstrates the relative truth of Deleuze's conclusions (his division of cinema into movement- and time-image), and gestures towards the numerous other philosophical conceptions of time that could potentially be argued of different world cinemas.

Deleuze's History of Cinema

As outlined in Chapter 1, for Deleuze the movement-image creates an indirect image of time. It renders visible the virtual whole of time (Bergson's duration), in a spatialized form. This process is most apparent in the action-image, in which the sensory-motor continuity of the protagonist creates the impression of spatial and temporal continuity across the otherwise discontinuous spaces juxtaposed by the editing. By contrast, the time-image provides a direct image of the virtual movement of time. Accordingly, in the time-image the montage of discontinuous spaces appears to move around a protagonist whose sensory-motor continuity is insufficient to master this movement of world. Instead of time subordinate to movement, of time actualized through movement as in the space-time of the movement-image, we obtain a glimpse of the open and changing virtual whole of time, shifting without a central, sensory-motor (human) focus.

Scholars have generally interpreted the relationship between movement- and time-images following one of two schools of thought. D. N. Rodowick, Angelo Restivo and Patricia Pisters[3] all variously agree that the movement- and time-image depict different ways of thinking, marking a shift in our relationship to time, truth and the image. For these scholars, the history that the two cinema books create charts a rupture, or epistemic shift, rather than a linear narrative of progression from movement- to time-image. By contrast, in his contribution to *The Brain is the Screen* (2000), András Bálint Kovács argues that – despite Deleuze's claims to the contrary[4] – Deleuze's two cinema texts provide a linear history of cinema. Kovács states:

> Even though he never says outright that film history is tantamount to the emergence of modern cinema, that this is the "aim" of film history, Deleuze's entire taxonomy anticipates the shift from classical to modern.[5]

According to Kovács, for Deleuze the time-image is the zenith of cinema's development, the end point of its linear progression through classical to modern cinema (from organic to crystalline regimes). Therefore, the time-image precedes the movement-image not only in Deleuze's thinking about cinema (such that the writing of a book entitled *Cinema 1* presupposes the writing of a second volume) but also in the sense that the time-image marks cinema's development to its ultimate goal, which entails the emergence of cinema's latent potential. Kovács quotes Deleuze to this effect, stating:

> The categories that Deleuze uses to define modern cinema – as I suggested, mental images or direct time-images – were already given at the beginning of cinema, virtually present in the image. As Deleuze writes, "The direct time-image is the phantom which has always haunted the cinema, but it took modern cinema to give a body to this phantom."[6]

Even so, this position does not necessarily contradict that of Restivo, Rodowick and Pisters. Rather like Jean-François Lyotard's view that 'a work can become modern only if it is first postmodern' (a position mentioned in passing by Restivo),[7] the possibility of the time-image always existed along with the movement-image. Thus the *Cinema* books can be considered to be numbered both to represent a linear, historical progression (*Cinema 1* followed by *Cinema 2*) or, if you prefer, a typology (*Cinema 1* and *Cinema 2* therefore being equally well described as *Cinema A* and *Cinema B*). Interestingly, David Deamer has even gone so far as to argue that while *Cinema 1* takes an 'almost evolutionary' approach (rather like that noted by Kovács), *Cinema 2* takes an 'ahistorical' one[8] – which Deamer seems to conceive of in much the same manner as Rodowick, Pisters and Restivo – as though the couplet were *Cinema 1, Cinema B*.

In either case, then, it is possible to follow Deleuze's stance, and see the emergence of the time-image in European cinema as a consequence of the conditions that arose in the immediate wake of the Second World War, when the time-image came to illustrate a shift in our image of thought. However, as I have argued in preceding chapters, for various context-specific reasons the progression from movement- to time-image – while marking a definite historical crisis in Deleuze's understanding of cinema – can also be interpreted differently. In the case of popular Indian cinema these categories can be seen to co-exist in a single cinema throughout its entire history, a fact that questions their very existence *as* categories, or any form of progression from one to the other (be it linear, or epistemic shift). Indeed, following on from the discussion that began in relation to Argentine cinema in Chapter 2, popular Indian cinema further illustrates how Deleuze's use of World War Two as a demarcation point between the two images was more a product of the types of cinema he focused on than its role as a universally influential historical event.

As discussed in Chapter 1, pre-war time-images undoubtedly existed, for some commentators even in early silent cinema. As noted in the introduction, Deleuze acknowledges the existence of the time-image in the films of Japanese director, Yasujiro Ozu (whose pre-war films are absent from *Cinema 1*), who he credits as 'the inventor of opsigns and sonsigns'.[9] Yet Deleuze avoids any attempt to understand why this might have occurred in 1930s Japan, noting only that the post-war European directors did not learn from Ozu. Deleuze thus gives the impression of considering Ozu as an unexplained, isolated precursor to the post-war European shift in thought marked by the time-image.

Yet if World War Two is not such a defining event in terms of dividing movement- from time-images, how are we to conceive of their coexistence? In *Deleuze, Cinema and National Identity* (2006), I drew on *A Thousand Plateaus* (1980) – which Deleuze cowrote with Félix Guattari before *Cinema 1* and *Cinema 2* – to argue that the movement- and time-images exist as interactive planes (the movement-image a reterritorialized plane of organization and the time-image a deterritorialized plane of consistency). This interactive model is one way to explain why cinema history contains examples of movement- and time-images that cross the great divide between *Cinema 1* and *Cinema 2*, and indeed, why numerous films contain aspects of both images. Seen in this light, the possibility of both types of image always exists, and it is a question of degree as to how de- or reterritorialized they are, how close to the limit conditions of the movement- or the time-image.[10]

It is possible, then, to conclude that even though it is usually the reterritorialized form of the movement-image that is dominant, cinema always contains within it the deterritorializing possibility of the time-image. This Deleuze himself seems to acknowledge when, as Kovács notes, in *Cinema 2* he described the time-image as 'the phantom which has always haunted the cinema', and as an image that is 'virtual, in opposition to the actuality of the movement-image'.[11] Indeed, prior to this, in *Cinema 1*, Deleuze introduced the crisis of the action-image in the post-war era saying: 'But can a crisis of the action-image be presented as something new? Was this not the constant state of cinema?'[12]

Time-images, then, while evidence of the potential that has always existed for a destabilizing of the movement-image (the principle behind the thinking of Rodowick, Pisters, Restivo), are not necessarily also evidence of a radical shift of episteme. Indeed, Deleuze's rather brief mention of World War Two as defining moment suggests that this may have been somewhat incidental to his thinking, which may well have been more absorbed in the construction of his taxonomy of images After all, as I have shown from Chapter 2 onwards, other parts of the world have their own defining moments, distinct from World War Two, that are equally disruptive to their cinemas (dictatorships, economic crises, geopolitical transformations under globalization, etc.). For this reason I would argue that Deleuze's categories of the movement- and the time-image are a product of his selection of certain films for discussion, and his lack of engagement (albeit perhaps due to the lack of global circulation and critical recognition that many films received in the 1980s) of certain others. Not least of these was popular Indian cinema.

Had Deleuze engaged with the existence of popular Indian cinema – a major force in many parts of the world throughout the twentieth and into the twenty-first century – then the distinction he draws between movement- and time-image would have appeared very different. As the popular Indian aesthetic that is most widespread today can be said to have solidified in the 1930s (from a national cinema dating back to the end of the nineteenth century[13]), the distinction Deleuze draws between movement- and time-image around the turning point of World War Two appears very much that of a European cinephile whose experience of cinema is confined to the circulation of classical Hollywood and (predominantly) European art films in the international arena. This distinction fails to take into account the numerous different national experiences of cinema, especially indigenous popular genre films, which exist around the world. Thus, although in *Deleuze, Cinema and National Identity* I analysed how the model of interactive planes can help us understand the ways in which filmmakers use time to construct narratives of national identity, I wish to take quite a different direction in this chapter.

Popular Indian cinema muddies any clear distinction between movement- and time-image. Defying easy categorization, it goes beyond illustrating the perpetual coexistence of the possibility for de- and reterritorialization offered by the two images. Rather, it demonstrates an altogether different way of organizing images (a different way of manifesting cinema's plane of immanence) to those of either the movement- or the time-image. This is because popular Indian cinema does not conceive of a temporal whole (duration) in precisely the same way as Deleuze defined the movement- (indirect expression of the whole) and the time-image (direct expression of the whole) from his Bergson-inspired position. Accordingly, whether it is a direct or indirect view of time is no longer a question that can be asked or answered, as what I am calling the *masala*-image is constructed on the basis of a different view of time altogether.

As I will demonstrate, detailed consideration of popular Indian film, in terms of form and reception, acknowledges the different national, cultural, historical and aesthetic conditions that shape its organization of images. Deleuze's Eurocentric focus on certain cinemas, then, is shown to be the cause of the initial polarizing of cinema into the movement- and time-image. Accordingly, his use of this model as evidence of either an epistemic shift or an evolutionary progression becomes extremely difficult to extrapolate into a globally applicable conclusion once popular Indian cinema is considered.

Popular Indian Cinema

In order to grasp the culturally specific reasons behind the emergence of popular Indian cinema's distinctive organization of images, it is necessary to first summarize the major points surrounding the popular Indian aesthetic and its consumption.

The most apparent influences on popular Indian cinema are two sacred texts of the Hindu faith, the *Ramayana* and the *Mahabharata*. The structures of these epic texts greatly influence the popular Indian film narrative. Rather than the clearly defined linear narrative of the classical Hollywood form (the action-image in its large form (SAS')), the narrative of popular Indian cinema, like that of the epic texts, incorporates 'endless digressions, detours [and] plots within plots'.[14] It is the interweaving of many storylines that popular Indian cinema derives from this epic narrative tradition, and it is primarily this that leads to the length of popular Indian films.

In popular Indian film the narrative drive is secondary to the progression of a series of often seemingly disconnected episodes, like song and dance routines, fight scenes, comic sequences, moments of family melodrama, tearful confrontations between lovers, and so on. In 1985 Rosie Thomas noted that the origins of this aesthetic in Sanskrit philosophy ensure that it is non-Aristotelian in its rejection of 'the unities of time and place and the dramatic development of narrative'.[15] The Hollywood action-image follows the guiding principles of continuity editing, and stresses the need to maintain a unity of time and place to the narrative. By contrast, the popular Indian film narrative is not constrained by the need for the coherent fictional world demanded of narrative realism. Instead, popular Indian film's distinctive aesthetic offers a narrative that is a '"ridiculous" pretext for spectacle and emotion',[16] thereby providing the viewer with the pleasure of experiencing a *masala* (the term means a blending of flavours or moods), from which I am taking the name *masala*-image.

Thomas argues that the pleasure to be had from viewing a popular Indian film is not derived from finding out what will happen at the end, but from seeing how the story gets to the end.[17] The epics from which popular Indian films gain their structure are part and parcel of an oral storytelling tradition. Historically they functioned to keep a communal record of cultural history among a predominantly illiterate rural populace. Hearing the same story told repeatedly, the pleasure is in hearing the familiar embellished, or otherwise rendered slightly differently each time. Similarly, in popular Indian cinema, the pleasure is gained from seeing how the same story is told differently, rather than the way it ends. This is generally already known, or is almost entirely predictable, to the viewer. This understanding of the popular Indian film narrative also explains why they are consumed differently from Hollywood films. Audiences in India are more likely to watch a popular Indian film several times over, singing along with the songs if they know them. This is unlike the consumption of films in most Western cultures, where they are usually only seen once, in comparative silence, at least in the cinema. As was the case with the attraction-image, then, understanding the context of reception impacts greatly on our comprehension of the film's form and narrative.

As K. Moti Gokulsing and Wimal Dissanayake clarify in *Popular Indian Cinema* (1998)[18] along with the *Ramayana* and the *Mahabharata* there are several other major influences that give popular Indian film its distinctive aesthetic. First, Sanskrit theatre. This is the classical Indian theatre from which popular Indian films inherited the episodic narrative, dance spectacles and various stylistic acting conventions. Indian folk theatre also contributes, peasant productions that continued the 'style and techniques of the classical theatre after its decline in the tenth century'.[19] Then there is Parsi theatre, a commercially-oriented theatre at once realist and fantastic, and popular throughout India in the nineteenth century.[20] Hollywood is also an influence, but its storylines are lifted, then Indianized[21] – usually through an infusion of emotion – to be incorporated within the distinctive popular Indian film aesthetic. Like the spaghetti western, then, popular Indian cinema exists in relation to the dominant US model (although it is extremely debateable how dominant Hollywood is on the Indian subcontinent), but is also an Indianized version of this mode, as opposed to an inferior copy of it. Finally, in recent years MTV has joined the mix, especially its quicker editing style, pop video camera angles, faster paced camera movements, and focus on teenage protagonists.[22]

The combination of these aesthetic influences creates the circuitous, episodic narrative progression of the popular Indian film. However, as was the case with the spaghetti western and the Hong Kong action movie, this is not the entire story. The industrial context also impacts upon the aesthetic. As M. Madhava Prasad argues in *Ideology of the Hindi Film* (1998), due to the segmentation of the production process into a series of independently produced constitutive parts ('the story, the dance, the song, the comedy scene, the fight, etc.'[23]) the structure of the Indian film industry does not facilitate the construction of a linear narrative like that of the action-image. Rather, the story is simply one more part in the whole, a fact that is reflected in the fragmented production process.

It might immediately be objected that, the above notwithstanding, Deleuze's *Cinema* books were not directly concerned with narrative as such, which he considered to stem from the manner in which different cinemas expressed the whole through montage. Why should it be of any great concern, then, that popular Indian cinema – deriving from these context-specific influences – is marked by a different kind of narrative structure to that of other cinemas? Yet the narrative structure of popular Indian cinema is of crucial importance in this discussion. First, in line with Deleuze's position, because it illustrates how popular Indian cinema's different organization of images, its different montage, constructs a different whole from which this distinct narrative stems. Secondly, although he at times seemed to disavow it, because Deleuze's history of cinema also charted a history of different cinematic narratives, thereby ensuring that the different narrative structure of popular Indian cinema throws a new light onto this "historical" development.

In *Cinema 2*, Deleuze reiterates and develops upon his position from *Cinema 1*, with regard to the relationship between montage and narrative, stating:

> So-called classical narration derives directly from the organic composition of movement-images [*montage*] . . . according to the laws of a sensory-motor schema. . . . [t]he modern forms of narration derive from the compositions and types of the time-image. Narration is never an evident given of images, or the effect of a structure which underlies them: it is a consequence of the visible images themselves, of the perceptible images in themselves, as they are initially defined for themselves.[24]

As Rodowick clarifies in *Gilles Deleuze's Time Machine* (1997), in this Deleuze is differentiating his own semiotics of cinema from Christian Metz's position (predominantly engaging with *Film Language* (1967) rather than Metz's later work *Language and Cinema* (1974)), that cinema can be understood to function like a language. Note, for example, Deleuze's apparent opposition to the idea that narrative can be considered the 'effect of a structure which underlies' images, a critique which he makes more explicit later in *Cinema 2*.[25] Instead, for Rodowick, 'Deleuze argues for understanding filmic narration as immanent to filmic signs and images'.[26] It is in this sense, then, that narration stems from montage (the expression of the whole), as far as Deleuze's semiotics of cinema considers different images to facilitate the expression of different narratives. Kovács is again instructive on this point, noting that:

> Deleuze concludes that the cinema is always in some sense narrative, that it cannot avoid telling a story – though the kind of story it tells will vary radically . . . Indeed, it is the very mutation of storytelling that informs Deleuze's categories. He defines his categories qua different types of images according to the different narrative conceptions that emerge during the history of cinema. Images are made up of different kinds of signs whose "combinations" render different kinds of narratives.[27]

Thus, in Chapter 6 of *Cinema 2*, Deleuze describes the Nietzschian-inspired 'powers of the false' that appear in the time-image as illustrative of the difference between its 'crystalline narration', and the sensory-motor narrative of the movement-image.[28] The centrality of narrative to Deleuze's categories is apparent, then, especially in his positioning of the Second World War as a defining moment in the development of cinema from movement- to time-image. It is also clear very early on in *Cinema 1*, where he determines the beginnings of cinema to start with D. W. Griffith's unified organic conception of the whole. As I demonstrated in Chapter 1, this moment coincides with the consolidation of continuity editing as central to the development of classical Hollywood cinema that aimed, above all else, for clarity of narrative.

Deleuze seems to consider narrative a product of montage because it is montage that expresses the whole. The type of narrative produced, then, is a result of the way in which images are combined (and their immanent narratives displayed), suggesting once again the tacit assumption on Deleuze's part of an ideological conception of the whole that differs between different national cinemas. Hence, as I explored in relation to the attraction-image, it is extremely difficult to disentangle the relationship between montage (expression of the whole), narrative and ideology in Deleuze's work, and this is before we even begin to consider the additional contextual factors listed above that have shaped the narrative of popular Indian cinema.

For this reason, understanding the uniqueness of the narrative of popular Indian cinema is extremely important. A product of the intertwining of various influential, contextually determined, aesthetic, cultural, social and industrial influences, due to its episodic narrative (that functions by blending together a range of different flavours or moods), popular Indian cinema does not exactly correspond to Deleuze's categories of movement- or time-image. As I will argue momentarily, if there is a whole to be found structuring the narrative of the *masala*-image (whether visible directly or indirectly), it is perhaps best described as a *dharmic* whole, and as such is very different to anything Deleuze identified in the *Cinema* books.

Masala-image (*dharmic* whole)

In *Cinema of Interruptions* (2002), Lalitha Gopalan dubbed popular Indian action cinema a 'cinema of interruptions'[29] in some ways akin to the early silent cinema of attractions. Gopalan notes that from its inception as a silent form, popular Indian cinema 'developed in a whirl of anti-colonial struggles that included an impulse to forge an independent cultural form by both reinterpreting tradition and making technology developed in the West indigenous'.[30] Gopalan goes on to argue the case for the 'interrupted pleasures' offered by this aesthetic, noting how – far from simplistically interrupting the pleasure of watching a seamless narrative progress – these moments of interruption serve to both 'block and propel the narrative in crucial ways'.[31] Reading Gopalan's introduction to *Cinema of Interruptions* it is apparent that she is writing to convince an audience that considers the classical Hollywood narrative normative, the problem that arises from this being the presupposition that the classical Hollywood narrative is somehow *un*interrupted in comparison – in spite of the major disruptions to time that belie the narrative fluidity constructed by continuity editing.

Yet this assumption is of particular relevance for this discussion of popular Indian cinema in relation to the movement- and the time-image. On the one hand, the series of spectacles or interruptions through which the popular Indian film haltingly or circuitously progresses suggests precisely a movement of world. The various spectacles seem to move around the characters, catching them up and causing the narrative – at once blocked and propelled – to progress circuitously. In this sense popular Indian films at times seem akin to time-images. On the other hand, popular Indian film narratives typically foreground the sensory-motor continuity of the protagonists. The most obvious examples are the physical moments common to nearly all popular Indian films, the dance routines, slapstick moments, fights, and other action scenes. In this sense they seem much closer to the movement-image.

Indeed, in terms of their overall narrative structure popular Indian films typically uphold the status quo, and are often described in terms that evoke the overarching SAS' structure of the Hollywood action-image. As Tejaswini Ganti states:

> Hindi films present a moral universe, the disruption of which initiates the narrative action. The disruption can have taken place in a previous generation or be very subtle and communicated briefly, but restoring order or resolving the disruption is usually the goal of the narrative.[32]

Yet this situation is not as simple as it may appear. In *Bollywood Cinema* (2002), Vijay Mishra seemingly agrees with Ganti's position, describing the manner in which the apparently conservative popular Indian cinema constructs 'texts that function as metatexts of tradition and dharmik values'.[33] Even so, this overarching structure that tends towards the status quo also facilitates the controlled exploration of a series of possible transgressions. Mishra continues:

> The relay through dharma-adharma-dharma allows for transgressive eruptions to take place from within so that the unspeakable, the anti-dharmik, may be articulated. Hence pleasures of transgression are entertained as the spectator identifies with any number of ideologically unstable elements with the foreknowledge that the order will be re-established.[34]

Although this progression – 'dharma-adharma-dharma' – may appear somewhat akin to classical Hollywood's SAS' structure (or at least, SAS), it is distinct from this linear narrative due to its emphasis on *dharma*, a somewhat simplified version of which could be argued to provide the conception of the whole which informs popular Indian cinema's narrative structure.

Dharma is an extremely complex concept that has different implications across various religions. The manner in which Mishra deploys the term relates to the notion, integral to Hinduism, of the existence of *dharma* as, if we follow Gavin Flood's definition, a 'cosmic, eternal principle' that relates to 'the world of human transaction'.[35] In *Indian Popular Cinema*, Gokulsing and Dissanayake similarly explain the centrality of *dharma* to popular Indian cinema, noting that:

> *Dharma* . . . is a metaphysical concept, embracing as it does the abstract principle of the social order. It has, however, practical consequences – namely, "the obligation and the tendency to act in a particular way in specified situations." . . . [i]n the popular imagination it has been simplified to mean the maintenance of the social order and the acceptance of one's prescribed life and the performance of one's duties accordingly.[36]

At once a conception of the whole (they note, in line with Flood, a 'Cosmic Moral Social order'[37]) and a guide or law concerning one's actions within it ('the performance of one's duties'), *dharma* provides the definition of whole and the impetus for action (especially when temporarily disrupted by the 'transgressive eruptions' of *adharma*) in popular Indian cinema. Accordingly, if we follow Mishra and Gokulsing and Dissanayake in viewing popular Indian cinema in this manner, we can argue that popular Indian cinema is marked by a different temporal, or at the very least, cosmological, schema to both movement- and time-image. In this instance it is not Bergson's duration, but a *dharmic* whole that we find, proceeding through the mutual interaction between movement of world and movement of people, embracing both the cosmic principle and the human ramifications of *dharma*. Although such a use of the term is something of a simplification of *dharma* per se,[38] and I am not aiming to Orientalise popular Indian cinema in an essentialist sense (such that Indian cinema is somehow defined by *dharma* in the same way as, for instance, Ozu's Japanese films have been by various US authors in relation to the concept of Zen, the underlining Western bias structuring such arguments having been convincingly critiqued by Mitsuhiro Yoshimoto[39]) it would seem to make sense to evoke this particular concept to describe popular Indian cinema, particularly due to its central structuring presence in the *Ramayana* and the *Mahabharata*.[40]

There is not room to explore the temporal ramifications of popular Indian cinema's *dharmic* whole in depth here. Suffice it to say, however, that what sets it apart from Deleuze's image categories is that it is influenced by a different form of time. As Anindita Niyogi Balslev outlines in *A Study of Time in Indian Philosophy* (1983), there is no one Indian view of time, but rather, 'an enormous divergence from school to school, tradition to tradition'.[41] Indeed, as there are many popular cinemas in India, not all of them Hindi, it would be wrong to generalize for all Indian cinemas. Yet as

Balslev acknowledges, 'the idea of a world-cycle . . . is a general feature of Indian mythology and philosophy',[42] even if this may refer to a temporal, or at other times a broader, cosmological, world-cycle. In any case, a cyclical form of time is integral to Hinduism.[43] For this reason it is at least useful to consider how the tensions and shifts between order and chaos, and determinism and freedom that are thought to be experienced within such a cyclical view of the cosmos, including within Hinduism,[44] create a fluctuating narrative whole that is specific to popular Indian cinema. In this way we can see that, although its images are organized in such a way as to suggest what might appear to be movement- and time-images, these are in actual fact better understood as *masala*-images, as a series of unique moments that, blended together, construct a *dharmic* whole.[45]

For this reason, popular Indian cinema offers one example of how an alternative view of time, manifest in a cinema from a very specific cultural and aesthetic tradition, can help us reconsider the universal applicability of Deleuze's conclusions in the *Cinema* books. I stress this conception of the whole to demonstrate not *the* alternative to Deleuze's Bergson-inflected image categories, but *an* alternative. In contrast to Deleuze's Bergsonian view of time, this cyclical worldview provides a different source for the movement of world that characterizes popular Indian cinema. The perpetual shifting between movement of character and movement of world suggests a cyclical view of the relationship between human actions and the greater shifting of the cosmos within which human actions are caught up. This is why it is not sufficient to simply argue that time-images intermittently emerge as interruptions in popular Indian cinema. Rather, its organization of images creates what seem at times to be time-images, but which can equally be considered the result of an altogether different worldview. This helps explain why the potentially transgressive eruptions (*adharma*) of the popular Indian film, which Mishra identified, are both facilitated and contained within a larger movement of world (*dharma*).

Perhaps the most obvious difference between the classical Hollywood narrative of the action-image (SAS') and the progression from *dharma* through *adharma* to *dharma*, is the greater time-span, that is opened up between beginning and end of the popular Indian film, within which to explore potential ideological transgressions. This is the case both literally in terms of the film's length (typically of three to four hours) and in terms of narrative complexity and spectacle. Encompassed by its overarching cyclical narrative development the popular Indian film narrative proceeds in a circuitous route, its various spectacles, interruptions or eruptions both blocking and propelling the narrative in a manner determined by the numerous interweaving plotlines that are themselves typical of the *Ramayana* and the *Mahabharata.*[46]

As a result, the narrative development is not exactly that of situation through action to changed situation (SAS'). However, nor is if precisely SSS or AAA. In fact, this kind of terminology, used by Deleuze when exploring the action-image, becomes as redundant as it does when exploring the time-image. Due to the mutual interweaving of movement of characters and movement of world, popular Indian cinema develops in the form that is not reducible to such a formulation. Thus Gopalan's slightly problematic choice of the term 'interruptions' (even though it tacitly suggests that a supposedly *un*interrupted mainstream Hollywood film is the norm) is extremely helpful. It is because the popular Indian film narrative progresses through various spectacular interruptions – themselves the product of its specific emergence in India – that it can be understood to organize its images, and therefore construct its narrative, differently to the (uninterrupted) movement-image.

In popular Indian cinema, sensory-motor continuity (typical of the movement-image) meets a general movement of world usually associated with the time-image. Here the *masala*-image is different from the attraction-image in that, rather than a reactive protagonist (who must become equal to situations as they "happen along"), character actions propel the narrative at times, even though at others they are not equal to the movement of world that periodically sweeps them along. Indeed, in the *masala*-image, actions do not always become equal to situations, a factor which delays or interrupts any smooth movement from situation, through action, to changed situation. At some points a song and dance sequence (or other spectacle) may progress the narrative. At others such a spectacle may be a moment in which the narrative appears to tread water (possibly to contemplate an appropriate course of actions in relation to *dharma*) and it is during the sensory-motor actions that follow in which decisive progress is made. Here, as in the time-image, 'it is as if the action floats in the situation, rather than bringing it to a conclusion or strengthening it'.[47] Moreover, characters never know when a new situation is going to suddenly emerge and derail their forward momentum. Hence, as the narrative progresses through its spectacular interruptions these two movements either mesh, or one or the other comes to the fore. This fluid interchange of movements seems to imply a shift or flux of movement- and time-images, but in actual fact popular Indian cinema's organization of images is neither of these.

To summarize the argument so far, the *masala*-image is different from both movement- and time-image because it organizes images in an altogether different manner. This is due to the different conception of the whole on which it is predicated, and this is, in turn because it comes from a different aesthetic, cultural, national and historical context than the movement- or the time-image. In popular Indian cinema, spatial and temporal disconti- nuity exists and is celebrated within an overarching progression that circu- itously proceeds through digression and multiplicity. Yet this occurs not because of any radical shift in "our" thinking about narrative time after an event like World War Two, but because of the specific aesthetic tradition from which the popular Indian narrative stems.

A Real Song and Dance

To more fully understand the difference between the popular Indian film aesthetic and the movement- and time-image, a focused consideration of the place of the spectacle or interruption in the popular Indian film narra- tive is necessary. Although this spectacle can take a number of forms I will address the song and dance sequence, a staple of the majority of popular Indian films.

As in a Hollywood musical, in popular Indian films numerous scenes take place in everyday situations (a house, a street, a restaurant) where characters burst into song, and the whole world corresponds. It is also common for a song to transport characters in a popular Indian film to other locations entirely, often to exotic places with no relationship to the diegetic world. This has increasingly been the case as popular Indian films target the huge international market of the South Asian diaspora (often referred to as Non Resident Indians, or NRIs), by shooting on location in diverse parts of the world.

In *Global Bollywood* (2008), Sangita Gopal and Sujata Moorti note that even during the silent era Indian audiences used to spectacular theatrical forms, typically containing song and dance numbers, were attracted to see films 'accompanied by live performances by dancing girls, jugglers and muscle men'.[48] Not surprisingly, then, the song (and laterally the song and dance) have been integral components of popular Indian cinema since the first sound pictures. The first Indian talkie, *Alam Ara* (1931) contained seven songs.[49] The immediate popularity of the film song was such that in the following year *Indrasabha* (1932) contained over 70 songs,[50] causing Anustup Basu to argue that 'the entire sound track of the film can be con- sidered to be a singular, constitutive body of musical narration'.[51] In 1933 alone '75 Hindi films were produced, all with songs and dances',[52] and in *Indian Film* (1963), Erik Barnouw and S. Krishnaswamy point out that:

> In 1931 and 1932, at what seemed a dark moment in Indian film history, song and dance – in part derived from a tradition of folk music-drama – played an important role in winning for the sound film an instant and widening acceptance.[53]

Today the majority of critics agree that, as Gokulsing and Dissanayake put it, after the early 1930s: 'Music and fantasy came to be seen as vital elements of the filmic experience'.[54] For example, Nasreen Munni Kabir states:

> *Alam Ara*, India's first sound film . . . borrowed the basic structure from the plays of the Parsee Theatre, which featured a number of songs based on Hindustani light-classical music. . . . After the success of these early song-filled movies, music became an essential component, featuring in all popular cinema.[55]

The *masala* aesthetic, then, was conceived and developed in the silent era, solidified in the 1930s, and by the 1940s the accepted formula was 'a star, six songs, three dances'.[56] Therefore, although popular Indian cinema as we know it today is perhaps more accurately dated to the post-war independence period, especially during the Golden Age of popular Indian cinema of the 1950s, and although here images akin to those Deleuze categorized as time-images do seem to appear, this is not a phenomenon that should be unproblematically assimilated within the overall schema of the epistemic shift envisaged by Deleuze's categories. The evocation by the above critics of folk and theatrical traditions as key influences on popular Indian cinema again illustrates the need to understand the popular Indian film aesthetic as distinct from both the movement- and the time-image because of its specific cultural origins.

As noted previously, the non-Aristotelian narrative of popular Indian cinema offers its audience the pleasure of spectacles for their own sake, a process in which the role of the song and dance is integral. As Kabir puts it: 'The average Hindi film does not pretend to offer a unique storyline . . . [W]hile a new twist to a familiar Bollywood storyline helps a film to succeed, if the audience is looking for originality, they know it is principally to be found in the score. The song and dance sequences are the most important moments.'[57] So, if the narrative's interruptions are the whole point of the narrative, exactly what type of image is seen in the song and dance sequence?

On the one hand, song and dance sequences could be said to loosely fall into the category of movement-image. This can be seen if we briefly consider Rodowick's example of the movement-image, of Buster Keaton's moving body in the dream sequence of *Sherlock Jr.* (1924), which demonstrates how in the movement-image the protagonist's body unifies the discontinuous spaces through which he passes, because his unbroken sensory-motor continuity enable him to act upon what he sees. Rodowick notes:

> When Keaton finds himself on a rock by the ocean, he dives, only to land headfirst in a snowbank. Keaton's movements from one shot to the next link incommensurable spaces through what modern mathematics calls a 'rational' division. The interval dividing any two spatial segments serves simultaneously as the end of the first and the beginning of the second. In Keaton's film, every division, no matter how unlikely and nonsensical, is mastered by this figure of rationality where the identification of movement with action assures the continuous unfolding of adjacent spaces. The consequence of this identification is the subordination of time to movement.[58]

In this way the action-image moves from situation through action to changed situation in a linear progression, the protagonist's command of space ensuring movement occurs in an entirely causal fashion. After all, in the movement-image we see an indirect image of time, of time edited around the protagonist's ability to act upon what they see. Similarly, the continuous organic movement of the actors in the song and dance sequence can be said to unify the disparate and disconnected environments through which the sequence often moves. On this view, in terms of Deleuze's findings in *Cinema 1* concerning the representation of time in various pre-war European cinema movements, the popular Indian film – like the early Soviet, French and German movement-images – can be said to use montage in the song and dance sequence to provide an indirect image of time. It might be tempting, then, to consider the *dharmic* whole to describe another form of movement-image that exists alongside the organic conception of the whole of the US action-image, the dialectic notion of the whole of Soviet montage, etc.

On the other hand, we could view such moments as time-images, as instances of fantasy, of sensory-motor suspension where the narrative pauses, or digresses, and the world moves around the protagonist, transporting them elsewhere even though they themselves do not move. When Deleuze discusses the musical in *Cinema 2* it is in precisely this fashion. Overcoming the seeming paradox of sensory-motor movements like singing and dancing occurring in the pause between perception and action, in *Cinema 2*, Deleuze sees this physical movement taking place within a larger movement of world:

> [W]hat counts is the way in which the dancer's individual genius, his subjectivity, moves from a personal motivation to a supra-personal element, to a movement of world that the dance will outline. This is the moment of truth where the dancer is still going, but already a sleepwalker, who will be taken over by the movement which seems to summon him: this can be seen with Fred Astaire in the walk which imperceptibly becomes dance . . . as well as with [Gene] Kelly in the dance which seems to have its origin in the unevenness of the pavement.[59]

In the song and dance sequence, then, the movement of world catches up or overtakes the sensory-motor movements of the characters. In fact, Deleuze also discusses *Sherlock Jr* in *Cinema 2*, to demonstrate the difference between the recollection-image (a virtual image of the past that becomes actual in the present, and therefore closer to the movement-image) and the dream-image (as in *Sherlock Jr*) which is closer to the time-image because it perpetually defers its actualization into another virtual movement.[60] In Rodowick's analysis of this scene the protagonist's sensory-motor actions are used to unify the elliptically edited spaces of the continuity system, hence, a movement-image. In Deleuze's, an independent movement of world ensures that the sensory-motor actions of the protagonist are forever deferred. Keaton is always one step behind the movement of world, the trajectory SAS' is impossible to complete, and therefore this dream-image is considered closer to the time-image. Admittedly Deleuze notes that the dream-image is explicitly figured as such in *Sherlock Jr*, and it does not provide the indiscernibility of virtual (dream) and actual (reality) that is captured in the purest form of the time-image, the crystal of time. Even so, this analysis of movement in *Sherlock Jr* demonstrates how the song and dance sequence in popular Indian cinema, which is characterized by a far more blurred transition from reality to fantasy than the classical Hollywood film, appears closer to the time-image than the movement-image.

Yet the popular Indian film is not a musical in the generic sense as we would describe a Hollywood musical like *Singin' in the Rain* (1952). Leaving aside

Mishra's argument that Bollywood cinema constitutes a sort of meta-genre,[61] the dominant genres remain: devotional, romantic, stunt, historical, social, and family films, all of which would typically include song and dance sequences among their attractions/interruptions.[62] Therefore, what happens in the popular Indian film song and dance number is not simply a moment of spectacle in an otherwise linear narrative, a time-image blended into the overarching structure of a movement-image.

Rather, in popular Indian cinema the contrasting movements of character and world alternatively mesh or alternate in importance or dominance, as the film's narrative progresses. The discontinuous montage often found in the song and dance sequence is thus symptomatic of the larger episodic progression of the popular Indian narrative, which weaves its way through numerous times and spaces, relying on a certain amount of sensory-motor continuity provided by its characters, while these characters are themselves periodically "caught up" by the *dharmic* movement of the narrative world. The episodic arrival of the song and dance sequence provides the clearest evidence of this. Here the point of change from one type of movement to another illustrates that it is a matter of degree or speed of movement as to which one dominates at any time. For the remainder of the chapter I will examine examples of song and dance sequences from three key moments in the history of popular Indian cinema that will illustrate this working of the *masala*-image.

Toofani Tarzan (1936)

Toofani Tarzan/Tempestuous Tarzan was a jungle adventure made by Wadia Movietone, one of the studios to achieve success during the 1930s, mainly through the production of stunt films.[63] As Thomas has shown at length, such action films were extremely popular at the time (a fact sometimes forgotten in histories of popular Indian cinema that tend to emphasize the dominance of the social) and were, 'at their core, sites of negotiation of a new Indian modernity'.[64] Examining this example from the early days of talkie production in India gives an indication of the initial development of the *masala*-image.

For the most part, *Toofani Tarzan*, whose overarching storyline is that of the Tarzan legend, proceeds through a series of episodes that often bear no immediately causal relationship to the one preceding or following it. These include: a daring hot air balloon ride through a thunderstorm; various performing animals fighting, doing tricks or generally looking menacing; elephant rides; elephant charges; slapstick comedy routines; stunt sequences (inevitably including Tarzan (John Cavas) swinging on a vine); Tarzan's daring kidnap of Leela (Gulshan) and their ensuing romance; action scenes (including Tarzan wrestling with an imprisoned King Kong); a tribal ambush or two; a set piece song around a campfire; Leela's love song; and so on. Constantly interrupted by these spectacles the narrative haltingly unfolds of Tarzan's grandfather arriving from the city to seek out his long lost grandson.

This particular example of the cinema of interruptions is very reminiscent of the early silent cinema of attractions, with its circus or cabaret-like appeal to the spectator's attention over the short time span of a sequence of novelty acts. It could also be compared to the original US Tarzan movies, or indeed, Laurel and Hardy movies, Buster Keaton films and so on. However, as with all popular Indian films that borrow from the Hollywood movement-image – for example it declares lead actor, John Cavas the 'Indian Eddie Polo', a reference to the US star of 1930s stunt film serials[65] – *Toofani Tarzan* is an Indianized version of its predecessor. Aside from the emergence of this film out of the specific context of the circus-like viewing conditions of silent Indian cinema, what marks *Toofani Tarzan* as primarily different from Hollywood cinema is that its interweaving storylines work to disrupt any sense of linear flow to the narrative's progression. The most obvious example of this is the repeated, unannounced appearance of Tarzan's insane mother Uma (Nazira) at various points in the film, a character who, Thomas states, Indian audiences would recognize as being 'coded as a kali figure, the goddess of creation and destruction'.[66] Such recurring storylines illustrate how the causal narrative progression we might expect of the movement-image (such as a Hollywood Tarzan movie) is constantly interrupted both by the narrative's episodic progression and its deliberately expansive – in terms of narrative progression – intertwining plotlines, in a manner drawn from the tradition of the religious epics.

One specific point in the film that distils the intermeshing movements of character and world is Leela's love song. Towards the end of *Toofani Tarzan*, Leela, Tarzan's Indianized Jane, sings a song while bathing in a jungle pool. This is an interruption that occurs rather abruptly after most of the safari caravan have been captured by tribal natives. The switch of mood is apparent, as we suddenly leave the distressed captives to focus on the rather happier aspect of Leela, singing of falling in love in the forest. Here the independent movement of narrative world typical of the cinema of interruptions is evident. It is also seen to function on a much smaller scale in Leela's song, in the movement of world that takes place around her.

As Leela treads water and sings her song of love, she temporarily becomes the centre of both the jungle and the narrative. Her partial sensory-motor immobility stills the narrative, and we pause for a moment to revel in the spectacle of her song.

Leela is shot from various angles around the pool, and is intercut with shots of a bird nesting in an overhead tree, an inquisitive chimp which climbs into a nearby tree to watch her (point of view shots of Leela are provided for both animals), elephants bathing and grazing nearby, the surrounding mountains, a shot of the coast, and finally the arrival of Moti (Tarzan's faithful dog) who returns Leela to the narrative by stealing her clothes and running into the jungle with them. These discontinuous spaces, intercut with Leela singing in the pool, pass before the spectator's gaze without the sensory-motor continuity of the movement-image. As an expression of the movement of world around the character they are more akin to the time-image, but in actual fact are illustrative of a movement of world particular to the *dharmic* whole. Leela's song, after all, illustrates her character's exploration of her desire for Tarzan, which contrasts with the peril faced by her father, which she will encounter momentarily. The song is an interruption that enables a momentary contemplation of individual expression before a return to familial loyalty, a moment of *adharma* before a *dharmic* movement of world returns her to a sensory-motor trajectory. In this it demonstrates the episodic interplay between movement of world and character movement typical of the *masala*-image. As the narrative picks up again with Leela's chasing of Moti, we return to what appears to be, in Deleuzian terms, the sensory-motor regime of the movement-image.

What is most important to note in this example from the 1930s is that this is the norm in the popular Indian cinema of interruptions, in which the narrative progresses circuitously through a series of spectacles, long before the Second World War. As I noted above, if we consider films like *Toofani Tarzan* in the light of Deleuze's discussion of the pre-war American, Soviet, French and German montage schools with which he starts *Cinema 1*, it might be possible to think of popular Indian cinema as constructing another type of movement-image. However, I would argue instead that the *dharmic* whole exists somewhere between the indirect (movement-image) and direct (time-image) expressions of the whole that Deleuze conceives of, popular Indian cinema resisting such easy categorization within such a Bergson-inspired worldview. Thus a considered investigation of the context from which popular Indian cinema emerged (in particular in terms of its *dharmic* conceptualization of the whole) challenges the notion that Bergson's work could be applied to cinema (in a global sense) in the manner that Deleuze does when exploring movement and time.

To round off this discussion of *Toofani Tarzan*, illustrating the closeness of montage, narrative and ideology, the interchange of movements of character and world in the *masala*-image also facilitates a broader examination of ideological concerns. This includes various ways of conceiving of identity, including national, gendered, diasporic, and so on. In the case of *Toofani Tarzan*, the interplay of these movements enables an exploration of the interaction taking place in India at that time between tradition and modernity. Thomas describes the scene in question as illustrative of Leela's position in the film as a facilitator of a larger exploration of fluid, ' "modern" identities', stating:

> Leela is an intriguing mix of 'modern' independence, coquettish help-lessness and unconstrained sexuality. She encompasses two facets of decadent city femininity: the vanity and 'falseness' signalled by her obsessional attachment to her make-up bag, and the assertive toughness of a woman in slacks who stands up to men, wields a gun and defies her father to choose her own sexual partner. The movie transforms her into a free spirit in a miniskirt whose hedonistic sexuality becomes, through a series of moves and denials, acceptably identified with the innocence of the jungle. Thus, for example, an erotic bathing scene, in which she (purportedly) bathes nude while singing a sensual song about "a burning rising in my body", is immediately followed by a comedy gag in which Moti the dog steals her clothes, and then her kidnap by the cannibals. [67]

For Thomas, Leela's assertive femininity opens the space for the playing out of a 'modern' sense of identity. While she is at home in the city, Leela is also ultimately able to accommodate herself to life in the jungle. The interplay between her different possible identities – assertive city dweller, jungle wife – interacts with the different movements evident in the film. While on safari with her father and his entourage, in her pistol-toting, pith helmet, boots and trousers guise, she drives the narrative through her sensory-motor actions. Once kidnapped by Tarzan, however, she becomes subject to the movement of world enacted by the jungle, and is threatened by tigers and crocodiles, each time saved and carried off by the commanding sensory-motor presence of Tarzan. In the scene in question, the movement of world that "catches her up" in a song offers an opportunity to explore a 'modern', expressive female identity (semi-naked, and with 'a burning

rising in my body') and then seemingly disavows this potential as Moti leads
Leela into the clutches of the cannibals from which she will be rescued by
Tarzan (*adharma – dharma*). Ultimately, then, the montage of jungle spaces,
Moti the dog, the cannibals (and finally Tarzan), are the agents who shift
events around her as she literally treads water in the centre of the image.
In one context, her sensory-motor continuity is assured. In the other,
the movement of world pauses her trajectory, in this particular instance
enabling the film and its audience to gaze upon her lyrical exploration of
her modern identity.

Typical of popular Indian cinema, then, in *Toofani Tarzan* the song is
used to help mediate national identity, in this case 'India's encounter with
modernity'.[68] In the context of the growth of the nationalist movement
in 1930s India, the two movements at play in the *masala*-image facilitate an
exploration of the versatility and potential of 'modern' female identity in
India. At the film's conclusion, Leela learns to overcome the movement of
world in the jungle. This she achieves through the modern relationship she
develops with Tarzan, which Thomas describes as 'fundamentally – and
quite radically – one of mutual interdependence'.[69] This union sees them
disappear into the jungle together at the film's close, Leela's running figure
uniting the spaces of the montage as she flees her father in the pursuit
of Tarzan, illustrating her regaining of sensory-motor control over the
jungle's, and the film's, movement of world. *Dharma* is thus restored, with
Tarzan and Leela recreating the previous jungle pairing of Tarzan's parents
before their idyllic life was disrupted.

At the beginning of the film, Tarzan's father, Ramu is killed by a rampag-
ing pride of lions, his scientific breakthrough (a chemical formula capable
of conferring immortality) left in the hands of the child Tarzan. His love
marriage to wife Uma is unblessed by his millionaire father. With Leela and
Tarzan's love union finally blessed by Ramu's millionaire father at the close
of the film, alternating character movement and movement of world have
led the narrative back to resolution in *dharma*, figured in this case as a cohe-
sive interdependence between modern world (city girl Leela) and traditional life (jungle man Tarzan), a union that enables Leela's *adharmic*
desires to be reconciled in what is in some way a more conventional, albeit
modern, marital relationship.

In this example from the 1930s we can see how, rather than movement-
or time-image, the *masala*-image organizes images in a manner that seems
at once to evoke both of Deleuze's categories, but is in fact neither of them.
In its slippages into interruption, the movement of world comes to the fore,
and literally takes over from the character. With the return to narrative,

however, sensory-motor movement of character drives events forward. What is important to note is that this is the norm in the popular Indian cinema of interruptions, in which the narrative progresses circuitously through a series of spectacles.

Awaara (1951)

The second example of the *masala*-image is *Awaara/Vagabond*, starring Raj Kapoor (the son of prolific actor Prithviraj Kapoor, who plays the role of Raj's father in the film) and his often paired romantic lead, Nargis, who is most famous for starring in *Mother India* (1957). *Awaara* was a smash hit, popular all over India and various parts of Europe (especially in the USSR), the Middle East, Africa and Asia.[70] Its widespread fame has led Dina Iordanova to argue that *Awaara* may be the most successful film in the history of cinema.[71] The international popularity of Indian films like *Awaara* in the 1950s is usually considered to be due to their ability to distinguish themselves from Hollywood cinema, in particular through their structure[72] and the means to which it can be employed to consider experiences common to various audiences worldwide.

Awaara opens as a court room drama. Its story unfolds in flashback in a manner that could very well suggest the Bergsonian view of time as a 'Being-memory'[73] which we all inhabit, and which characterizes cinema of the time-image. However, what is revealed through the playing out of these flashbacks is not an open and enduring whole of time (or even an indirect expression of it), but rather, the *dharmic* cycle of the whole.

Drawing on the melodramatic tradition of the epic religious texts,[74] and indeed, popular Indian cinema's various theatrical predecessors, *Awaara* focuses its narrative around a familial conflict that spans two generations. Judge Raghunath (Prithviraj Kapoor) becomes suspicious that his wife's pregnancy may be a consequence of a short period of captivity she spent at the hands of the bandit, Jagga (K. N. Singh). In actual fact, the child is legitimate, although Jagga initially intended rape in revenge for Raghunath's previous conviction of him for a crime (of which he was innocent) on the strength of his father and his grandfather's lives as bandits. Nevertheless Raghunath throws his pregnant wife out of the house, and she brings up her son, Raj (Raj Kapoor) in a Mumbai slum. There Jagga initiates him in the ways of the criminal underworld, in order to disprove Raghunath's belief in the caste system. There is a great deal more to the plot, including the romance between Raj and Raghunath's charge, Rita (Nargis), who were (coincidentally) childhood friends. The film begins at the point at which Raj is in court for the murder of Jagga and the attempted murder of Raghunath. Raj's mother has died under the wheels of Raghunath's car. Rita is questioning Raghunath in the dock as defence counsel for Raj. The flashback that follows fills in the narrative, and Raj is ultimately condemned not to death, but to three years imprisonment.

The question at the heart of this nature versus nurture story is whether a judge's son is destined to be a judge, and a criminal's son a criminal, or whether individuals are a product of their milieu, with at least the potential to determine their own future through their actions. The convoluted cycling of the narrative plays out the conundrum of whether an individual is destined to become what they are due to their caste status or whether they are a product of their circumstances. Put another way, *Awaara* explores whether individuals have the power to influence their situation through sensory-motor actions, or are subject to the greater movement of world. The coincidences that bring the family back together, themselves typical of the melodrama, ensure that *Awaara*'s examination of the role of caste and personal freedom within newly independent India appears on the surface to be a familial story. However, the whole that is created is *dharmic*, both at the level of the family and the nation. For this reason, although most critical writing on *Awaara* emphasizes the extraordinary nine-minute-long dream sequence that occurs part way through the film (it contains three songs and took three months to film), by contrast it is the theme song from *Awaara*, Awaara Hoon (I am a Tramp), that is particularly instructive for this discussion.

In Awaara Hoon, Kapoor's character, Raj, just released from prison, happily sings of his identity as a thief and vagabond. The song begins with a close-up of Raj's feet, which wander through the city streets. As he wanders, he picks the pockets of those he encounters. Once spotted, Raj runs away from his pursuer, stealing a bicycle that momentarily runs away from him as he attempts to mount it. From the bicycle he daringly mounts a moving truck, dismounting only once his attempts to flirt with its dancing female passengers fail. Picking himself up off the ground he finds himself back in the slums on the outskirts of the city, the area of his upbringing. Like Keaton in *Sherlock Jr*, Kapoor moves through discontinuous spaces, his skill as a thief and an acrobat and the movement of his singing figure serving to unify these spaces in the style of a movement-image. Yet it is ultimately the movement of the world that encircles and "catches him up". After all, his sensory-motor movements are attempts to escape from or match these movements – those of his pursuers, the bicycle or the truck that briefly carries him along – ensuring that this moment of spectacle appears more like a time-image. In actual fact, however, this chase visualizes the meshing and unmeshing of the competing movements of characters and world of popular Indian cinema.

Due to the coincidence of the golden age of popular Indian cinema in the 1950s with Indian independence, it would be tempting to view examples of what look to be time-images in *Awaara* (and indeed, other works of 1950s popular Indian cinema) as deterritorializations of the movement-image in the service of national identity creation. This was as I did of films from Asia, Europe and the USA, in *Deleuze, Cinema and National Identity*. Most obviously, the Chaplinesque underclass thieves and tramps played by Raj Kapoor in such films as *Awaara* are particularly reminiscent of Deleuze's wandering seer of the time-image, and these characters were specifically engaged in an examination of how India's new national character should develop.[75] As Yves Thoraval has it:

> A large section of the post-war audience was made up of uprooted people drawn to the cities by the economic boom in urban areas. These people literally had to invent new ties of solidarity and community feeling that rose above traditional extended family or caste ties, which had governed life in the countryside. Raj Kapoor was at the very crest of a wave of "optimism" that ran through Indian cinema at that time, bearing the hopes for change of a newly independent India.[76]

If we were to follow this logic, in Awaara Hoon, Raj's momentary exclusions from the movement of world emphasizes his ambiguous relationship to the rapidly developing movements of modernity in India. His narrative wanders circuitously through the city because automobile transportation is limited to him, as is his access to the circulation of wealth, both of which at times "catches him up", and at times passes him by.

Yet, if we consider the *dharmic* background to popular Indian cinema, and its cyclical temporal model, the wandering of Raj that Kapoor portrays in *Awaara* is less that of a seer in the time-image than it is that of an "interrupted" character whose movements alternate between decisive action (typical of the movement-image) and the aimless wandering (typical of the time-image's seer). This alternation exists, however, because Raj is situated in a *dharmic* whole. Kapoor's Raj wanders amidst the narrative malaise (interruption) of *adharma*, mixing with the urban poor, including assorted low-life thieves (pick pockets, scam artists, etc.), murderers, gamblers, vampish women and so on, in search of a new *dharmic* conception of India that will reconcile the broader, *dharmic* movements that divided his family/nation.

Although the demographic shift noted by Thoraval, and its resultant impact on traditional social values and structures, was a recurring pattern in post-war countries worldwide, even so, as the above analysis of *Toofani Tarzan* demonstrates, even in the 1930s – long before independence in 1947 – the cinema of interruptions clearly existed in India, defying categorization as either movement- or time-image. Therefore, although it is possible to see popular Indian cinema as containing deterritorializing moments of the time-image, which are used in the post-war era to examine national identity, this process (formal and ideological) has been a facet of the popular Indian cinema aesthetic since at least the 1930s. Instead, these movements can still be understood as examining a specific moment in national history, but doing so in a manner typical of popular Indian cinema, through consideration of the *dharmic* whole and its component parts. As Mishra puts it:

> Within the oppositional simplicity of the popular, Raj Kapoor presents the colonial and the postcolonial as a simple opposition: do children of thieves grow up to be thieves and children of well-to-do parents grow up to be decent citizens regardless of their upbringing? Can the colonial bourgeoisie never change in a postcolonial world order? In a very real sense the matter rests there because the film really endorses neither.[77]

These oppositions, reminiscent of those Deleuze identifies as structuring the duel at the heart of the action-image, are, instead, constitutive of a *dharmic* whole. In this instance, they are used to question existing assumptions pertaining to the caste system in the new, post-independence context, in relation to the "duel" that occurs between human actions and destiny (movements of characters and world respectively). For this reason, as Michael H. Hoffheimer has demonstrated, in the postcolonial era *Awaara* depicted the Indian legal institution as both modern enough to resolve public conflicts and 'as a traditional institution capable of restoring the moral social order or *dharma*'.[78] Hence, Raj must be convicted for murder, but so too must his father realize his complicity (he was the one who cast Raj out into this life after all) for the family to be reunited and *dharma* restored. In the absence of the colonizers, then, India was depicted as a family/nation capable of resolving its own perpetual struggles of *dharma*, of the cyclical interactions of the cosmic moral social order and individual actions. Although the movements of de- and reterritorialization we see on screen do enable a negotiation of national identity, then, this is not an interplay of movement- and time-image, but of *dharma* and *adharma*.

Dilwale Dulhania Le Jayenge (1995)

Finally, to demonstrate that this argument functions throughout the twentieth century, a concluding example is drawn from the 1990s. *Dilwale Dulhania Le Jayenge/The Brave Heart Will Take the Bride* was a smash hit that exemplified the international aim of popular Indian cinema after the impact on India of 'economic liberalization'[79] and its subsequent appeal to the massive global market of NRIs. From the days of silent cinema, Indian movie entrepreneurs reached out to the Indian diaspora in recognition of its potential as a market for popular Indian cinema.[80] In the 1990s, however, *Dilwale Dulhania Le Jayenge* was at the forefront of a movement characterized by higher production values and a blockbuster format that, Wimal Dissanayake notes, 'opened a transitional pathway from nationalist capitalism to postmodernist multinational capitalism and consumerism'.[81] Accordingly, *Dilwale Dulhania Le Jayenge* is a film in two parts that compares and contrasts life in the diaspora (first half) with life in contemporary India (second half). In doing so it demonstrates both the shared values, and the opportunities – both romantic and economic – that are increasingly available in both contexts.

In *Dilwale Dulhania Le Jayenge* the difficulty of attributing movement- or time-image status to the popular Indian film is again apparent. In the main the narrative is defined by the sensory-motor actions of its protagonists. The first half of the film in particular sees its carefree young NRI protagonists, Raj Malhotra (Shah Rukh Khan) and love interest Simran Singh (Kajol) backpacking across the discontinuous spaces of tourist Europe. Typical of the movement-image, their physical presence in these spaces provides continuity across the montage of different national landscapes, as it does in the second half that takes place in Punjab. In the song and dance sequences of the first half of the film, however, the movement of world takes precedence, the discontinuous montage overtaking them, leaving them to sing and dance in the suspended sensory-motor interval. Here the lovers are moved rapidly through costume changes as they visit various towns, travel on trains, appear on snow-covered mountain tops, swim in indoor swimming pools, wander streets at night, all the time singing and dancing. Typically for popular Indian cinema, the difference between these two moments, however, are simply a matter of degree, or speed of movement of world, and the subsequent interaction that is created with character movement.

Dilwale Dulhania Le Jayenge's theme song, Tujhe Dekha, is especially interesting in this respect. It takes place at the beginning of the second half of the film, and in it what initially appears to be a Bergsonian model of time emerges as Raj and Simran revisit the European locations in a song of mutual memory, and re-realize their initially stilted courtship as though it had been a time of mutual love and uninterrupted happiness. The song begins in a vast field of mustard, with yellow flowers stretching out of the frame. As Raj and Simran sing they are transported back in time through their memories of Europe (and through various scenes from earlier in the film) revisiting a church, train, hotel room, lush green countryside, lake, bridge and snow covered mountains before returning to the Punjabi mustard field. Several of these virtual movements include costume changes, the overall impression being of the two lovers slipping between Deleuzian sheets of the past.

Reliving the recent past as though it were a time of unbridled love and happiness (whereas in reality it was a time of halting, if good natured courtship) the past is coloured by their recent realization of love in the present. The virtual past and the actual present oscillate, becoming indiscernible in the moment of the song, as we might expect of the time-image. However, as the song returns to the mustard field in Punjab, the popular Indian film narrative – which proceeds circuitously due to the cyclical notion of time it derives from the *dharmic* whole, and its resultant interruptions – here literally progresses circuitously, as the narrative's past is revisited and advanced in the present. Once again the larger movement of world of the narrative of interruptions catches up the characters, but here it returns them to previous moments of the narrative, enabling these moments to become active once again. This momentary interruption to the narrative's progress ensures that the characters' movements re-mesh with those of the narrative world. In addition to the general fluidity of movements of world and movements of character, then, in the song and dance sequence the narrative of the popular Indian film advances precisely due to the alternation between past and present.

Although we could consider this process to be akin to the falsifying narration of a Nietzschian powers of the false, that Deleuze aligns with the Bergsonian model of time (via Jorge Luis Borges' notion of the labyrinth of time) in *Cinema 2*, it can equally be understood as an example of the world-cycle of popular Indian cinema's *dharmic* whole. Taking such a view, *Dilwale Dulhania Le Jayenge* can be seen to examine the possible interplay between the sensory-motor desires of the two diasporic lovers and the *dharmic* movements of world, by reconsidering their agency during a recent past in Europe. In short, events are replayed such that their previous sensory-motor ability is now suspended and reframed by the dominating movement of world. Noticeably this takes place in such a way as to offer an alternative view of the recent past in the NRI from the perspective of NRI characters who have since been transported to India and face separation due to an immanent arranged marriage. In this reconsideration of the past they are not activating a Nietzschian powers of the false, but realizing their existence within the larger *dharmic* movement of world. They are acknowledging their awareness of the relative agency of human actions within broader, cyclical temporal or cosmological shifts, a realization they experience in a present in which their love is threatened, in circumstances that shed a rosier light on events in the recent past.

This realization is, in turn, used to comment upon the interaction between the NRI diaspora and India, as postcolonial diasporic life moves these characters between the two locations. Tujhe Dekha brings together the two movements of the film to intertwine Europe and India, past and present, and transnational (indeed, global) capital flows and traditional Indian values. A recent history of economically successful diasporic energies is thus recontextualized in relation to the return of these flows to India, and indeed, to the economic resurgence of India. In this respect, Purnima Mankekar's observations on the film are particularly pertinent: 'In a context marked by liberalization and intensified transnational flows of migrants and of capital, *Dilwale Dulhania Le Jayenge*'s representations of the homeland signal the reconstitution of postcolonial Indian nationalism.'[82] In such a context:

> [P]ostcoloniality does not designate a moment of unambiguous rupture with the colonial past but, instead, signifies the ubiquitous presence of the colonial past in the present. This understanding of postcoloniality rests on the premise that decolonisation does not occur along a linear trajectory (as in the teleological fantasies of anticolonial nationalists), but that it constitutes a series of discontinuous and uneven processes and is characterized by multiple temporalities.[83]

In the intertwining of the film's movements, *Dilwale Dulhania Le Jayenge* engages a postcolonial Indian present with a recent narrative past spent in the diaspora, echoing the 'discontinuous and uneven processes' and 'multiple temporalities' through which postcolonial identities are continuously reformed in the present, precisely by the movement of characters between the two locations seen in the film. In Tujhe Dekha in particular, the narrative's past, the possibility of potential "liberation" from traditional restraints, is revisited in the homeland. In the song's re-playing of the recent past it appears as though the European diaspora houses the possibility of romantic rejuvenation, alongside the promise of financial injection offered by the return of the NRIs to India. Yet this occurs in such a manner that the film also acknowledges that traditional Hindu values were upheld while the characters travelled across Europe, the romance remaining chaste in spite of the threateningly "liberating" context. Ultimately, then, the song and dance "remembers" time in Europe differently, becoming a moment of suspension akin to that of Leela in the water in *Toofani Tarzan*, a time of diasporic identity exploration prior to a return to a renegotiated "normality" in India. This moment, however, is tied to a much larger, *dharmic* movement of world in which the nation's postcolonial identity develops through 'discontinuous and uneven processes', through the multiple, interacting temporalities of India and diaspora, rather than through the powers of the false.

In this way, as Gayatri Gopinath notes, *Dilwale Dulhania Le Jayenge* reassures the 'transnational viewership, both in India and the diaspora, that globalization and "traditional" Indian values go hand in hand'.[84] The Indian homeland is reinvigorated by the diaspora, as the movement of world (also here a postcolonial, economic movement across the globe) reactivates the film's past, to examine the changing face of Indian and NRI identities. As in *Toofani Tarzan* and *Awaara*, then, in *Dilwale Dulhania Le Jayenge* the return to *dharma* sees a coexistence of tradition and modernity that at once (re) establishes the status quo and yet ensures progression within the cycle. By the film's conclusion, in line with Gopinath's perspective, the recent past offered by Raj and Simran's time in Europe has entered into an apparently more productive interaction with the Indian present, as they return to the diaspora as a couple with the blessing of their parents. This is not so much a crystalline interaction between indiscernible virtual and actual facets of time, however, as it is a postcolonial movement towards narrative resolution peculiar to popular Indian cinema in the 1990s (a product of its twin target audiences, national and NRI) and its *dharmic* conception of the – in this instance for domestic and diasporic audiences – (trans)national whole.

Conclusion: Deleuze Needs Spectacles

The *masala*-image illustrates that Deleuze's fixing of cinema into the two categories (movement-/time-image) does not account for different cinematic traditions – based on different conceptions of time or cosmology – that have a different relation to the whole. Accordingly, Deleuze's conceptualizing of the indirect and direct expression of the whole in cinema needs to be reconsidered. Deleuze's image categories are two different perspectives on the image that point, by definition, towards many more possible images. The philosophical underpinnings that Deleuze identifies (Bergson et al.) are not absolutes, and nor are movement- and time-image exhaustive categories.

Rather than an epistemic shift or an evolutionary progression marking a development from movement- to time-image, popular Indian films express the existence of a different organization of images, based on a different conception of the whole. This is the *masala*-image that is created from the culturally specific aesthetic traditions that inform popular Indian cinema. Due to its unique organization of images, popular Indian cinema expresses both the movement of world (Deleuze's time-image) and the sensory-motor movement of characters in the world (Deleuze's movement-image) as part of a broader cinema of spectacular interruptions. Although both movement- and time-image can be identified if we look for them in popular Indian films, these images should be understood as part of something altogether different from Deleuze's reterritorializing categories, which were derived from a knowledge of cinema predominantly limited to Hollywood and European cinema. In this instance, by contrast, the whole is constructed from *dharmic* cycles. For this reason it would be erroneous to consider popular Indian cinema as another kind of movement- or time-image, as it does not offer either an indirect or a direct expression of (Bergson's) duration, but something altogether different.

Deleuze needs spectacles, then, in order to see better that the categories of movement- and time-image are too restrictive when we consider the wealth of different cinemas that exist which do not precisely conform to either definition. These different types of cinema, products of specific contexts of production and reception, throw open the field of enquiry to new interpretations.

Conclusion

The Continuing Adventures of Deleuze and World Cinemas

This book has taken Deleuze on his travels, both historically and geographically, from the earliest days of cinema in late nineteenth century France; through popular Indian films (from the 1930s to the 1990s); European spaghetti westerns of the Cold War era; East Asian cinemas negotiating globalization at the close of the twentieth century; and early twenty-first century films as diverse as the Los Angeles-set Hollywood blockbusters of Michael Mann, and Marcelo Piñeyro's historically revisionist Argentine melodrama, *Kamchatka* (2002). These extremely varied examples have enabled me to critique, revise and refine several of the concepts and conclusions from Deleuze's *Cinema* books. In so doing, I have demonstrated the importance of considering historical context (including specific industrial, cultural and aesthetic conditions) when applying Deleuze's ideas to different kinds of films from around the world. Simultaneously, I have argued for the need to be open to the possibility that different films, both films from different countries and different kinds of films (different types of popular genres for example), can enable us to develop the work Deleuze started. In short, I have made the case that if Deleuze's *Cinema* books are to have continued relevance into the twenty-first century his conclusions need to be "advanced", very often in the sense of developed beyond their existing form, in conjunction with the study of a world of cinemas.

In this process, in order to make sense of cinema worldwide as we are increasingly coming to know it, the *Cinema* books begin to come adrift from their original philosophical moorings (the underpinning ideas of Henri Bergson, Charles Sanders Peirce, Friedrich Nietzsche, Baruch Spinoza, etc). Deleuze's interpretation of these various philosophical predecessors was always somewhat unique to Deleuze, the most pertinent to this study being his own particular take on Bergson. Strict adherence to the ideas of these predecessors as they influence Deleuze's philosophy would inevitably mean that Deleuze's ideas are perpetually reaffirmed, rather than reconsidered, with any number of cinemas that do not conform to his categories remaining "undiscovered" by such a narrow Deleuzian methodology. It would be extremely un-Deleuzian to pay such close respect to these philosophical influences that we continually repeat and reaffirm the conclusions of the *Cinema* books (forming in this instance the "tree" of Deleuze's thought) by perpetually uncovering and validating the existence of these "roots" as determining cause of all further conclusions regarding cinema. Rather, we should explore the rhizomatic forest that is the world of cinemas, refusing to focus on any one privileged tree in favour of a considered study of the spreading multiplicity. As Édouard Glissant argues in *The Poetics of Relation* (1997), 'the rhizome maintains . . . the idea of rootedness but challenges that of a totalitarian root'.[1] Accordingly, each of the world cinemas that Deleuze's ideas encounters entails a consideration of their context-specific roots, but this process in turn uproots the *Cinema* books from their initial ground. Taking this approach we can deterritorialize the *Cinema* books and thereby enable their repetition in difference when they come into contact with the cinemas otherwise "Othered" from their pages.

As I noted in the introduction, although my approach might seem in a certain respect to move "beyond" Deleuze in a manner that is more determined by the films explored than the philosophical starting point (in fact for many, including myself, the preferred manner of working with film theory or film philosophy), from another point of view such a move might be interpreted as a continuation of Deleuze's own project, to uncover the building blocks of cinema, but working with a broader conception of (the world of) cinema than Deleuze had. We might argue that although Deleuze went a long way towards discovering cinema's DNA in the movement- and time-image, further work remains to be done in this respect in relation to the broader conception of cinema we now have.

This project, then, attempts to construct a Deleuzian assemblage that is less about Deleuze and other philosophers, and more about Deleuze and a world of cinemas. The new assemblage consists of Deleuze's *Cinema* books plus the raw material of world cinemas as a socio-historical phenomenon. The major advantage of this approach is that it takes us one step closer towards a freeing of Deleuze's *Cinema* books from accusations of Eurocentrism (all too easy to make in relation to the films he discusses and the universalizing conclusions regarding time that he draws from them), even if it is, I acknowledge, only a small step in that direction, rather than any definitive conclusion.

Next Stops: Africa . . . then . . .

In light of the above, *Deleuze and World Cinemas* could be said to offer a partially completed page to Dudley Andrew's proposed 'Atlas of World Cinema', perhaps a philosophical (or certainly a Deleuzian) page or 'view', to add to those isolated by Andrew: the 'political, demographic, linguistic, topographical, meteorological, marine, historical',[2] etc. As with all Atlases, however, there remains a major question mark over exactly whose view such a project provides on the world of cinemas, the interlinked spectres of Eurocentrism, Orientalism, the ethnographic gaze and (intellectual and cultural) imperialism immediately resurfacing whenever any such process of mapping is evoked. Yet, the continuing negotiation of this recurrent problem notwithstanding, which further parts of the map can be shaded in? Put another way, where will Deleuze's cinematic travels touch down next?

African cinemas, and I should stress that I mean cinemas from specific African nations, and not Africa as a homogenous film-producing continent, are not discussed in this book. However, as I hope I have by now demonstrated, I have not neglected films from, say, Egypt, Morocco, Algeria, Senegal, Mali, Burkina Faso, Nigeria, South Africa (not to mention Russia, Poland, Brazil, Peru, Uruguay, Mexico, Canada, Thailand, Vietnam, Scotland, Denmark, Australia, New Zealand just to choose a random selection of cinemas from various continents) and a host of others, and yet included the mainstream Hollywood director Michael Mann, because I have a skewed sense of the term world cinemas. The omission of African cinemas is partly due to the fact that there is only so much that one scholar can do on their own. Covering the diverse cinemas that I have often requires a bungee-like stretch to the very limits of my knowledge. However, their absence is also because various African cinemas have already been discussed using Deleuze's ideas. Beyond Rodowick's discussion of Ousmane Sembene's *Borom Sarrett* (1966) in *Gilles Deleuze's Time Machine* (1997), Andrew is one intrepid explorer who has crossed this territory, riding on the back of Deleuze, and drawing on Gayatri Chakravorty Spivak's well-known critique of Deleuze in 'Can the Subaltern Speak?' to note precisely the problems raised by the Eurocentric philosopher's viewpoint on this cinematic terrain.[3] Indeed, Andrew is joined by Patricia Pisters who, taking off from Deleuze's *Cinema* books, examines several contemporary African films (*Lumumba* (2000), *Tanger, le rêve des brûleurs/Tangier, The Burner's Dream* (2003), *Viva Laldjérie/ Viva Algeria* (2004)) to explore the challenges and advances they offer to a Deleuzian analysis of political films.[4]

Undoubtedly there is still much to be said about Africa's many cinemas, especially Nollywood (Nigeria's incredibly productive film industry), in relation to Deleuze's *Cinema* books. Such scholarship, when it arrives, will surely enable us to reconsider his ideas yet further. The same could be said, for that matter, of numerous types of indigenous films (sometimes referred to in debates surrounding 'fourth cinema'[5]) from around the globe, such as Aboriginal or '*Blak*' films from Australia,[6] Maori films from New Zealand,[7] and so on. This is particularly so due to their potential to offer different conceptions of time to work with, some of which may pre-exist the models Deleuze discusses in the *Cinema* books. It is at this point, however, that it becomes clear how mammoth a task it would be to fill in this page of the Atlas, with books and anthologies to be written on continents (such as *Deleuze and African Cinemas*, or perhaps more likely independent volumes entitled *Deleuze and North African Cinemas* and *Deleuze and Sub-Saharan African Cinemas*), and in many cases on nations and/or new waves (as only one for instance, *Deleuze and Iranian Cinema*) as well as any number of directors (perhaps starting with the most pertinent, *Deleuze and Yasujiro Ozu*). This is before we consider the books that could be written on genres (to join Anna Powell's *Deleuze and Horror Film* (2005)), and doubtless various other potentially transnational ways of considering cinema. Indeed, the major challenge to Deleuze's anthropocentric notion of cinema may well lie in the different kinds of time and space now made possible by new digital media.[8]

As such a comprehensive movement in relation to any one thinker seems unlikely, perhaps the more modest hope might be for an openness to the relevance of Deleuze's ideas in such contexts, even if (or perhaps rather, precisely because) engagement with cinemas absent from the *Cinema* books will undoubtedly ask questions of Deleuze's conclusions. Therefore although this book does not claim to be exhaustive, as I have demonstrated through several case studies, despite the difficulties associated with the use of Deleuze with different cinemas there are a wealth of world cinemas just waiting to help us explore the potential that exists for the application, reconsideration and transformation of Deleuze's ideas.

It may now be time to discuss the philosophical issues Deleuze raises in his *Cinema* books, especially concerning time, in a "post-Deleuzian" manner when engaging them with world cinemas. After all, if the ideas and concepts of Deleuze's *Cinema* books are to continue to exist as a useful form of currency it is in these Othered cinemas that we must look for their eternal return.

Notes

Introduction

[1] Gilles Deleuze & Félix Guattari, *A Thousand Plateaus*, trans. Brian Massumi (London: Athlone, [1980] 1987), p. 4.

[2] Stephanie Dennison & Song Hwee Lim, 'Situating World Cinema as a Theoretical Problem', Stephanie Dennison & Song Hwee Lim (eds), *Remapping World Cinema* (London: Wallflower, 2006), pp. 1–15, p. 1; Toby Miller, 'Preface', Linda Badley, R. Barton Palmer & Steven Jay Schneider (eds), *Traditions in World Cinema* (Edinburgh: Edinburgh University Press, 2006), pp. xi–xvi, p. xi.

[3] David Martin-Jones, *Scotland: Global Cinema* (Edinburgh: Edinburgh University Press, 2009), p. 16.

[4] Dina Iordanova, 'Rise of the Fringe', Dina Iordanova, David Martin-Jones & Belén Vidal, *Cinema at the Periphery* (Detroit, MI: Wayne State University Press, 2010), pp. 23–45, p. 23.

[5] Lúcia Nagib, 'Towards a Positive Definition of World Cinema', Stephanie Dennison & Song Hwee Lim (eds), *Remapping World Cinema*, pp. 30–7, p. 34.

[6] Nagib, p. 34.

[7] For a summary of this body of work see David Martin-Jones & Damian Sutton, *Deleuze Reframed* (London: I. B. Tauris, 2008), pp. 51–64.

[8] Laura U. Marks, *The Skin of the Film* (Durham, NC: Duke University Press, 2000); Hamid Naficy, *An Accented Cinema* (Princeton, NJ: Princeton University Press, 2001).

[9] Dudley Andrew, 'An Atlas of World Cinema', Stephanie Dennison & Song Hwee Lim (eds), *Remapping World Cinema*, pp. 19–29, p. 26.

[10] D. N. Rodowick, *Gilles Deleuze's Time Machine* (Durham, NC: Duke University Press, 1997), pp. 162–9; Patricia Pisters, *The Matrix of Visual Culture* (Stanford, CA: Stanford University Press, 2003), pp. 72–4 & p. 93

[11] Janice Tong, '*Chungking Express*', Chris Berry (ed.), *Chinese Films in Focus* (London: BFI, 2003), pp. 47–55.

[12] Shohini Chaudhuri & Howard Finn, 'The Open Image', *Screen*, 44: 1 (2003), pp. 38–57.

[13] Kenneth W. Harrow, 'Women with Open Eyes, Women of Stone and Hammers', Kenneth W. Harrow (ed.) *African Cinema* (Trenton, NJ & Asmara Eritrea: Africa World Press, Inc., 1999), pp. 225–40 and Kenneth W. Harrow, *Postcolonial African Cinema* (Bloomington, IN: Indiana University Press, 2007, pp. 115–39; Hamid Naficy, 'Veiled vision/powerful presences', Rose Issa & Sheila Whitaker (eds), *Life and Art* (London: BFI, 1999), pp. 44–65.

[14] Dudley Andrew, 'La réception américaine', François Dosse and Jean-Michel Frodon (eds), *Gilles Deleuze et les images* (Paris: Cahiers du cinéma, 2008), pp. 145–59.

[15] Gilles Deleuze, *Difference and Repetition*, trans. Paul Patton (London: Athlone, [1968] 1994), p. xxi.

[16] Jacques Rancière, *Film Fables*, trans. Emiliano Batista (Oxford: Berg [2001] 2006), pp. 107–23.

[17] Rosi Braidotti, 'The Becoming-Minoritarian of Europe', Ian Buchanan & Adrian Parr, *Deleuze and the Contemporary World* (Edinburgh: Edinburgh University Press, 2006), pp. 79–94, p. 79.

[18] Ibid., p. 80.

[19] Dipesh Chakrabarty, *Provincialising Europe* (Princeton & Oxford: Princeton University Press, 2000), pp. 5–6.

[20] D. N. Rodowick, *Reading the Figural* (Durham, NC: Duke University Press, 2001), pp. 170–202.

[21] Chakrabarty, p. 7.

[22] Gilles Deleuze, *Cinema 2*, trans. Hugh Tomlinson & Robert Galeta (London: Continuum, [1985] 2005), pp. 13–16.

[23] For an indepth discussion of Deleuze and Japanese cinema, see David Deamer, *The Spectre of Impossibility*. Unpublished Doctoral Thesis. (Manchester Metropolitan University, 2008

[24] Chakrabarty, pp. ix–xv.

[25] I am grateful to William Brown for this suggestion that the *Cinema* books be considered attempts to discover cinema's DNA.

[26] Ella Shohat & Robert Stam, *Unthinking Eurocentrism* (New York: Routledge, 1994).

[27] Walter D. Mignolo, *Local Histories/Global Designs* (Princeton: Princeton University Press, 2000), p. 279.

[28] Arjun Appadurai, *Modernity at Large* (Minneapolis: Minnesota University Press, 1996); Manuel Castells, *The Rise of the Network Society* (Oxford: Blackwell, 1996); Ulf Hannerz, *Transnational Connections* (London: Routledge, 1996); Zygmunt Bauman, *Globalization* (Cambridge: Polity, 1998); Michael Hardt & Antonio Negri, *Empire* (Cambridge, MA: Harvard University Press, 2000).

[29] Shohini Chaudhuri, *Contemporary World Cinema* (Edinburgh: Edinburgh University Press, 2005) p. 2.

Chapter 1

[1] Tom Gunning, 'The Cinema of Attractions', Thomas Elsaesser (ed.) *Early Cinema* (London: BFI, 1990), pp. 56–62.

[2] I draw this name from Gunning's 'Cinema of Attractions'. David Deamer refers to the period of 1896–1914 as that of the 'attraction image' in a diagram in his doctoral thesis: David Deamer, *The Spectre of Impossibility*. Unpublished Doctoral Thesis. (Manchester Metropolitan University, 2008), p. 562. My use of this term is different. It develops in relation to early silent film in the period 1895–1906/7, but is also applicable beyond that time. It should not be confused with Deleuze's 'attractional images', which refer to cinematic figures that function as metaphors (even though both Gunning and Deleuze are drawing upon Sergei Eisenstein's expression 'montage of attractions'). See Gilles Deleuze, *Cinema 1*, trans. Hugh Tomlinson & Barbara Habberjam (London: Continuum, [1983] 2005), p. 187 for 'attractional images', and pp. 33–42 for Deleuze's discussion of montage and

Eisenstein (on p. 37 he acknowledges the spectacular nature of attraction, but not in relation to the static shot early silent films I discuss after Gunning). Nor is my term the same as David Deamer's development of the category 'attraction-image', with regard to the relationship between the two forms of the action-image: David Deamer, 'Cinema, chronos/cronos', Jeffrey A. Bell & Claire Colebrook (eds), *Deleuze and History* (Edinburgh: Edinburgh University Press, 2009), pp. 161–87, p. 163 and p. 182.

3 John Mullarkey, *Refractions of Reality* (London: Palgrave Macmillan, 2009), pp. 97–100.

4 Ronald Bogue, *Deleuze on Cinema* (New York: Routledge, 2003), p. 3; Henri Bergson, *Matter and Memory* (New York: Zone Books, [1896] 1988), p. 9.

5 Bogue, p. 3 and pp. 11–39; Henri Bergson, *Creative Evolution,* trans. Arthur Mitchell (New York: Dover Publications Inc., [1907] 1998), p. 4.

6 Deleuze, *Cinema 1,* p. 1.

7 Ibid., p. 2.

8 Tom Gunning, 'Non-Continuity, Continuity, Discontinuity', Thomas Elsaesser (ed.) *Early Cinema*, pp. 86–94, p. 89.

9 Deleuze, *Cinema 1,* p. 3.

10 Deleuze, *Cinema 1,* p. 1.

11 Ibid., p. 8 and p. 13.

12 Ibid., p. 8.

13 Ibid., p. 61.

14 Ibid., p. 64.

15 Mullarkey, p. 89.

16 Deleuze, *Cinema 1,* p. 29.

17 Ibid., p. 32.

18 Ibid., p. 31.

19 Ibid.

20 Ibid.

21 Ibid., p. 32.

22 Ibid., p. 146.

23 Jacques Rancière, 'Entretien avec Jacques Rancière', *Cahiers du cinéma,* 268–9 (1976). Translated into English and reprinted as: Jacques Rancière, 'Interview: The Image of Brotherhood', *Edinburgh 77 Magazine* Vol. 2 (1977) pp. 26–31.

24 Deleuze, *Cinema 1,* p. 152.

25 Benedict Anderson, *Imagined Communities* (London: Verso, 1983), p. 6.

26 Deleuze, *Cinema 1,* pp. 153–5.

27 David Martin-Jones, *Deleuze, Cinema and National Identity* (Edinburgh: Edinburgh University Press, 2006), pp. 121–55.

28 Deleuze, *Cinema 1,* p. 32.

29 David Bordwell, Janet Staiger & Kristin Thompson, *The Classical Hollywood Cinema* (London: Routledge, 1985), pp. 128–53.

30 Laura Mulvey, 'Visual Pleasure and Narrative Cinema', Philip Rosen (ed.), *Narrative, Apparatus, Ideology* (New York: Columbia University Press, 1986), pp. 198–209.

31 Amy Herzog, 'Becoming-Fluid', D. N. Rodowick (ed.), *Afterimages of Gilles Deleuze's Film Philosophy* (Minneapolis, MN: Minnesota University Press, 2009), pp. 259–79, p. 260.

32 Gunning, 'The Cinema of Attractions', p. 56.

[33] Marshall Deutelbaum, 'Structural Patterning in the Lumière Films', John Fell (ed.) *Film Before Griffith* (Berkeley, CA: University of California Press, 1983), pp. 299–310; André Gaudreault, 'Film, Narrative, Narration, Elsaesser (ed.) *Early Cinema*, pp. 68–75.

[34] Noël Burch, 'A Primitive Mode of Representation?', Elsaesser (ed.) *Early Cinema*, pp. 220–7, p. 222.

[35] Tom Gunning, 'Now You see It, Now You Don't', Richard Abel (ed.), *Silent Film* (London: Athlone, 1996), pp. 71–84, pp. 80–1.

[36] Deleuze, *Cinema 1*, p. xi.

[37] Deleuze, *Cinema 1*, pp. 25–6.

[38] Ibid., p. 3.

[39] Ibid., p. 26.

[40] Ibid., p. 20.

[41] D. N. Rodowick, *Gilles Deleuze's Time Machine* (Durham, NC: Duke University Press, 1997), p. 214.

[42] Damian Sutton, *Photography, Cinema, Memory* (Minneapolis, MN: Minnesota University Press, 2009), p. 85.

[43] Gilles Deleuze, *Cinema 2: The Time-Image*, trans. Hugh Tomlinson & Robert Galeta (London: Continuum, [1985] 2005), p. xiii.

[44] Deleuze, *Cinema 2*, p. 56.

[45] Gunning concurs with Noël Burch's groundbreaking work on early silent cinema in which he discussed its 'unicity' of framing. Noël Burch, Primitivism and the Avant-Gardes', Rosen (ed.), *Narrative, Apparatus, Ideology*, pp. 483–506, p. 486.

[46] Tom Gunning, ' "Primitive Cinema" A Frame-up? Or The Trick's on Us', Elsaesser (ed.) *Early Cinema*, pp. 95–103, pp. 97–8.

[47] Gunning, 'Now You see It, Now You Don't', p. 81.

[48] Deleuze, *Cinema 1*, p. 15 & p. 30.

[49] Deleuze, *Cinema 1*, pp. 27–28; Deleuze, *Cinema 2*, pp. 102–112.

[50] Elizabeth Ezra, *Georges Méliès* (Manchester: Manchester University Press, 2000), p. 36.

[51] Deleuze, *Cinema 1*, p. 20 & 24; Deleuze, *Cinema 2*, p. 33.

[52] Gunning, 'Now You see It, Now You Don't', p. 80.

[53] Deleuze, *Cinema 1*, p. 172.

[54] Ezra, p. 117.

[55] Ibid., pp. 117–33.

[56] Ibid., p. 117.

[57] Gunning, ' "Primitive Cinema" A Frame-up? Or The Trick's on Us', p. 99.

[58] Gunning, 'The Cinema of Attractions', p. 60.

[59] Christopher Wagstaff, 'Italian Genre Films in the World Market', Geoffrey Nowell Smith & Steven Ricci (eds), *Hollywood and Europe* (London: BFI, 1998), pp. 74–85.

[60] Dimitris Eleftheriotis, *Popular Cinemas of Europe* (New York: Continuum, 2001), pp. 106–7.

[61] Ibid., p. 106.

[62] Richard Dyer & Ginette Vincendeau's *Popular European Cinema* (London: Routledge, 1992).

[63] Christopher Frayling, *Spaghetti Westerns* (London: I. B. Taurus, 1981), p. xxiii.

[64] Christopher Wagstaff, 'A Forkful of Westerns', in Richard Dyer & Ginette Vincendeau, *Popular European Cinema* (London: Routledge, 1992), pp. 245–61, pp. 249–51.

⁶⁵ Ibid., p. 253.

⁶⁶ Burch, Primitivism and the Avant-Gardes', p. 489.

⁶⁷ Wagstaff, 'A Forkful of Westerns', p. 253.

⁶⁸ Christopher Frayling, 'Django', *Monthly Film Bulletin*, 53: 635, pp. 55–6, p. 55.

⁶⁹ Maggie Günsberg notes the similarity between spaghetti westerns and the pre-cinematic origins of the western genre, in the comic strip and the Wild West shows of the late nineteenth century (Maggie Günsberg, *Italian Cinema* (New York: Palgrave Macmillan, 2005), p. 183), and Marcia Landy in the theatrical tradition of the comic opera (Marcia Landy, *Cinematic Uses of the Past* (Minnesota: University of Minnesota Press, 1996), p. 87.).

⁷⁰ James Chapman, *Cinemas of the World* (London: Reaktion Books, 2003), p. 293.

⁷¹ Eleftheriotis, p. 128.

⁷² Ibid., pp. 123–4.

⁷³ Ibid., pp. 126–7.

⁷⁴ Ibid., p. 124.

⁷⁵ Deleuze, *Cinema 1*, p. 172.

⁷⁶ Eleftheriotis, p. 122.

⁷⁷ Bogue, p. 91.

⁷⁸ Christopher Frayling, *Sergio Leone* (London: Faber & Faber, 2000), p. 309.

⁷⁹ Frayling, *Spaghetti Westerns*, p. 232.

⁸⁰ Howard Hughes, *Once Upon a Time in the Italian West* (London: I. B. Tauris, 2006), p. 100.

⁸¹ Henry Heller, *The Cold War and the New Imperialism* (New York: Monthly Review Press, 2006), pp. 193–238.

⁸² Ibid., pp. 214–18; Thomas Borstelmann, *The Cold War and the Colour Line* (Cambridge, MA: Harvard University Press, 2001), pp. 234–5.

⁸³ Greg Grandin, *The Last Colonial Massacre* (Chicago: University of Chicago Press, 2004), p. 174.

⁸⁴ Landy, *Cinematic Uses of the Past*, p. 82.

⁸⁵ Eleftheriotis, p. 115.

⁸⁶ Robert Stam & Louise Spence, 'Colonialism, Racism and Representation – An Introduction', *Screen*, 24: 2 (1983), pp. 2–20.

⁸⁷ Frayling, *Spaghetti Westerns*, pp. 192–216.

⁸⁸ Ken Nolley, 'The Representation of Conquest', Peter C. Rollins and John E. O'Connor (eds) *Hollywood's Indian* (Lexington: The University Press of Kentucky, 1998), pp. 73–90, p. 85.

⁸⁹ Heller, pp. 207–8.

⁹⁰ Eleftheriotis, p. 127.

⁹¹ Ibid., p. 115.

⁹² Talitha Espiritu, 'Multiculturalism, Dictatorship and Cinema Vanguards', Ella Shohat and Robert Stam (eds), *Multiculturalism, Postcoloniality, and Transnational Media* (New Brunswick: Rutgers University Press, 2003), pp. 279–98, p. 287.

⁹³ Zygmunt Bauman, *Globalization* (Cambridge: Polity, 1998), pp. 89–93.

⁹⁴ Neil Campbell, 'Forget the Alamo', Paul Grainge (ed.), *Memory and Popular Film* (Manchester: Manchester University Press, 2003), pp. 162–79, pp. 166–7.

⁹⁵ Interview on the Argent Films Ltd DVD, *Keoma* (2008).

⁹⁶ Deleuze, *Cinema 2*, p. 96.

Chapter 2

[1] This expression does not refer to Deleuze and Guattari's work on the novella, Gilles Deleuze and Félix Guattari. *A Thousand Plateaus* trans. Brian Massumi (London: Athlone, [1980] 1987), pp. 192–207.

[2] For a discussion of the Bergsonian distinction between the virtual past that is and the actualized past that was in relation to national identity, see: David Martin-Jones, *Deleuze, Cinema and National Identity* (Edinburgh: Edinburgh University Press, 2006), pp. 50–84.

[3] Michael J. Lazzara, 'Filming Loss', *Latin American Perspectives,* 36: 5 (2009), pp. 147–57, p. 148; Alison Landsberg, 'Prosthetic Memory', Paul Grainge (ed.), *Memory and Popular Film* (Manchester: Manchester University Press, 2003), pp. 144–61; Robert Burgoyne, *Film Nation*, Revised Edition (Minneapolis, MN: Minnesota University Press, 2010), pp. 104–19.

[4] Gilles Deleuze, *Cinema 1* (London: Continuum, [1983] 2005), p. 209.

[5] Ibid., p. 210.

[6] Ibid., p. 212.

[7] Ibid., pp. 209–15.

[8] Ibid., p. 214.

[9] Ibid., p. 216.

[10] Gilles Deleuze, *Cinema 2* (London: Continuum, [1985] 2005), p. 2.

[11] Ibid., p. 6.

[12] Ibid., p. 2.

[13] Ibid., p. 3.

[14] Ibid., p. 6.

[15] Ibid., p. 17.

[16] Ibid., p. 4.

[17] Ibid., p. xi.

[18] Ibid., p. 19.

[19] André Bazin, 'Germany Year Zero', Bert Cardullo (ed.) *Bazin at Work* (New York: Routledge, 1997). pp. 121–4, p. 121; Marina Werner, 'Through a Child's Eyes', Duncan Petrie (ed.) *Cinema and the Realms of Enchantment* (London: BFI, 1993), pp. 36–62, p. 42.

[20] Karen Lury, *The Child in Film* (London: I. B.Tauris, 2010), p. 109.

[21] Paul Sutton, 'The *bambino negato* or missing child of contemporary Italian cinema', *Screen*, 46: 3 (2005), pp. 353–72, pp. 357–8.

[22] Peter Bondanella, *The Films of Roberto Rossellini* (Cambridge: Cambridge University Press, 1993), pp. 45–63; Julia Hallam with Margaret Marshment, *Realism and Popular Cinema* (Manchester: Manchester University Press, 2000), p. 40

[23] Rosalind Galt, *The New European Cinema* (New York: Columbia University Press, 2006), p. 190.

[24] For example, a Deleuzian analysis of post-war rubble films that stresses their reconstruction of post-war masculinities: Jaimey Fisher, 'On the Ruins of Masculinity', Laura E. Ruberto & Kristi M. Wilson (eds), *Italian Neorealism and Global Cinema* (Detroit, MI: Wayne State University Press, 2007), pp. 25–53, p. 47.

[25] Emma Wilson, 'Children, Emotion and Viewing in Contemporary European Cinema', *Screen*, 46: 3 (2005), pp. 329–340, p. 330.

[26] Ibid., p. 331.

[27] Dimitris Eleftheriotis, 'Early Cinema As Child', *Screen*, 46: 3 (2005), pp. 315–28, p. 317.

[28] Thomas Elsaesser, *European Cinema* (Amsterdam: Amsterdam University Press, 2005), p. 509.

[29] Rob Stone, *Spanish Cinema* (Essex: Pearson Education Ltd, 2002), p. 89.

[30] Paul Julian Smith, 'Between Metaphysics and Scientism', Peter William Evans (ed.), *Spanish Cinema* (Manchester: Manchester University Press, 1999), pp. 93–114, p. 100.

[31] Diana Taylor, *Disappearing Acts* (Durham: Duke University Press, 1997), pp. 139–82.

[32] Catherine Grant, 'Still Moving Images', Alex Hughes & Andrea Noble (eds), *Phototextualities* (Alberquerque: University of New Mexico Press, 2003), pp. 63–86, p. 66.

[33] Ibid., p. 67.

[34] Deleuze, *Cinema 2*, p. 52.

[35] Ibid.

[36] Interview on Argentine Home Video DVD (2007).

[37] Herman Melville, *Moby Dick* (London: Penguin [1851], 1994), p. 70.

[38] Interview on Argentine Home Video DVD (2007).

[39] H.I.J.O.S website: http://www.hijos-capital.org.ar/ (20/11/08).

[40] Constanza Burucúa, *Confronting the 'Dirty War' in Argentine Cinema, 1983–1993* (Woodbridge: Tamesis, 2009), pp. 4–5.

[41] Ibid., p. 166.

[42] John King, 'María Luisa Bemberg and Argentine Culture, John King, Sheila Whitaker, Rosa Bosch (eds), *An Argentine Passion* (London: Verso, 2000), pp. 1–32, p. 23.

[43] Burucúa, p. 165.

[44] David Pion-Berlin, *The Ideology of State Terror* (Boulder: Lynne Reinner, 1989), pp. 47–60.

[45] Nick Caistor, 'Argentina: 1976–1983', John King & Nissa Torrents (eds), *The Garden of Forking Paths* (London: British Film Institute, 1987), pp. 81–91, p. 82.

[46] Luis Alberto Romero, *Argentina in the Twentieth Century* (Pennsylvania, PA: Pennsylvania State University Press, 2002), pp. 221–30; Pion-Berlin, pp. 111–23; Laura Tedesco, *Democracy in Argentina* (London: Frank Cass, 1999), pp. 23–46.

[47] Different figures exist, placing the number somewhere between 30 per cent and 37 per cent. Tedesco, p. 27 – 30 per cent; Patricia Marchak, *God's Assassins* (Montreal and Kingston: McGill-Queen's University Press, 1999), p. 155 – 37 per cent.

[48] Romero, p. 319.

[49] Ibid., p. 320.

[50] Pion-Berlin, p. 105.

[51] Tedesco, p. 169.

[52] Ibid., p. 157.

[53] Ibid., pp. 171–3.

[54] Romero, p. 231.

[55] Ibid., p. 324; Pion-Berlin, p. 98 and p. 111.

[56] Carlos H. Waisman, 'Argentina', Larry Diamond et al. (eds), *Democracy in Developing Countries* (Boulder: Lynne Rienner, 1999), pp. 71–130.

[57] Romero, pp. 285–96; Tedesco, pp. 82–7.

[58] Romero, p. 218.

[59] Joanna Page, *Crisis and Capitalism in Contemporary Argentine Cinema* (Durham, NC: Duke University Press, 2009), pp. 180–94.

[60] David William Foster, 'Family Romance and Pathetic Rhetoric', Deborah Shaw (ed.) *Contemporary Latin American Cinema* (New York: Rowman and Littlefield, 2007), pp. 105–16, p. 105.

[61] Luisela Alvaray, 'National, Regional, and Global', *Cinema Journal*, 47: 3 (2008), pp. 48–65.

[62] Ibid., p. 55.

[63] Tamara L. Falicov, *The Cinematic Tango* (London: Wallflower, 2007), pp. 102–3.

[64] Anna Marie de la Fuente, 'Latin Lovers', *Screen International*, 1435 (2004), pp. 12–14, p. 14.

[65] Foster, 'Family Romance and Pathetic Rhetoric', p. 113.

[66] Ibid., p. 114.

[67] Carlos H. Waisman, 'Argentina', Larry Diamond et al. (eds), *Democracy in Developing Countries* (Boulder: Lynne Rienner, 1999), pp. 71–130.

[68] Pion-Berlin, p. 119; Tedesco, p. 37, p. 56 and p. 172.

[69] Tedesco, p. 172.

[70] For an introduction to terms such as 'imperfect cinema', 'third cinema' and an 'esthetic of hunger': Michael T. Martin (ed.), *New Latin American Cinema: Volume One* (Detroit, MI: Wayne State University Press, 1997)

[71] Foster, 'Family Romance and Pathetic Rhetoric', p. 114.

[72] Burucúa, pp. 72–191.

[73] David Harvey, *A Brief History of Neoliberalism* (Oxford: Oxford University Press, 2005), pp. 118–19.

[74] Walter D. Mignolo, *Local Histories/Global Designs* (Princeton, NJ: Princeton University Press, 2000), p. 279.

[75] John King, *Magical Reels* (London: Verso, 2000), p. 90.

[76] Greg Grandin, *The Last Colonial Massacre* (Chicago, IL: Chicago University Press, 2004), p. 188.

[77] Mark Jancovich, *Rational Fears* (Manchester: Manchester University Press, 1996), p. 2..

[78] Phil Powrie, 'On the Threshold Between Past and Present', Justine Ashby & Andrew Higson (eds), *British Cinema, Past and Present* (London: Routledge, 2000), pp. 316–26, p. 323.

[79] Eduardo Rojas, 'Canto castrato', *El Amante Cine*, 127 (2002), pp. 29.

Chapter 3

[1] Gilles Deleuze, *Cinema 1*, trans. Hugh Tomlinson & Barbara Habberjam (London: Continuum, [1983] 2005), p. 153.

[2] Friedrich Nietzsche, *Untimely Meditations*, trans. R. J. Hollingdale (Cambridge: Cambridge University Press, 1997), p. 68.

[3] Deleuze, *Cinema 1*, p. 155.

[4] Ibid., pp. 244–5, n. 13.

[5] Gilles Deleuze, *Cinema 2*, trans. Hugh Tomlinson & Robert Galeta (London: Continuum, [1985] 2005), p. 208.

[6] For a discussion of the emergence of this term see David Martin-Jones, *Deleuze, Cinema and National Identity* (Edinburgh: Edinburgh University Press, 2006), p. 6.

[7] Deleuze, *Cinema 2*, p. 213.

[8] Ibid., p. 173.

[9] Ibid., p. 162 and p. 174.

[10] Ibid., p. 207.

[11] Ibid., pp. 207–15.

[12] Gilles Deleuze, *The Fold*, trans. Tom Conley (London: Athlone, [1988] 1993), p. 3.

[13] Ibid., p. 62.

[14] David Rodowick, *Gilles Deleuze's Time Machine* (Durham, NC: Duke University Press, 1997), 221, n. 6; Tom Conley, 'The Film Event', Gregory Flaxman (ed.), *The Brain is the Screen* (Minneapolis, MN: University of Minnesota Press, 2000), pp. 303–25, pp. 315–17.

[15] Michael Goddard, 'The Fold', Thomas Lamarre & Kang Nae-hui (eds) *Impacts of Modernities* (Hong Kong: Hong Kong University Press, 2004), pp. 209–28, p. 224.

[16] Timothy Murray, *Digital Baroque* (Minneapolis, MN: University of Minnesota Press, 2008), p. 239.

[17] Giuliana Bruno, 'Pleats of Matter, Folds of the Soul', D. N. Rodowick (ed.), *Afterimages of Gilles Deleuze's Film Philosophy* (Minneapolis, MN: Minnesota University Press, 2009), pp. 213–33, p. 213.

[18] Ronald Bogue, *Deleuze on Cinema* (New York: Routledge, 2003), p. 198.

[19] Ibid., p. 182.

[20] Laura U. Marks, 'Invisible Media,' Anna Everett & John T. Caldwell (eds), *New Media* (New York: Routledge, 2003), pp. 33–46; Laura U. Marks, 'Information, Secrets, and Enigmas', *Screen*, 50: 1 (2009), pp. 86–98.

[21] Laura U. Marks, 'Experience – Information – Image', Dina Iordanova, David Martin-Jones and Belén Vidal (eds), *Cinema at the Periphery* (Detroit, MI: Wayne State University Press, 2010), pp. 232–53.

[22] Scott Nygren, *Time Frames* (Minneapolis, MN: Minnesota University Press, 2007), pp. 99–114.

[23] Ibid., p. 111.

[24] Rodowick, p. 177.

[25] Ibid., p. 178.

[26] Kyung Hyun Kim, *The Remasculinization of Korean Cinema* (Durham, NC: Duke University Press, 2004), p. 270.

[27] Chi-Yun Shin & Julian Stringer (eds), *New Korean Cinema* (Edinburgh: Edinburgh University Press, 2005); Frances Gateward (ed.), *Seoul Searching* (New York: State University of New York Press, 2007).

[28] Kyung-Sup Chang, 'Compressed Modernity and its Discontents', *Economy and Society*, 28: 1 (1999), pp. 30–55, p. 30.

[29] David Martin-Jones, *Deleuze, Cinema and National Identity* (Edinburgh: Edinburgh University Press, 2006), pp. 205–19.

[30] David Martin-Jones, 'Traces of Time in *Traces of Love* (2006)', *Asian Cinema*, 18: 2 (2007), pp. 252–70.

[31] Anthony Leong (2002), *Korean Cinema* (Victoria: Trafford Publishing, 2002), pp. 117–54.

[32] Art Black, 'Coming of Age', Steven Jay Schneider (ed.), *Fear Without Frontiers* (London: FAB Press, 2003), pp. 185–203, p. 190.

[33] Chang, p. 48.

[34] Official figures state approximately 200, while unofficial estimates range up to 2000.

[35] McHugh & Abelmann, 'Introduction', McHugh & Abelmann (eds) *South Korean Golden Age Melodrama*, (Detroit, MI: Wayne State University Press, 2005), pp. 1–15, p. 13.

[36] Ibid., p. 2.

[37] John Mercer & Martin Schingler, *Melodrama* (London: Wallflower, 2004), p. 97.

[38] Abelmann, *The Melodrama of Mobility* (Honolulu: University of Hawaii Press, 2003), p. 23.

[39] McHugh & Abelmann, 'Introduction', McHugh & Abelmann (eds) *South Korean Golden Age Melodrama*, p. 4.

[40] Hae-joang Cho Han, 'You Are Trapped in an Imaginary Well', *Inter Asia Cultural Studies*, 1: 1 (2000), pp. 49–69, p. 51

[41] Abelmann, *The Melodrama of Mobility*, p. 10.

[42] Chang, p. 31.

[43] David Martin-Jones, *Deleuze, Cinema and National Identity* (Edinburgh: Edinburgh University Press, 2006), p. 113.

[44] Chang, p. 31.

[45] Seungsook Moon, *Militarized Modernity and Gendered Citizenship in South Korea* (Durham, NC: Duke University Press, 2005), p. 102.

[46] Ibid.

[47] Laura Kendall, 'Introduction', Laura Kendall (ed.), *Under Construction* (Honolulu: University of Hawaii Press, 2002), pp. 1–24, p. 17.

[48] Seungsook Moon, 'The Production and Subversion of Hegemonic Masculinity', Kendall (ed.), *Under Construction*, pp. 79–113, p. 79.

[49] Cho, 'You Are Trapped in an Imaginary Well', p. 63.

[50] Ibid.

[51] Deleuze, *Cinema 2*, p. 46.

[52] Moon, *Militarized Modernity*, p. 68.

[53] Ibid., p. 44.

[54] Cho, 'You Are Trapped in an Imaginary Well", p. 62.

[55] Moon, 'The Production and Subversion of Hegemonic Masculinity', p. 84.

[56] Cho, 'You Are Trapped in an Imaginary well', p. 62.

[57] Soyoung Kim, 'The birth of the local feminist sphere in the global era', *Inter Asia Cultural Studies*, 4: 1 (2003), pp. 10–24, pp. 17–18.

[58] Ibid., p. 17.

[59] Moon, *Militarized Modernity*, p. 148.

[60] Ibid., p. 180.

[61] Kendall, 'Introduction', Kendall (ed), *Under Construction*, p. 14; and, Moon, 'The Production and Subversion of Hegemonic Masculinity', pp. 80–81.

[62] Seungsook Moon, 'Begetting the Nation', Elaine H. Kim and Chungmoo Choi (eds), *Dangerous Women* (London: Routledge, 1998), pp. 33–66, p. 53.

[63] Moon, *Militarized Modernity*, pp. 158–159.

[64] Ibid., p. 163.

[65] So-hee Lee, 'Female Sexuality in Popular Culture', Kendall (ed.), *Under Construction*, pp. 141–64, p. 158.

[66] Kim, 'Lethal Work', p. 203. .

[67] Haejoang Cho, 'Living with Conflicting Subjectivities', Kendall (ed.), *Under Construction*, pp. 165–95, p. 190.

[68] Chris Berry, 'What's Big About the Big Film?', Julian Stringer (ed.) *Movie Blockbusters* (London: Routledge, 2003), p. 224.

[69] Darcy Paquet, 'Resurrection of the Korean Blockbuster', *Screen International*, 1422 (2003), pp. 12–13, p. 13.

[70] Leong, *Korean Cinema*, p. 13.

[71] Jan Noh, 'KOFIC to send Korean filmmakers overseas', *Screen Daily Stories*, (19/04/06), http://www.screendaily.com/story.asp?storyid=25878&tl=True (19/04/06)

[72] Darcy Paquet, 'International Production', *Screen International*, 1347 (2002), 19.

[73] Darcy Paquet, 'Korean Film Newsletter', 13 (2002), http://www.koreanfilm.org/news14.html and Darcy Paquet, 'Korean Film Newsletter', 14 (2002), http://www.koreanfilm.org/news13.html (21/12/09).

Chapter 4

[1] David Martin-Jones, *Deleuze, Cinema and National Identity* (Edinburgh: Edinburgh University Press, 2006), pp. 128–9.

[2] Gilles Deleuze, *Cinema 1*, trans. Hugh Tomlinson & Barbara Habberjam (London: Continuum, [1983] 2005), p. 112.

[3] Ibid., p. 99.

[4] Gilles Deleuze, *Cinema 2*, trans. Hugh Tomlinson & Robert Galeta (London: Continuum, [1985] 2005), p. xi.

[5] Deleuze, *Cinema 1*, pp. 100–1.

[6] Claire Colebrook, *Deleuze* (London: Continuum, 2006), p. 58.

[7] Deleuze, *Cinema 1*, p. 113.

[8] Ibid., p. 106.

[9] Ibid., p. 114.

[10] D. N. Rodowick, *Gilles Deleuze's Time Machine* (Durham, NC: Duke University Press, 1997), pp. 65–6.

[11] Ibid., p. 66.

[12] Ronald Bogue, *Deleuze on Cinema* (London: Routledge, 2003), p. 80.

[13] Deleuze, *Cinema 1*, p. 114.

[14] Ibid., pp. 122–6.

[15] Ibid., p. 123.

[16] Ibid.

[17] Ibid., p. 124.

[18] Ibid., p. 212 and p. 216.

[19] Rodowick, *Gilles Deleuze's Time Machine*, p. 73.

[20] Deleuze, *Cinema 2*, p. 56.

[21] Ibid., p. 5.

22 Ibid., p. 4.

23 Ibid., p. 17.

24 Ibid., p. 19.

25 Ackbar Abbas, *Hong Kong* (Minnesota: Minnesota University Press, 1997), p. 1.

26 Ibid., p. 7.

27 Ibid., p. 3.

28 Martin-Jones, *Deleuze, Cinema and National Identity*, pp. 188–95.

29 Abbas, p. 49.

30 Ibid., p. 49

31 Ibid., pp. 25–6.

32 Ibid., p. 62.

33 Julian Stringer, 'Your Tender Smiles Give Me Strength" *Screen*, 38: 1 (1997), pp. 25–41; Abbas, p. 34.

34 Jenny Kwok Wah Lau, 'Besides Fists and Blood', Poshek Fu & David Desser, *The Cinema of Hong Kong* (Cambridge: Cambridge University Press, 2000), pp. 158–75, p. 162.

35 Ka-Fai Yau, 'Cinema 3', *Cultural Studies*, 15: 3–4 (2001), pp. 543–63.

36 Stephen Chan Ching-kiu, 'The Fighting Condition in Hong Kong Cinema', Meaghan Morris, Siu Leung Li & Stephen Chan Ching-kiu (eds) *Hong Kong Connections* (Durham, NC: Duke University Press, 2005), pp. 63–80; Esther C. M. Yau, 'Introduction', Esther C.M. Yau (ed.) *At Full Speed* (Minneapolis, MN: University of Minnesota Press, 2001), pp. 1–30; Kwai-cheung Lo, 'Transnationalization of the Local in Hong Kong Cinema of the 1990s', in Yau (ed.), pp. 261–76.

37 David Harvey, *A Brief History of Neoliberalism* (Oxford: Oxford University Press, 2005), p. 120.

38 Ibid., pp. 120–51.

39 Martin-Jones, *Deleuze, Cinema and National Identity*, pp. 85–120.

40 Laura U. Marks, *The Skin of the Film* (Durham, NC: Duke University Press, 2000), p. 27.

41 Mark Shiel, 'Cinema and the City in History and Theory', in Mark Shiel & Tony Fitzmaurice (eds), *Cinema and the City* (Oxford: Blackwell, 2001), pp. 1–18, p. 12.

42 Martine Beugnet, *Cinema and Sensation* (Edinburgh: Edinburgh University Press, 2007), p. 143.

43 Ibid., pp. 150–1.

44 Ibid., pp. 143–4.

45 Marc Augé, *Non-Places*, trans. John Howe (London: Verso, 1995). Deleuze attributes the any-space-whatever to Pascal Augé, creating some confusion over whether there are one or two Augés. See: www.langlab.wayne.edu/CStivale/D-G/DuellingAuge.html (04/05/09). Although the two ideas are quite similar, despite Réda Bensmaïa's confidence in linking Augé's non-places and Deleuze's any-space-whatever (Réda Bensmaïa, 'L'espace quelconque comme personage conceptuel', *iris*, 23 (1997), pp. 25–35) and although Deleuze would presumably have been aware of Marc Augé's work, it seems likely that Deleuze was drawing on the work of Pascal Auger. The website for Paris VIII (Deleuze's former employer) suggests that Pascal Auger was a student of Deleuze's: http://www.univ-paris8.fr/deleuze/article.php3?id_article=174 (03/07/09).

46 Augé, *Non-Places*, pp. 31–2.

[47] Ibid., p. 34 and p. 78.

[48] Marc Augé, *A Sense for the Other*, trans Amy Jacobs (Stanford, CA: Stanford University Press, 1998), p. 105.

[49] Ian Buchanan, 'Space in the Age of Non-Place', Ian Buchanan & Gregg Lambert (eds), *Deleuze and Space* (Edinburgh: Edinburgh University Press, 2005), pp. 16–35, p. 28.

[50] Deleuze, *Cinema 2*, p. 4.

[51] Mike Featherstone, 'Localism, Globalism and Cultural Identity', Rob Wilson & Wimal Dissanayake (eds), *Global/Local* (Durham, NC: Duke University Press, 1996), pp. 46–77, p. 46; Roland Robertson, 'Glocalization', Mike Featherstone & Scott Lash (eds), *Global Modernities* (London: Sage, 1995), pp. 25–44, p. 40.

[52] David Morley & Kevin Robins, *Spaces of Identity* (London: Routledge, 1995), p. 116.

[53] Deleuze, *Cinema 1*, p. 90.

[54] Rodowick, *Gilles Deleuze's Time Machine*, p. 70.

[55] Deleuze, *Cinema 1*, pp. 164–81.

[56] Ibid., pp. 164–9.

[57] David Bordwell, *Planet Hong Kong* (Cambridge, MA: Harvard University Press, 2000), pp. 180–185.

[58] David Bordwell, 'Aesthetics in Action', Esther C. M. Yau (ed.) *At Full Speed*, pp. 73–94, p. 78.

[59] Deleuze, *Cinema 1*, p. 124.

[60] Steve Tsang, *A Modern History of Hong Kong* (London: I. B. Tauris, 2007), p. 189 and p. 199.

[61] Ibid., p. 188.

[62] Ibid., p. 175.

[63] Ibid., pp. 175–9.

[64] Ibid., p. 274.

[65] David Petersen & Elfed Vaughan Roberts, 'The Hong Kong Business Environment Since 1997', Robert Ash, Peter Ferdinand, Brian Hook & Robin Porter (eds), *Hong Kong in Transition* (London: RoutledgeCurzon, 2003), pp. 13–33, p. 14.

[66] Tsang, p. 175.

[67] Gary McDonogh & Cindy Wong, *Global Hong Kong* (London: Routledge, 2005), p. 90.

[68] Saskia Sassen, *The Global City* (Princeton: Princeton University Press, 1991), p. 9 and pp. 197–244; Saskia Sassen, *Cities in a World Economy* (Thousand Oaks, CA: Pine Forge Press, 1994), pp. 99–117; Saskia Sassen, *Globalization and its Discontents* (New York: The New Press, 1998), pp. 137–51.

[69] David Harvey, *A Brief History of Neoliberalism* (Oxford: Oxford University Press, 2005), pp. 118–119; David Harvey, *The Spaces of Global Capitalism* (London: Verso, 2006), p. 31.

[70] Robert H. Wade, 'Should We Worry about Income Inequality', David Held & Ayse Kaya (eds), *Global Inequality* (Cambridge: Polity Press, 2007), pp. 104–31, p. 124.

[71] Ibid., p. 110.

[72] Tsang, p. 192.

[73] Lok Sang Ho & Robert Ash, 'Introduction', in Lok Sang Ho & Robert Ash (eds), *China, Hong Kong and the World Economy* (London: Palgrave, 2006), pp. 1–16, p. 1.

[74] James K. Galbraith, 'Global Inequality and Global Macro Economics', Held & Kaya (eds), *Global Inequality*, pp. 148–75, p. 153; Harvey, *A Brief History of Neoliberalism*, pp. 123–51; Tsang, p. 245.

[75] Galbraith, p. 153.

[76] Kui-yin Cheung & C. Simon Fan, 'Economic Integration between Hong Kong and Mainland China', in Ho & Ash (eds), *China, Hong Kong and the World Economy*, pp. 186–99, p. 188.

[77] Tsang, p. 178; McDonogh & Wong, p. 95.

[78] McDonogh & Wong, p. 92.

[79] Cheung & Fan, p. 189.

[80] Mike Davis, *Planet of Slums* (London: Verso, 2006), pp. 20–49.

[81] Ibid., p. 63.

[82] Tsang, p. 199.

[83] McDonogh & Wong, p. 98.

[84] John K. Keung, 'Government Intervention and Housing Policy in Hong Kong', *Third World Planning Review*, 7: 1 (1985), pp. 23–44, p. 39.

[85] Ibid., pp. 30–1.

[86] Ibid., p. 40.

[87] McDonogh & Wong, p. 96.

[88] Ibid., pp. 98–9.

[89] Gina Marchetti, *Andrew Lau and Alan Mak's Infernal Affairs – The Trilogy* (Hong Kong: Hong Kong University Press, 2007), pp. 66–75.

[90] D. J. Dwyer & V. F. S. Sit, 'Small-Scale Industries and Problems of Urban and Regional Planning', *Third World Planning Review*, 8: 2 (1986), pp. 99–120, p. 107, p. 112 and p. 115; McDonogh & Wong, p. 98.

[91] Michael J. Shapiro, *Cinematic Geopolitics* (London: Routledge, 2009), p. 10.

[92] Ibid., p. 11.

[93] Ibid.

[94] Mark Gallagher, *Action Figures* (New York: Palgrave Macmillan, 2006), p. 180.

[95] Bordwell, *Planet Hong Kong*, p. 58.

[96] Steve Fore, 'Jackie Chan and the Cultural Dynamics of Global Entertainment', Sheldon Hsiao-peng Lu (ed.), *Transnational Chinese Cinemas* (Honolulu: University of Hawai'i Press, 1997), pp. 239–62, pp. 243–4.

[97] Yingchi Chu, *Hong Kong Cinema* (London: Routledge, 2003), p. 81.

[98] Ramie Tateishi, 'Jackie Chan and the Reinvention of Tradition', *Asian Cinema*, 10: 1 (1998), pp. 78–84, p. 78.

[99] Fore, 'Jackie Chan and the Cultural Dynamics of Global Entertainment', p. 242.

[100] Ibid., p. 247.

[101] Steve Fore, 'Life Imitates Entertainment', Yau (ed.) *At Full Speed*, pp. 115–41, p. 128.

[102] Kenneth Chan, 'Mimicry as Failure', *Asian Cinema*, 15: 2 (2004), pp. 84–97, p. 85.

[103] This stunt was potentially fatal, as the lights were not rigged to a low voltage source as they should have been, and Chan was lucky to escape with only skinned hands. Fredric Dannen & Barry Long, *Hong Kong Babylon* (London: Faber & Faber, 1997), pp. 19–20.

Chapter 5

[1] Gilles Deleuze, *Cinema 2*, trans. Hugh Tomlinson & Robert Galeta (London: Continuum, [1985] 2005), p. 56.

[2] David Martin-Jones, *Deleuze, Cinema and National Identity* (Edinburgh: Edinburgh University Press, 2006), pp. 5–10.

[3] D. N. Rodowick, *Gilles Deleuze's Time Machine* (New York: Duke University Press, 1997), p. xiv.

[4] Tom Ambrose, 'L.A. Story', *Empire*, 221 (2007), pp. 152–60, p. 157.

[5] Peter Mitchell, 'When Dion met Michael', *Inside Film*, 70 (2004), pp. 26–7, p. 26.

[6] F. X. Feeney & Paul Duncan (eds), *Michael Mann* (Los Angeles: Taschen, 2006), pp. 160–3.

[7] Nick James, *Heat* (London: BFI, 2002), p. 9, p. 13, p. 26.

[8] Peter Galvin, 'Collateral', *Inside Film*, 70 (2004), p. 63.

[9] Mark Olsen, 'It Happened One Night', *Sight and Sound*, 14: 10 (2004), pp. 14–15, p. 15.

[10] Richard T. Kelly, 'Collateral', *Sight and Sound*, 14: 10 (2004), p. 50.

[11] Michael J. Anderson, 'Before Sunrise, or Los Angeles Plays Itself in a Lonely Place', *Senses of Cinema*, 33 (2004): http://archive.sensesofcinema.com/contents/04/33/collateral.html (29/06/09)

[12] Feeney & Duncan, p. 81.

[13] James, pp. 67–8.

[14] Feeney & Duncan, p. 99.

[15] Gilles Deleuze, *Cinema 1*, trans. Hugh Tomlinson & Barbara Habberjam (London: Continuum, [1983] 2005), p. 170.

[16] Ibid., p. 172.

[17] Ibid., pp. 149–50.

[18] Ibid., p. 168.

[19] Mark Bould, *Film Noir* (London: Wallflower, 2005), p. 29.

[20] Previously I noted the reterritorializing force of a national narrative in contemporary US action-images. Martin-Jones, *Deleuze, Cinema and National Identity*, pp. 121–87.

[21] Deleuze, *Cinema 2*, p. 66.

[22] Ibid., p. 66.

[23] Ibid., pp. 66–94.

[24] Ibid., p. 72 and p. 79.

[25] Ibid., pp. 67–9.

[26] Ronald Bogue, *Deleuze on Cinema* (New York: Routledge, 2003), p. 124.

[27] Ibid., pp. 132–3.

[28] Rodowick, *Gilles Deleuze's Time Machine*, p. 73.

[29] Deleuze, *Cinema 2*, p. 70.

[30] Ibid., p. 71.

[31] Ibid.

[32] Ibid.

[33] Ibid., pp. 82–3.

[34] Deleuze, *Cinema 1*, p. 43,

[35] Deleuze, *Cinema 2*, p. 69.

[36] Deleuze, *Cinema 1*, p. 146.

37 Ibid., p. 145.

38 Mike Davis, *City of Quartz* (London: Verso, [1990] 2006), p. vi.

39 'By 1992, the L.A. Customs District, once a trade backwater, was handling $122 billion in global trade, dramatically up from $6.2 billion in 1972.' Steven P. Erie, *Globalizing L.A.* (Stanford: Stanford University Press, 2004), p. 77.

40 Davis, *City of Quartz*, p. vii.

41 Ibid., pp. 135–8.

42 Erie, p. 9.

43 Ibid., p. 11.

44 Ibid., p. xi and p. 5.

45 Ibid., p. 4.

46 Ibid., p. 78.

47 Edward W. Soja, *Postmodern Geographies* (London: Verso, 1989), p. 193.

48 Davis, *City of Quartz*, p. 129.

49 Ibid., p. xiv.

50 Ibid., p. 230.

51 Ibid., pp. 223–63.

52 Ibid., p. 252.

53 Erie, p. 116.

54 Martine Beugnet, *Cinema and Sensation* (Edinburgh: Edinburgh University Press, 2007), pp. 143–144.

55 Ibid., p. 165.

56 Soja, p. 222.

57 Edward Dimendberg, *Film Noir and the Spaces of Modernity* (Cambridge, MA: Harvard University Press, 2004), pp. 102–8 & pp. 172–206.

58 Alain Silver & James Ursini, *L.A. Noir* (Santa Monica: Santa Monica Press, 2005), p. 132.

59 James Naremore, *More than Night* (Berkeley, CA: University of California Press, 1998), p. 220.

60 Silver & Ursini, p. 133.

61 Ibid., p. 134.

62 Erie, p. 23.

63 In 1994 LAX claimed it was responsible for $43 billion in economic activity, around 10 per cent of the output of the entire region, and by 2001, LAX would become the 'world's third busiest passenger and fourth busiest air-cargo facility.' Erie, p. 173 and p. 14.

64 Ibid., p. 117.

65 Davis, *City of Quartz*, p. 251.

66 Norman M. Klein, *The History of Forgetting* (London: Verso, 1998), pp. 263–91.

67 James, p. 34.

68 Feeney & Duncan, p. 99; Ambrose, p. 159.

69 Les Paul Robley, 'Hot Set', *American Cinematographer*, 77: 1 (1996), pp. 46–50, p. 47.

70 Simon Gray, 'Tricks of the Trade', *American Cinematographer*, 84: 6 (2003), pp. 121–2, p. 121.

71 Silver & Ursini, p. 132.

72 Robley, p. 48.

[73] Beugnet, p. 8.

[74] Ibid., p. 61.

[75] Thom Andersen, 'Collateral Damage', *Cinemascope*, 20 (2004), pp. 48–51, p. 51. Mann notes that his expressive use of locations rendered the geography askew, for instance when he situated El Rodeo amidst oil refineries nearby San Pedro and Wilmington: Mark Olsen, 'Paint it Black', *Sight and Sound*, 14: 10 (2004), pp. 16–17, p. 16.

[76] Deleuze, *Cinema 2*, p. 86.

[77] Deleuze, *Cinema 1*, p. 172.

[78] Klein, p. 79.

[79] Davis, p. 104.

[80] Elana Zilberg, '*Falling Down* in *El Norte*', *Wide Angle*, 20: 3 (1998), pp. 182–09; Jude Davies, 'Gender, ethnicity and cultural crisis in *Falling Down* and *Groundhog Day*', *Screen* 36: 3 (1995): 214–32.

[81] Dave Hare, 'The Shape of Light', *Metro*, 155 (2007), pp. 134–40, p. 137.

[82] Peter Mitchell, 'When Dion met Michael', pp. 26–7, p. 26–7.

[83] Andersen, *Collateral Damage*, p. 51.

[84] Jay Holben, 'Hell on Wheels', *American Cinematographer*, 85: 8 (2004), pp. 40–51, p. 46.

[85] Dave Hare, 'The Shape of Light', *Metro*, 155 (2007), pp. 134–40, p. 138.

[86] Holben, pp. 46–7.

[87] Deleuze, *Cinema 1*, p. 127.

[88] Mitchell, p. 27.

[89] Deleuze, *Cinema 2*, p. 71.

[90] David H. Fleming, '*Drugs, Danger, Delusions (and Deleuzians?)*' Unpublished Doctoral Thesis (University of St Andrews, 2009), pp. 218–19.

Chapter 6

[1] 'Bollywood' specifically refers to Hindi cinema, produced by the film industry focused around Mumbai. An internationally recognized term, nevertheless it tends to homogenize the numerous regional Indian cinemas (in certain cases not Hindi cinemas) under one heading. Moreover, it is debateable when popular Indian cinema became known as 'Bollywood' cinema, the term potentially causing confusion as to the time period under discussion. In this chapter, although it discusses the influence of Hinduism to a large extent, I retain the term popular Indian cinema.

[2] Gilles Deleuze, *Cinema 2*, trans. Hugh Tomlinson & Robert Gelata (London: Continuum, [1985] 2005), p. 56.

[3] David Rodowick, *Gilles Deleuze's Time Machine* (Durham, NC: Duke University Press, 1997), pp. 175–80; Angelo Restivo, 'Into the Breach', Gregory Flaxman (ed.), *The Brain is the Screen* (Minneapolis, MN: University of Minnesota Press, 2000), pp. 171–92, p. 171; Patricia Pisters, *The Matrix of Visual Culture* (California: Stanford University Press, 2003), p. 16.

[4] Gilles Deleuze, *Cinema 1*, trans. Hugh Tomlinson & Barbara Habberjam (London: Continuum, [1983] 2005), p. xi and p. xix.

[5] András Bálint Kovács, 'The Film History of Thought', in, Gregory Flaxman (ed.), *The Brain is the Screen* (Minneapolis, MN: University of Minnesota Press, 2000), pp. 153–70, p. 156.

[6] Ibid.

[7] Restivo, p. 172.

[8] David Deamer, 'Cinema, chronos/cronos', Jeffrey A. Bell & Claire Colebrook (eds), *Deleuze and History* (Edinburgh: Edinburgh University Press, 2009), pp, 161–87, p. 172.

[9] Deleuze, *Cinema 2*, p. 13.

[10] David Martin-Jones, *Deleuze, Cinema and National Identity* (Edinburgh: Edinburgh University Press, 2006), pp. 19–49.

[11] Deleuze, *Cinema 2*, p. 40.

[12] Deleuze, *Cinema 1*, p. 209.

[13] Valentina Vitali, *Hindi Action Cinema* (Oxford: Oxford University Press, 2008), p. 4

[14] K. Moti Gokulsing & Wimal Dissanayake, *Indian Popular Cinema* (Stoke on Trent: Trentham Books, 1998), p. 17.

[15] Rosie Thomas, 'Indian Cinema: Pleasures and Popularity', *Screen* 26: 3–4 (1985): pp. 116–31, p. 130.

[16] Ibid., p. 123.

[17] Ibid., p. 130.

[18] Gokulsing & Dissanayake, pp. 18–22.

[19] Ibid., p. 20.

[20] M. Madhava Prasad, *Ideology of the Hindi Film* (Oxford: Oxford University Press, 1998), p. 30.

[21] Thomas, 'Indian Cinema', p. 121 and Vijay Mishra, *Bollywood Cinema* (London: Routledge, 2002), p. 18.

[22] Gokulsing & Dissanayake, p. 22.

[23] Prasad, p. 43.

[24] Deleuze, *Cinema 2*, p. 26.

[25] Ibid., p. 132.

[26] Rodowick, *Gilles Deleuz's Time Machine*, p. 41.

[27] András Bálint Kovács, 'The Film History of Thought', Gregory Flaxman (ed.), *The Brain is the Screen* (Minneapolis: University of Minnesota Press, 2000), pp. 153–70, p. 154.

[28] Deleuze, *Cinema 2*, p. 124.

[29] Lalitha Gopalan, *Cinema of Interruptions* (London: British Film Institute, 2002), p. 3.

[30] Ibid., p. 17.

[31] Ibid., p. 21.

[32] Tejaswini Ganti, *Bollywood* (London: Routledge, 2004), p. 138.

[33] Mishra, p. 5.

[34] Ibid.

[35] Gavin Flood, *An Introduction to Hinduism* (Cambridge: Cambridge University Press, 1996), p. 57.

[36] Ibid., pp. 54–5.

[37] Gokulsing & Dissanayake, p. 54.

[38] Flood, pp. 51–74.
[39] Mitsuhiro Yoshimoto, 'Melodrama, Postmodernism and Japanese Cinema', Wimal Dissanayake, (ed.), *Melodrama and Asian Cinema* (Cambridge: Cambridge University Press, 1993), pp. 101–26, pp. 113–16. Mitsuhiro Yoshimoto, *Kurosawa* (Durham: Duke University Press, 2000), pp. 9–16.
[40] Flood, pp. 105–9.
[41] Anindita Niyogi Balslev, *A Study of Time in Indian Philosophy* (Wiesbaden: Otto Harrassowitz, 1983), p. 23.
[42] Ibid., p. 145.
[43] Yong Choon Kim, *Oriental Thought* (New Jersey: Rowman and Littlefield, 1973), p. 10; Flood, pp. 20–1; Arvind Sharma, *Hinduism and its Sense of History* (Oxford: Oxford University Press, 2003), pp. 93–5.
[44] Julius Lipner, *Hindus* (London: Routledge, 1994), pp. 86–88, p. 197 and p. 211.
[45] By evoking this cyclical model I am not attempting to propagate the centuries old myth (strengthened under British Imperial rule) that India lacks a conception of its own history (Flood, pp. 20–1). I do not wish to position India as somehow 'ahistorical', or 'the West's irrational "other"' (Flood, pp. 103–4) by positing a linear conception of history for the West and a seemingly cyclical one for India that is implicitly considered non-progressive in comparison. As contemporary film scholarship clearly demonstrates, popular Indian cinema is clearly involved in the negotiation of Indian history.
[46] Flood, pp. 105–9.
[47] Deleuze, *Cinema 2*, p. 4.
[48] Sangita Gopal & Sujata Moorti 'Introduction', Sangita Gopal and Sujata Moorti (eds), *Global Bollywood* (Minneapolis, MN: University of Minnesota Press, 2008), pp. 1–60, p. 19
[49] Gopalan, p. 19.
[50] Gokulsing & Dissanayake, p. 14; and Nasreen Munni Kabir, *Bollywood* (London: Channel 4 Books, 2001), p. 157.
[51] Anustup Basu, 'The Music of Intolerable Love', Gopal and Moorti (eds), *Global Bollywood*, pp. 153–76, p. 155.
[52] Ganti, p. 209.
[53] Erik Barnouw & S. Krishnaswamy, *Indian Film* (Oxford: Oxford University Press, [1963] 1980), p. 73.
[54] Gokulsing & Dissanayake, p. 13.
[55] Kabir, p. 155.
[56] Michael H. Hoffheimer, '*Awāra* and the Post-colonial Origins of the Hindu Law Drama', *Historical Journal of Film, Radio and Television*, 26: 3 (2006), pp. 341–59, p. 342.
[57] Kabir, p. 15.
[58] Rodowick, *Gilles Deleuze's Time Machine*, p. 3.
[59] Deleuze, *Cinema 2*, p. 58.
[60] Ibid., p. 55.
[61] Mishra, p. 32.
[62] Gokulsing & Dissanayake, pp. 23–4.
[63] Barnouw & Krishnaswamy, p. 110.

[64] Rosie Thomas, 'Not Quite (Pearl) White', Raminder Kaur & Ajay J. Sinha (eds) *Bollyworld* (New Delhi: Sage Publications, 2005), pp. 35–69, p. 50.

[65] Barnouw & Krishnaswamy, p. 110.

[66] Rosie Thomas, 'Zimbo and Son Meet the Girl with the Gun', in David Blamey & Robert D'Souza (eds), *Living Pictures* (London: Open Editions, 2005), pp. 27–44, p. 36.

[67] Ibid., p. 36.

[68] Gopal & Moorti, p. 18.

[69] Thomas, 'Zimbo and Son Meet the Girl with the Gun', p. 37.

[70] Barnouw & Krishnaswamy, pp. 159–60.

[71] Dina Iordanova, 'Indian Cinema's Global Reach', *South Asian Popular Culture, 4: 2 (2006)*, pp. 113–40, p. 114.

[72] Gopal & Moorti, p. 28.

[73] Deleuze, *Cinema 2*, p. 95.

[74] Hoffheimer, p. 349.

[75] Jyotika Virdi, *The Cinematic Imagination* (New Brunswick: Rutgers University Press, 2003), pp. 92–100.

[76] Yves Thoraval, *The Cinema of India* (Delhi: Macmillan India Ltd, 2000), p. 85.

[77] Mishra, p. 107.

[78] Hoffheimer, p. 342.

[79] Ravinder Kaur, 'Viewing the West through Bollywood', *Contemporary South Asia* 1: 2 (2002), pp. 199–209, p. 202.

[80] Gopal and Moorti, pp. 32–33.

[81] Wimal Dissanayake, 'Globalization and Cultural Narcissism', *Asian Cinema*, 15: 1 (2004), pp. 143–150, p. 149.

[82] Mankekar, Purnima (1999), 'Brides Who Travel', *Positions*, 7: 3, pp. 731–61, p. 754.

[83] Ibid., p. 735.

[84] Gavatri Gopinath, *Impossible Desires* (Durham, NC: Duke University Press, 2005), p. 190.

Conclusion

[1] Édouard Glissant, *The Poetics of Relation* (Ann Arbor, MI: University of Michigan Press, 1997), p. 11.

[2] Dudley Andrew, 'An Atlas of World Cinema', Stephanie Dennison & Song Hwee Lim (eds), *Remapping World Cinema* (London: Wallflower, 2006), pp. 19–29, p. 20.

[3] Dudley Andrew, 'The Roots of the Nomadic', Gregory Flaxman (ed.), *The Brain is the Screen* (Minneapolis, MN: University of Minnesota Press, 2000), pp. 215–49, p. 217.

[4] Patricia Pisters, 'Arresting the Flux of Images and Sounds', Ian Buchanan & Adrian Parr (eds), *Deleuze and the Contemporary World* (Edinburgh: Edinburgh University Press, 2006), pp. 175–93, pp. 180–91.

[5] Duncan Petrie, 'Cinema in a Settler Society', Dina Iordanova, David Martin-Jones & Belén Vidal (eds), *Cinema at the Periphery*, (Detroit, MI: Wayne State University Press, 2009), pp. 67–83, p. 79.

[6] Faye Ginsburg, 'Peripheral Visions', Iordanova et al (eds), *Cinema at the Periphery* pp. 84–103, p. 85.

[7] Duncan Petrie, Iordanova et al (eds), *Cinema at the Periphery*, pp. 67–83.

[8] Barbara Filser, 'Gilles Deleuze and Future Cinema', Jeffrey Shaw & Peter Weibel (eds), *The Cinematic Imaginary After Film* (Cambridge, MA: The MIT Press, 2003), pp. 214–19; William Brown, 'Man without a movie camera – movies without men', Warren Buckland (ed.), *Film Theory and Contemporary Hollywood Movies* (New York: Routledge/AFI, 2009), pp. 66–85.

Select Bibliography

Abbas, Ackbar, *Hong Kong* (Minneapolis, MN: Minnesota University Press, 1997).

Abel, Richard (ed.), *Silent Film* (London: Athlone, 1996).

Abelmann, Nancy, *The Melodrama of Mobility* (Honolulu, HI: University of Hawaii Press, 2003).

Aguilar, Gonzalo, *Other Worlds* (London: Palgrave, 2008).

Anderson, Benedict, *Imagined Communities* (London: Verso, 1983).

Andrew, Dudley, 'An Atlas of World Cinema', Stephanie Dennison & Song Hwee Lim (eds), *Remapping World Cinema* (London: Wallflower, 2006), pp. 19–29.

Ash, Robert, Peter Ferdinand, Brian Hook & Robin Porter (eds), *Hong Kong in Transition* (London: Routledge, 2003).

Augé, Marc, *Non-Places*, trans. John Howe (London: Verso, 1995).

Augé, Marc, *A Sense for the Other*, trans. Amy Jacobs (Stanford, CA: Stanford University Press, 1998).

Badley, Linda, R. Barton Palmer & Steven Jay Schneider (eds), *Traditions in World Cinema* (Edinburgh: Edinburgh University Press, 2006).

Balslev, Anindita Niyogi, *A Study of Time in Indian Philosophy* (Wiesbaden: Otto Harrassowitz, 1983).

Barnouw, Erik & S. Krishnaswamy, *Indian Film* (Oxford: Oxford University Press, [1963] 1980).

Bergson, Henri, *Matter and Memory*, trans. Nancy Margaret Paul & W. Scott Palmer (New York: Zone Books, [1896] 1988).

Bergson, Henri, *Creative Evolution*, trans. Arthur Mitchell (New York: Dover Publications Inc., [1907] 1998).

Beugnet, Martine, *Cinema and Sensation* (Edinburgh: Edinburgh University Press, 2007).

Blamey, David & Robert D'Souza (eds), *Living Pictures* (London: Open Editions, 2005).

Bogue, Ronald, *Deleuze on Cinema* (New York: Routledge, 2003).

Bordwell, David, *Planet Hong Kong* (Cambridge, MA: Harvard University Press, 2000).

Buchanan, Ian & Gregg Lambert (eds), *Deleuze and Space* (Edinburgh: Edinburgh University Press, 2005).

Buchanan, Ian & Patricia MacCormack (eds), *Deleuze and the Schizoanalysis of Cinema* (London: Continuum, 2008).

Burch, Noël, 'Primitivism and the Avant-Gardes', Philip Rosen (ed.), *Narrative, Apparatus, Ideology* (New York: Columbia University Press, 1986), pp. 483–506.

Burch, Noël, 'A Primitive Mode of Representation?', Thomas Elsaesser (ed.) *Early Cinema* (London: BFI, 1990), pp. 220–7.

Burucúa, Constanza, *Confronting the 'Dirty War' in Argentine Cinema, 1983–1993* (Woodbridge: Tamesis, 2009).

Chakrabarty, Dipesh, *Provincialising Europe* (Princeton, NJ: Princeton University Press, 2000).

Chapman, James, *Cinemas of the World* (London: Reaktion Books, 2003).

Christie, Ian, *The Last Machine* (London: BFI, 1994).

Chu, Yingchi, *Hong Kong Cinema* (London: Routledge, 2003).

Colebrook, Claire, *Deleuze* (London: Continuum, 2006).

Davis, Mike, *City of Quartz* (London: Verso, [1990] 2006).

Davis, Mike, *Planet of Slums* (London: Verso, 2006).

Deleuze, Gilles, *Difference and Repetition*, trans. Paul Patton (London: Athlone, [1968] 1994).

Deleuze, Gilles, *Cinema 1*, trans. Hugh Tomlinson & Barbara Habberjam (London: Continuum, [1983] 2005).

Deleuze, Gilles, *Cinema 2*, trans. Hugh Tomlinson & Robert Galeta (London: Continuum, [1985] 2005).

Deleuze, Gilles, *The Fold*, trans. Tom Conley (London: Athlone, [1988] 1993).

Deleuze, Gilles & Félix Guattari, *A Thousand Plateaus*, trans. Brian Massumi (London: Athlone, [1980] 1987).

Dennison, Stephanie & Lisa Shaw, *Popular Cinema in Brazil* (Manchester: Manchester University Press, 2004).

Dennison, Stephanie & Song Hwee Lim (eds), *Remapping World Cinema* (London: Wallflower, 2006).

Dissanayake, Wimal, 'Globalization and Cultural Narcissism', *Asian Cinema*, 15: 1 (2004), pp. 143–50.

Dosse, François & Jean-Michel Frodon (eds), *Gilles Deleuze et les images* (Paris: Cahiers du cinéma, 2008).

Dyer, Richard & Ginette Vincendeau, *Popular European Cinema* (London: Routledge, 1992).

Eleftheriotis, Dimitris, *Popular Cinemas of Europe* (New York: Continuum, 2001).

Elsaesser, Thomas (ed.) *Early Cinema* (London: BFI, 1990).

Elsaesser, Thomas, *European Cinema* (Amsterdam: University of Amsterdam Press, 2005).

Erie, Steven P., *Globalizaing L.A.* (Stanford, CA: Stanford University Press, 2004).

Evans, Peter William (ed.), *Spanish Cinema* (Manchester: Manchester University Press, 1999).

Elena, Alberto & Marina Díaz (eds) *The Cinema of Latin America* (London: Wallflower, 2003).

Ezra, Elizabeth, *Georges Méliès* (Manchester: Manchester University Press, 2000).

Falicov, Tamara L., *The Cinematic Tango* (London: Wallflower, 2007).

Featherstone, Mike & Scott Lash (eds), *Global Modernities* (London: Sage, 1995).

Feeney, F.X. & Paul Duncan (eds), *Michael Mann* (Los Angeles: Taschen, 2006).

Flaxman, Gregory (ed.), *The Brain is the Screen* (Minneapolis, MN: University of Minnesota Press, 2000).

Frayling, Christopher, *Spaghetti Westerns* (London: I. B. Taurus, 1981).

Fu, Poshek & David Desser, *The Cinema of Hong Kong* (Cambridge: Cambridge University Press, 2000).

Galt, Rosalind, *The New European Cinema* (New York: Columbia University Press, 2006).

Ganti, Tejaswini Ganti, *Bollywood* (London: Routledge, 2004).

Gateward, Frances (ed.), *Seoul Searching* (New York: State University of New York Press, 2007).

Glissant, Édouard, *The Poetics of Relation*, trans. Betsy Wing (Ann Arbor, MI: University of Michigan Press, 1997).

Gokulsing, K. Moti & Wimal Dissanayake, *Indian Popular Cinema* (Stoke on Trent: Trentham Books, 1998).

Gopal, Sangita & Sujata Moorti (eds), *Global Bollywood* (Minneapolis, MN: University of Minnesota Press, 2008).

Gopalan, Lalitha, *Cinema of Interruptions* (London: BFI, 2002).

Gopinath, Gavatri, *Impossible Desires* (Durham, NC: Duke University Press, 2005).

Grieveson, Lee, & Peter Krämer (eds), *The Silent Cinema Reader* (London: Routledge, 2004).

Gunning, Tom, 'Non-Continuity, Continuity, Discontinuity', Thomas Elsaesser (ed.) *Early Cinema* (London: BFI, 1990), pp. 86–94.

Gunning, Tom, 'The Cinema of Attractions', Thomas Elsaesser (ed.) *Early Cinema* (London: BFI, 1990), pp. 56–62.

Gunning, Tom, 'Now You see It, Now You Don't', Richard Abel (ed.), *Silent Film* (London: Athlone, 1996), pp. 71–84.

Gunning, Tom, 'Tracing the Individual Body', Leo Charney and Vanessa R. Schwartz (eds), *Cinema and the Invention of Modern Life* (Berkeley, CA: University of California Press, 1995), pp. 15–45.

Hallam, Julia with Margaret Marshment, *Realism and Popular Cinema* (Manchester: Manchester University Press, 2000).

Hardt, Michael & Antonio Negri, *Empire* (Cambridge, MA: Harvard University Press, 2000).

Hart, Stephen & Richard Young (eds), *Contemporary Latin American Cultural Studies* (London: Hodder Arnold, 2003).

Hart, Stephen M., *A Companion to Latin American Film* (Woodbridge, Suffolk: Tamesis, 2004).

Harvey, David, *A Brief History of Neoliberalism* (Oxford: Oxford University Press, 2005).

Harvey, David, *The Spaces of Global Capitalism* (London: Verso, 2006).

Held, David & Ayse Kaya (eds) *Global Inequality* (Cambridge: Polity Press, 2007).

Heller, Henry, *The Cold War and the New Imperialism* (New York: Monthly Review Press, 2006).

Herzog, Amy, *Dreams of Difference, Songs of the Same* (Minneapolis, MN: University of Minnesota Press, 2009).

Ho, Lok Sang & Robert Ash (eds), *China, Hong Kong and the World Economy* (London: Palgrave, 2006).

Hughes, Howard, *Once Upon a Time in the Italian West* (London: I. B. Tauris, 2006).

Iordanova, Dina, David Martin-Jones & Belén Vidal, *Cinema at the Periphery* (Detroit, MI: Wayne State University Press, 2010).

James, Nick, *Heat* (London: BFI, 2002).

Jancovich, Mark, *Rational Fears* (Manchester: Manchester University Press, 1996).

Kabir, Nasreen Munni, *Bollywood* (London: Channel 4 Books, 2001).

Kaur, Raminder & Ajay J. Sinha (eds) *Bollyworld* (New Delhi: Sage Publications, 2005).

Kim, Elaine H. & Chungmoo Choi (eds), *Dangerous Women* (London: Routledge, 1998).

Kim, Kyung Hyun, *The Remasculinization of Korean Cinema* (Durham, NC: Duke University Press, 2004).

King, John & Nissa Torrents (eds), *The Garden of Forking Paths* (London: BFI, 1987).

King, John, Sheila Whitaker & Rosa Bosch (eds), *An Argentine Passion* (London: Verso, 2000).

King, John, *Magical Reels* (London: Verso, 2000).

Li, Siu Leung & Stephen Chan Ching-kiu (eds) *Hong Kong Connections* (Durham, NC: Duke University Press, 2005).

Lu, Sheldon (ed.), *Transnational Chinese Cinemas* (Honolulu, HI: University of Hawaii Press, 1997).

Lu, Sheldon & Emilie Yuen-Yu Yeh (eds) *Chinese Language Film* (Honolulu, HI: University of Hawaii Press, 2005).

Marks, Laura U., *The Skin of the Film* (Durham, NC: Duke University Press, 2000).

Martin, Michael T. (ed.), *New Latin American Cinema: Volume One* (Detroit, MI: Wayne State University Press, 1997).

Martin-Jones, David, *Deleuze, Cinema and National Identity* (Edinburgh: Edinburgh University Press, 2006).

Martin-Jones, David, 'Traces of time in *Traces of Love* (2006)', *Asian Cinema*, 18: 2 (2007), pp. 252–70.

Martin-Jones, David & Damian P. Sutton, *Deleuze Reframed* (London: I. B.Tauris, 2008).

Martin-Jones, David, *Scotland: Global Cinema* (Edinburgh: Edinburgh University Press, 2009).

Martin-Jones, David & Soledad Montañez, '*Bicycle Thieves*, or Thieves on Bicycles?', *Studies in Hispanic Cinemas*, 4: 3 (2007), pp. 183–98.

McDonogh, Gary & Cindy Wong, *Global Hong Kong* (London: Routledge, 2005).

McHugh, Kathleen & Nancy Abelmann (eds) *South Korean Golden Age Melodrama* (Detroit, MI: Wayne State University Press, 2005).

Mercer, John & Martin Schingler, *Melodrama* (London: Wallflower, 2004).

Mignolo, Walter D., *Local Histories/Global Designs* (Princeton, NJ: Princeton University Press, 2000).

Mishra, Vijay, *Bollywood Cinema* (London: Routledge, 2002).

Mullarkey, John, *Refractions of Reality* (London: Palgrave Macmillan, 2009).

Murray, Timothy, *Digital Baroque* (Minneapolis, MN: University of Minnesota Press, 2008).

Naficy, Hamid, *An Accented Cinema* (Princeton, NJ: Princeton University Press, 2001).

Nietzsche, Friedrich, *Untimely Meditations*, trans. R. J. Hollingdale (Cambridge: Cambridge University Press, 1997).

Nygren, Scott, *Time Frames* (Minneapolis, MN: Minnesota University Press, 2007).

Page, Joanna, *Crisis and Capitalism in Contemporary Argentine Cinema* (Durham, NC: Duke University Press, 2009).

Pion-Berlin, David, *The Ideology of State Terror* (Boulder: Lynne Reinner, 1989).

Pisters, Patricia, *The Matrix of Visual Culture* (Stanford, CA: Stanford University Press, 2003).

Pisters, Patricia, 'Arresting the Flux of Images and Sounds', Ian Buchanan & Adrian Parr (eds), *Deleuze and the Contemporary World* (Edinburgh: Edinburgh University Press, 2006), pp. 175–93.

Powell, Anna, *Deleuze and Horror Film* (Edinburgh: Edinburgh University Press, 2005).

Prasad, M. Madhava, *Ideology of the Hindi Film* (Oxford: Oxford University Press, 1998).

Rancière, Jacques, *Film Fables*, trans. Emiliano Battista (Oxford: Berg, [2001] 2006).

Rodowick, D. N., *Gilles Deleuze's Time Machine* (Durham, NC: Duke University Press, 1997).

Rodowick, D. N., *Reading the Figural* (Durham, NC: Duke University Press, 2001).

Rodowick, D. N. (ed.), *Afterimages of Gilles Deleuze's Film Philosophy* (Minneapolis, MN: Minnesota University Press, 2009).

Romero, Luis Alberto, *Argentina in the Twentieth Century* (Pennsylvania, PA: Pennsylvania State University Press, 2002).

Sassen, Saskia, *The Global City* (Princeton, NJ: Princeton University Press, 1991).

Sassen, Saskia, *Cities in a World Economy* (Thousand Oaks, CA: Pine Forge Press, 1994).

Sassen, Saskia, *Globalization and its Discontents* (New York: The New Press, 1998).

Shapiro, Michael J., *Cinematic Geopolitics* (London: Routledge, 2009).

Shaw, Deborah (ed.) *Contemporary Latin American Cinema* (New York: Rowman & Littlefield, 2007).

Shaw, Lisa & Stephanie Dennison (eds), *Latin American Cinema* (London: McFarland & Company Inc., 2005).

Shiel, Mark & Tony Fitzmaurice (eds), *Cinema and the City* (Oxford: Blackwell, 2001).

Shin, Chi-Yun & Julian Stringer (eds), *New Korean Cinema* (Edinburgh: Edinburgh University Press, 2005).

Shohat, Ella & Robert Stam, *Unthinking Eurocentrism* (London and New York: Routledge, 1994).

Shohini Chaudhuri, *Contemporary World Cinema* (Edinburgh: Edinburgh University Press, 2005).

Silver, Alain & James Ursini, *L.A. Noir* (Santa Monica, CA: Santa Monica Press, 2005).

Soja, Edward W., *Postmodern Geographies* (London: Verso, 1989).

Stam, Robert, *Tropical Multiculturalism* (Durham, NC: Duke University Press, 1997).

Stam, Robert & Louise Spence, 'Colonialism, Racism and Representation – An Introduction', *Screen*, 24: 2 (1983), pp. 2–20.

Stone, Rob, *Spanish Cinema* (Essex: Pearson Education Ltd, 2002).

Strauven, Wanda (ed.) *The Cinema of Attractions Reloaded* (Amsterdam: Amsterdam University Press, 2006).

Stringer, Julian (ed.) *Movie Blockbusters* (London: Routledge, 2003).

Sutton, Damian, *Photography, Cinema, Memory* (Minneapolis, MN: Minnesota University Press, 2009).

Taylor, Diana, *Disappearing Acts* (Durham, NC: Duke University Press, 1997).

Tedesco, Laura, *Democracy in Argentina* (London: Frank Cass, 1999).

Thomas, Rosie, 'Indian Cinema', *Screen*, 26:3–4 (1985), pp. 116–31.

Thomas, Rosie, 'Not Quite (Pearl) White', Raminder Kaur & Ajay J. Sinha (eds), *Bollyworld* (New Delhi: Sage Publications, 2005), pp. 35–69.

Thomas, Rosie, 'Zimbo and Son Meet the Girl with the Gun', David Blamey & Robert D'Souza (eds), *Living Pictures* (London: Open Editions, 2005), pp. 27–44.

Thoraval, Yves, *The Cinema of India* (Delhi: Macmillan India Ltd, 2000).

Tsang, Steve, *A Modern History of Hong Kong* (London: I. B. Tauris, 2007).

Virdi, Jyotika, *The Cinematic Imagination* (New Brunswick, NJ: Rutgers University Press, 2003).

Vitali, Valentina, *Hindi Action Cinema* (Oxford: Oxford University Press, 2008).

Wagstaff, Christopher, 'Italian Genre Films in the World Market', Geoffrey Nowell Smith & Steven Ricci (eds), *Hollywood and Europe* (London: BFI, 1998), pp. 74–85.

Wagstaff, Christopher, 'A forkful of westerns', Richard Dyer & Ginette Vincendeau (eds), *Popular European Cinema* (London: Routledge, 1992), pp. 245–61.

Wilson, Rob & Wimal Dissanayake (eds), *Global/Local* (Durham, NC: Duke University Press, 1996).

Yau, Esther C. M. (ed.) *At Full Speed* (Minneapolis, MN: University of Minnesota Press, 2001).

Index